MEET THE
RABBIS

(Drawing by Gae Lynn Duncan)

The Torah Is a Tree of Life

My child, do not forget my teaching. Focus your heart to observe my commandments . . .

MEET THE
RABBIS

*Rabbinic Thought and the
Teachings of Jesus*

BRAD H. YOUNG

HENDRICKSON PUBLISHERS

Meet the Rabbis: Rabbinic Thought and the Teachings of Jesus
© 2007 by Hendrickson Publishers, Inc.
P. O. Box 3473
Peabody, Massachusetts 01961-3473

ISBN 978-1-56563-405-3

Printed in the United States of America

Third Printing — May 2008

Scripture taken from the HOLY BIBLE, NEW INTERNATIONAL VERSION. Copyright © 1973, 1978, 1984 by International Bible Society. Used by permission of Zondervan Bible Publishers. All rights reserved. (Italics in quoted scriptures is author's emphasis.)

Scripture quotations taken from the New American Standard Bible®, Copyright © 1960, 1962, 1963, 1968, 1971, 1972, 1973, 1975, 1977, 1995 by The Lockman Foundation Used by permission. (www.Lockman.org)

Cover Art: Schiavone, Andrea (c. 1520–1563). "Christ Teaching in the Temple." Location: S. Giacomo dell'Orio, Venice, Italy. Photo Credit: Cameraphoto Arte, Venice/Art Resource, N.Y. Used with Permission.

Library of Congress Cataloging-in-Publication Data

Young, Brad, 1955–
    Meet the rabbis : rabbinic thought and the teachings of Jesus /
    Brad H. Young.
        p. cm.
    Includes bibliographical references and indexes.
    ISBN 978-1-56563-405-3 (alk. paper)
    1. Jesus Christ—Jewishness. 2. Jesus Christ—Teachings. 3. Rabbinical literature—Relation to the New Testament. 4. Sermon on the mount—Criticism, interpretation, etc. I. Title.
    BT590.J8Y69 2007
    232.9'06—dc22
                                                2007003328

Dedicated to the memory of Shony Alex Braun, masterful violinist, composer, and humanitarian, who survived the Holocaust and gave joy to millions through his magic fingers and charismatic personality.
(See Shony Alex Braun, *My Heart Is a Violin*
[Los Angeles: Shony Music, 2003])

Table of Contents

Part IV: Study Helps

List of Illustrations and Maps

The illustrations on pages 33, 51, 94, 158, and 216 are from Bernard A. Solomon, *The Zaddick Christ: A Suite of Wood Engravings.* Greenwood, S.C.: Attic, 1973. Used with permission.

Foreword

Rabbi Charles P. Sherman

Four decades ago, I entered Hebrew Union College's Jewish Institute of Religion in Cincinnati to begin training as a reform Rabbi. During the course of my studies there, I was truly blessed to have required courses in the Inter-Testamental Literature and Period taught by Dr. Samuel Sandmel. Dr. Sandmel was a true pioneer—a Rabbi who was one of the world's leading authorities on Christian Scripture. He provided his students with a methodology and a context for understanding texts with which we were, in general, unfamiliar. My rabbinate has certainly been enriched by what I began learning in Dr. Sandmel's courses and also from his books.

I believe that Dr. Brad H. Young's students in the Graduate School of Theology at Oral Roberts University are similarly blessed. They have the opportunity to study Jewish texts and thought, as well as to gain an understanding of the context for Christian Scripture, from a man who is both a scholar in Judaism and a faithful Christian. It has been my privilege to address Dr. Young's classes on numerous occasions, and I have been impressed with his students' curiosity about Judaism, as well as their openness and respect. I especially appreciate that Dr. Young believes Christians should not study rabbinic Judaism merely to understand more clearly the context of early Christianity, but also because Judaism is alive, well, and relevant today.

In this volume, Dr. Young introduces readers, who do not have to be scholars, to the Jewish context of Jesus' life and times. The author's impressive knowledge of the period and of Jewish texts, and his ability to summarize vast amounts and types of literature clearly and interestingly, makes this volume very readable. Dr. Young moves readers from the more to the less familiar gracefully. It is my hope that this volume will whet the appetite of Christians new to this approach so that they will read other volumes by Dr. Young, as well as other scholars who appreciate the importance of both Judaism and Jews, historically and today. Jewish readers will also learn from this book.

As one who has toiled for many years in the interfaith vineyards, I have said repeatedly that my own faith has been strengthened, broadened, and enriched by what I have learned from other faith traditions. Dr. Young exemplifies that same belief in his efforts to help faithful Christians "meet the Rabbis."

Rabbi Charles P. Sherman
Temple Israel
Tulsa, Oklahoma

Foreword

Dr. E. William Bean

In June, 2006 Dr. Brad Young took me to Bet Shearim during a study trip to Israel. Today this location is referred to as the tombs of the rabbis because of the rich archaeological remains of an enormous necropolis carved out of limestone with very impressive sarcophagi, many of which are resting in their original places. Moreover, in Jewish history Bet Shearim was known as an important center of Torah learning. Rabbi Judah Ha-Nasi, the compiler of the Mishnah lived, worked and was buried at Bet Shearim. This city had became the seat of the Sanhedrin. From this time on, the Bet Shearim burial grounds became an important site for Jewish history during the Mishnaic and Talmudic periods. The faith of the Jewish people flourished at Bet Shearim because of the spiritual and religious leaders who guided the community through hardship and adversity. But Dr. Young does not believe that the rabbis should be buried and forgotten.

It was at Bet Shearim during this trip to Israel that I learned about Dr. Young's forthcoming book, *Meet the Rabbis*. I was honored when Dr. Young asked me to write a foreword to this great work.

Twenty-one years ago I was introduced to the Jewish background of Christianity as well as to the close connection between rabbinic literature and the New Testament. At that time, I had already served as a minister of a major denomination for over twenty-four years. After a complete study on the subject, I began to teach people about the Semitic background to the New Testament. For over twenty-one years I have devoted my life to the study of the beginnings of Christian faith and have desired to become Jesus centric, language centric, culture centric, and Kingdom centric in my research and teaching.

In this new book, Dr. Young emphasizes that "Modern Christians selectively read the Gospels from the perspective of traditional church teachings." The perspective of the church changed rapidly after the destruction of Jerusalem in 70 C.E. The Body of the Lord drifted away from the Jewish roots that nourished the growing branch of the early church and began to become more influenced by Greco-Roman culture and to become Westernized in thinking and theology. When the Pharisees built a hedge around Torah, the church built a hedge around itself.

Dr. Young stresses that knowing rabbinic teachings and sources throws new light upon the teachings of Jesus, who lived in a world of the Eastern mind-set. He also mentions that to understand prayer, almsgiving, and fasting, the Christian should wholly concentrate on God. Learning about the world religion of Judaism does much to help us understand the start of Christianity.

According to Dr. Young we need "master teachers," not "master preachers." Dr. Young reminds us that when Jesus said, "Go into the world and make disciples" (Matt 28:19), the teaching of the *Ethics of the Fathers* (1:1) parallels this command with a similar statement, ". . . raise up many disciples." He adds, "For disciples to be made, there is first a need for master teachers." Dr. Young introduces his readers to Torah masters.

Dr. Young's work *Meet the Rabbis* has strengthened my beliefs, enhanced my faith, and given fresh insight into my studies. His statement that, "During the Yavneh period, the Torah teaching—'Follow justice and justice alone, so that you may live and possess the land the LORD your God is giving you' (Deut 16:20 NIV)—was interpreted to mean that everyone should follow the scholars of learning to the places where Torah is taught," has encouraged me to seek out the best of scholarship and to learn for meaningful life transformation. I need to learn from the rabbis. The church needs to learn from the rabbis. Everyone will benefit from learning about the substance and content of rabbinic Judaism.

The principle of the kingdom of heaven is expressed in this book. As we Christians move forward in the Lord's Movement we should keep in mind His words: "For I was hungry and you gave me something to eat, I was thirsty and you gave me something to drink, I was a stranger and you invited me in, I needed clothes and you clothed me, I was sick and you looked after me: I was in prison and you came to visit me" (Matt 25:35–36 NIV).

My father, Dr. Louis W. Bean, was a pastor of a large church and was a serious student of New Testament Greek and biblical scholarship. For years he admired the humanitarian work of Dr. Albert Schweitzer and was fascinated by his great contributions to the academic research on the beginnings of Christianity. My father and his congregation supported Dr. Schweitzer's work financially. Around 1960 in the last years of Dr. Schweitzer's life, my father was invited to travel to Lambaréné, French Equatorial Africa in order to spend time with Dr. Schweitzer.

This great humanitarian scholar already had received the Nobel Peace Prize in 1952 for his care of the sick and his missionary activities, and was recognized internationally for his academic achievements. My father was greatly moved by his experience with meeting Dr. Schweitzer. At the completion of his trip, my Dad asked Dr. Schweitzer what he could go back and tell Americans. Dr. Schweitzer thought for a minute and then said, "You go back and tell Americans to stake out a claim of human need about them and spend the rest of their lives pursuing that claim." Dr. Young so eloquently expresses this statement when he stresses helping those who are less fortunate, and studying the word of God. Dr. Schweitzer wrote the classic book, *The Quest for the Historical Jesus*.

Dr. Young worked with orthodox Jewish scholar Prof. David Flusser and Christian scholar Dr. Robert Lindsey in his own quest to understand the historical Jesus. While Dr. Schweitzer, Prof. Flusser, and Dr. Lindsey would not agree with each other concerning questions about Jesus and the Synoptic Gospels, they all stand together in agreement about pursuing the claim to meet the needs of the less fortunate in a suffering world. In fact, understanding the Jewish origins of Christianity makes this point crystal clear.

I personally can relate to my Dad's experience with Albert Schweitzer because I have had the privilege of meeting Prof. David Flusser and Dr. Robert Lindsey. Though one of these scholars was an orthodox Jew and the other an evangelical Christian, they worked together for the common good. They believed that Christians and Jews should be partners rather than rivals. They honored and esteemed each other, in spite of differences and because of each man's deep conviction of faith in the love of God. Prof. Flusser and Dr. Lindsey were building bridges of awareness in their studies for a greater understanding between the Christian community and the Jewish people. My desire over the past twenty years has been to pursue the claim that these two men established, i.e., to open up the world of the synagogue to the people of the church.

Dr. Young's new book is a contribution in this tradition of the quest to understand and appreciate the Jewish beginnings of Christian faith. He had the unusual and extremely fortunate opportunity to work closely with Prof. David Flusser and Dr. Robert Lindsey for many years and to bring the contributions of these scholars to a logical outcome. In his work, the quest for the historical Jesus reaches a new level. Dr. Young is able to honor and scientifically explore both early Judaism and Christianity, introducing readers to the spiritual message of rabbinic literature. His new book *Meet the Rabbis* does much more than take the reader to the tombs of the Jewish sages in Bet Shearim. Dr. Young helps his reader to encounter the Jewish people, their spiritual leaders and a living faith community. He helps his readers to value the impact ancient Judaism has had upon early Christianity and the New Testament. The Jewish sages must not be forgotten in their tombs. Everyone needs to meet the rabbis through Dr. Young's book.

Dr. E. William Bean
Centre for the Study of Biblical Research
Redlands, California

Preface

Meet the Rabbis is a project I have wanted to prepare for quite some time. I first encountered rabbinic thought and literature in 1978, as a foreign student at the Hebrew University. Taught in Modern Hebrew, the class was designed to meet the needs of Israeli students. As a Christian from the U.S., I was challenged to study ancient Jewish texts from a cultural and religious orientation very different than my own.

I was shocked to discover that the discipline of New Testament[1] studies, as I had so far been introduced to it at that point, for the most part ignored rabbinic literature. In fact, most Christians outside the academy do not know that such books exist! Even in the area of professional academic research, the evidence of rabbinic literature is marginalized. I must admit that I even felt a little anger that I had not been afforded the opportunity to study rabbinics in some area of my American university training in the Hebrew Bible and the Greek New Testament. A biblical studies undergraduate major in most academic programs will not be introduced to rabbinic thought and literature, leaving a gaping hole in Christian education.

The lack of comparative study of rabbinic literature and the New Testament is partly due to mutual ignorance. On the one hand, New Testament scholars do not always know Hebrew well and seldom have learned how to research rabbinic texts. On the other hand, rabbinic scholars are not always inclined to explore the New Testament even as a historical document of a sectarian faith during Second Temple period Judaism. Moreover, Christian scholarship is often characterized, sometimes unintentionally, by an anti-Jewish prejudice that sometimes emerges as blatant anti-Semitism. As an example, Kittel's massive ten-volume lexicon, the classic text of New Testament Greek first published in 1932, was originally funded by the Nazi Party in Germany. Kittel himself was a Nazi, and his anti-Semitism is a matter of

---

[1] Using the term "New Testament" does not imply that the Old Testament, which I prefer to call the Hebrew Bible, has been replaced or is no longer valid. Many Jewish readers prefer the term "Christian Scriptures" for the New Testament. For clarity, this book uses the more widely acknowledged titles: Old and New Testaments.

record. His views serve as a subjective foundation for his New Testament scholarship.[2] In his day he was the authority for Old Testament research and Judaic studies, and, because his influential work is still used as a reference today by many, his influence is still felt.

The present introduction is designed for the learner who has read the New Testament. Many Christians are not cognizant of the fact that much of the New Testament was written by Jewish authors for a Jewish audience. In fact, many aspects of the literary types in rabbinic texts are paralleled in the New Testament, especially in the Gospels.

My original title for this book, *Meet the Rabbis: An Introduction to Rabbinic Thought and Literature based on the Sermon on the Mount*, indicated that Christians would be the primary readers. This was somewhat misleading. Most individuals in the Western world today, regardless of whether they are Christians, atheists, agnostics, secular community leaders, or some other religious and political persuasions, are more knowledgeable of Jesus' ethical teachings in the Sermon on the Mount than they are of the the *Ethics of the Fathers* (commonly referred to by the Hebrew title, *Avot* or "Fathers") in a Jewish prayer book. I want readers to begin with what they know about the teachings of Jesus and, by an associative method, to introduce them to the world of Jewish Torah learning. Within this world we discover the authentic cultural background of Jesus' teachings in ancient Judaism. In fact, it is not a background, it is the original life setting. Jewish thought permeates the New Testament.

As a starting point, I have used parts of the New Testament, especially the Sermon on the Mount, as a springboard for probing rabbinic method. But this book is not a commentary for the Sermon on the Mount. It is an introduction to rabbinic thought and literature. In general overview, the book has three main sections in its layout: Introduction to Rabbinic Thought, Introduction to Rabbinic Literature, and Meet the Rabbis, a biographical description of influential rabbis from Talmudic sources.

I do not wish to imply that studying rabbinic thought and literature is primarily beneficial for the comparative research of early Christianity. Christians should not study rabbinics just to understand more clearly the New Testament environment. Rabbinic thought is relevant to every aspect of modern life. The literature explores the meaning of living life to its fullest, in right relationship with God and humanity. I believe that Christians particularly will enjoy studying the Talmud because ancient Judaism is the root that nourishes the branch. Here I have included some major key texts like the

---

[2] See Gerhard Kittel, *Theological Dictionary of the New Testament* (trans. G. Bromiley; 10 vols.; Grand Rapids: Eerdmans, 1964–1976).

Ethics of the Fathers and the Amidah Prayer, which I have translated for the readers. For greater precision, I have often made a fresh translation of the biblical text, as well. All unmarked Bible translations are my own.

The challenge of any introductory work is recognizing what to include and what to exclude, since it can only incorporate foundational elements. My hope is that this introduction will inspire further study. The bibliography and study diagrams such as the "Oral and Written Torahs" or "The Rabbis and their disciples" are meant to aid the learner in taking the next step. I sincerely hope that rabbinic thought and literature will become as meaningful to you as they have been to me.

Acknowledgments

Many people assisted in preparing this manuscript for publication. I greatly appreciate the diligent work carried out by Teresa Frankovic in transcribing a portion of this book from public lectures on cassette tape to a written form. I also express my gratitude to Joseph Frankovic who edited much of the text. His work goes far beyond the editing of the manuscript. Joseph offered valuable insights from his extensive knowledge of the subject matter. His scholarly understanding and ability to communicate have strengthened the present work immensely. My heartfelt appreciation goes to artist Gae Lynn Duncan, who drew the "Tree and Roots" illustration for me. I want to thank my dear wife, Gayle, who not only read the manuscript and prepared many reader helps, but also was a constant source of encouragement in producing this work. My friend and colleague Carl Johnson has been a steady source of encouragement. His skillful efforts have made publishing this document a joy.

Foremost among those whom I would acknowledge are my teachers and students. I am particularly grateful to Prof. David Flusser of the Hebrew University. His creative genius has challenged me. I mourn his loss and will never be able to express adequately my gratitude for his involvement in my life. I must express thanks to Prof. Yaakov Sussmann and Prof. Shmuel Safrai who have guided me in my study of rabbinic literature at the Hebrew University. Prof. Safrai has been an inspiration to me because of his personal commitment to excellence and his incredible knowledge. His phenomenal memory, original insights, and kindness to students are a model for all educators to emulate. His death leaves a tremendous void in scholarly research. His students will miss his kind smile and the excited gleam in his eyes when he discussed a text. Finally, I must thank my students—in the classrooms in which I taught in Israel, Sweden, Korea, Malaysia, England, and the United States—for asking probing questions that have taught me so much and helped me understand the meaning of interpreting a text in its authentic setting. Thank you for asking the right questions and being willing to answer them honestly.

Abbreviations

GENERAL

1QS	The Community Rule (from the Dead Sea Scrolls)
Ant.	Josephus, *Jewish Antiquities*
b.	Babylonian Talmud
ca.	circa
C.E.	Common Era
ch(s).	chapter(s)
hal.	halakhah
KJV	King James Version
m.	Mishnah
NASB	New American Standard Bible
NIV	New International Version
NJPS	*Tanakh: The Holy Scriptures: the New JPS Translation according to the Traditional Hebrew Text*
pl.	plural
prob.	probably
RSV	Revised Standard Version
sing.	singular
t.	Tosefta
y.	Jerusalem Talmud

BIBLE, HEBREW

Gen	Genesis
Exod	Exodus
Lev	Leviticus
Num	Numbers
Deut	Deuteronomy
Judg	Judges
1 Sam	1 Samuel
1–2 Kgs	1–2 Kings

Esth	Esther
2 Chr	2 Chronicles
Neh	Nehemiah
Ps	Psalms
Prov	Proverbs
Isa	Isaiah
Jer	Jeremiah
Hos	Hosea
Mic	Micah

BIBLE, DEUTEROCANONICAL

1–2 Macc	1–2 Maccabees
Sir	Sirach
Tob	Tobit

BIBLE, NEW TESTAMENT

Matt	Matthew
Rom	Romans
1 Cor	1 Corinthians
Gal	Galatians
Eph	Ephesians
1–2 Thess	1–2 Thessalonians
2 Tim	2 Timothy
Heb	Hebrews
Jas	James

RABBINIC WRITINGS

Avot	*Fathers, Ethics of the Fathers*
Avot R. Nat.	*Avot of Rabbi Nathan, Fathers according to Rabbi Nathan*
Pesik. Rab Kah.	*Pesikta of Rab Kahana*

SECONDARY LITERATURE

ASTI	*Annual of the Swedish Theological Institute*
BDAG	Danker, F. W., W. Bauer, W. F. Arndt, and F. W. Gingrich. *Greek-English Lexicon of the New Testament and Other Early Christian Literature.* 3d ed., Chicago, 2000

BDB	Brown, F., S. R. Driver, and C. A. Briggs. *A Hebrew and English Lexicon of the Old Testament.* Oxford, 1907
HUCA	*Hebrew Union College Annual*
JBL	*Journal of Biblical Literature*
JJS	*Journal of Jewish Studies*
JQR	*Jewish Quarterly Review*

An effort to standardize the transliteration of Hebrew has been made in the text and footnotes, though not for the actual titles or quotations taken from other works, which reflect those authors' methods. In general the General Purpose Style of the *SBL Handbook of Style* has been followed. For instance, the *aleph* and *ayin* are represented with a simple apostrophe ('). There are two exceptions. (1) The Hebrew letter *chet* (*khet*) is transliterated with *ch* to avoid confusion with the Hebrew letter *kaf,* which when aspirated is transliterated with *kh*. (2) In accord with common practice among scholars of rabbinic literature, the Hebrew letter *qof* is transliterated with a *k* rather than the standard *q* found in the *SBL Handbook of Style*. Thus an initial *kaf* and an initial *qof* would both be marked with a *k*.

PART I

Introduction to Rabbinic Thought

An introduction to rabbinic thought and literature centered on the Sermon on the Mount begins with the conceptual world that connects the Jewishness of Jesus and His teachings to the thinking of the ancient rabbis and their interpretation of the Bible. Both Jesus and the old rabbis begin with the Bible. Their thought patterns are Jewish to the core, and focus on living life to its fullest and most meaningful purpose based upon their understanding and interpretation of Scripture. The Sermon on the Mount is more familiar to most Christian readers than the rabbinic literature. Here we will begin with teachings more familiar to the general reader and move into less familiar terrain. Rabbinic thought opens up a fresh conceptual world and gives new insight into the Bible.

Torah Learning for Beginners

"We'll start at the very beginning," I told her as I opened the Bible to the Book of Genesis. "The Torah," I told her, "is different from all other studies. It is G-d's* blueprint for us so that we may learn how to live our lives. Each word, each letter, each punctuation mark and cantillation has layers and layers of meaning. The greatest minds have studied it over and over throughout their lives, and on each occasion, they find something new. The wisdom therein is infinite because it comes from an infinite source. It is not a book that can be simply read. It's a lifetime pursuit. Before we commence our studies, we are enjoined to pronounce the prayer asking G-d to grant us the privilege of understanding His holy words." And with that introduction I opened the Book and started to teach, "In the beginning, G-d created . . ."

> Rebbetzin Esther Jungreis, *The Committed Life* (New York: Cliff Books, 1998), 25–26. *Rebbetzin Esther Jungreis is giving the first Torah lesson to a well-educated, secular woman who is beginning her religious studies for her journey back to faith in God. Because Jungreis is Orthodox, she does not write out the name of God in reverence of the commandment not to take the name of God in vain.

CHAPTER 1

Introduction to Rabbinic Thought

Most Christians, as well as many educated people in Western society, are already familiar to some extent with the New Testament, especially the ethical and moral message Jesus preached in the Sermon on the Mount (see Matt 5–7; Luke 6:20b–49). For instance, they probably know that Jesus taught his disciples to "turn the other cheek" (Matt 5:39; Luke 6:29). The present work begins with such familiar passages from the teachings of Jesus and digs deeper into the teachings of the ancient rabbis of Israel. Some of these rabbis lived before Jesus and others lived after him. Both the Sermon on the Mount and the teachings of the rabbis in the Talmud are rooted in the rich soil of ancient Judaism, from the glorious days of the Second Temple period.

Many Christians are surprised to discover that Jesus was closely connected to the rabbinic movement in his thought and educational approach. To better understand this movement, we will begin with the thought patterns of the Jewish sages and move into the literary works that have been preserved over time. But we must first meet these rabbis. The books were written on their hearts long before they were compiled in writing. Students of rabbinic literature must explore the real-life experiences of the rabbis in order to fully appreciate their teachings.

Major themes from the Jewish conceptual frame of reference flow from the moral teachings of Jesus in the Sermon on the Mount. The original context of this sermon is not the pulpit of the Christian church on Sunday but rather the setting of Jewish learning and education in the land of Israel in the first century C.E. While the mentality of first-century Jews is very different from that of modern Christians, both ancient Judaism and modern Christianity grow from the same root. The root system of any tree is far more extensive than the branches themselves. Jesus focused attention on themes such as prayer, fasting, and almsgiving (Matt 6:1–18; Luke 11:2–13). His audience understood these activities to be expressions of their spirituality. To understand rabbinic thought and literature, one must first develop a passion for the spiritual life of the people who learned Torah and practiced it by reaching out to others in need.

The vast sea of Jewish literature teems with commentaries on the Bible and instructions on how to live a life that is pleasing to God within the community of faith. Here we will create a familiarity with the major works of rabbinic literature, from the basic Bible commentaries to the extensive discussions of the legal code in the Talmuds. The basic outline of the book will explore Jewish thought, examine rabbinic literature, introduce major rabbis, and discuss interpretations of the Sermon on the Mount from the time of Jesus to the present. Our study of this literature will include my translation of the *Ethics of the Fathers* (one of the most important documents for the study of ancient Judaism), charts with the names of major rabbis, lists of the tractates of the Oral Torah, including the Mishnah and Talmuds,[1] outlines for dating the major works of rabbinic literature, suggested reading lists, and the Amidah prayer of the synagogue that has been prayed in some form from antiquity to the present. We will explore the Great Sanhedrin, the Master-Mentor relationship, and the meaning of Torah in practical living. The discussion of rabbinic thought and literature is rooted in the study of these foundational works. We will move from the Temple in the time of Jesus to the synagogue of today.

Finally we will explore the lives and works of some of the rabbis, because Christians are more familiar with Augustine than with Rabbi Akiva. Rabbinic literature was written by scholars, educators, community leaders, preachers of the Word, and common people who passed carefully memorized teachings from one generation to the next. This process of memory and manuscript resulted from spiritual leaders who were caring for the needs of their communities of faith throughout a long and noble history. They were leaders of decisive action. Judaism, unlike Christianity, stresses action more than belief. Although Maimonides did develop the thirteen foundational principles of Jewish faith which stress belief, action, that is, practicing one's faith in ethical conduct and ceremonial worship takes priority over theological purity. We will see that the great leader Hillel the Elder was very close to Jesus in his teachings of Torah and its practical applications.

PERSPECTIVES ON ANCIENT JUDAISM

Our introduction to rabbinic thought begins with a well-known New Testament passage from Matthew's Gospel. From there we will enter less fa-

---

[1] The term Oral Torah (and synonyms, oral law, oral tradition, Mishnah) refer to the interpretation of the Written Torah, Genesis, Exodus, Leviticus, Numbers, and Deuteronomy, which, according to Jewish orthodox teachings, was revealed to Moses on Mount Sinai. The Oral Torah explains the meaning of the written word. The tradition was passed down from one generation to the next as an oral history.

miliar terrain. Taking this approach we will see firsthand how various aspects of Jesus' life and teachings can be brought into sharper focus by viewing them against the social and historical backdrop of first-century Judaism. To succeed at this task we need to equip ourselves with a social, historical, and religious framework through which we can view Jesus and compare him with other personalities, sects, and movements in his time. Then we may ask, what was so revolutionary about his message? What was original about it in relation to other sects and movements? What was normative about it in relation to other teachings of the day?

In Christian literature, including academic writings, I often encounter a prejudicial attitude against Judaism. The prejudice is usually directed at the Pharisees and their spiritual successors, the rabbis, in the form of sweeping generalizations. John Lightfoot's *Commentary on the New Testament from the Talmud and Hebraica*—a four-volume commentary spanning Matthew through 1 Corinthians first published between 1658–1674—stands out in my mind as an example of Christian literature containing an anti-Jewish bias. Lightfoot lived from 1602 to 1675. A Puritan who taught at Cambridge, Lightfoot wrote his commentary on the New Testament in Latin. In 1684 the Latin was translated into English, which underwent revision in 1859. Here is a sampling of the type of remarks a reader encounters throughout Lightfoot's commentary: "The Jews themselves stink . . . their writings stink as much amongst all." They are "of all impious men the most impious, of all cursed wretches the most cursed."[2] In another place he describes them "as being persons whose highest law the purse and profit was wont to be."[3] In 1979, Lightfoot's commentary was republished. Sadly, the publisher did not include a notice regarding Lightfoot's bigotry. Such anti-Semitism and anti-Judaism have been a severe problem in the history of Christian education and theology.[4]

Since Lightfoot's time, German scholars have also written comparative studies on the New Testament and Talmudic literature. The most famous of these works is Herman Strack and Paul Billerbeck's *Kommentar zum Neuen Testament aus Talmud und Midrasch.*[5] An excellent reference tool, this work

---

[2] Lightfoot on Matt 11:21. See John Lightfoot, *A Commentary on the New Testament from the Talmud and Hebraica Matthew—1 Corinthians* (4 vols.; Grand Rapids: Baker, 1979), 2:4, 193.

[3] Lightfoot on Matt 8:30. Lightfoot, *A Commentary,* 2:168.

[4] Marvin R. Wilson, *Our Father Abraham: Jewish Roots of Christian Faith* (Grand Rapids: Eerdmans, 1989), 87–103; and the classic work, Edward H. Flannery, *The Anguish of the Jews: Twenty-Three Centuries of Anti-Semitism* (Mahwah, N.J.: Paulist, 1985).

[5] Herman L. Strack and Paul Billerbeck, *Kommentar zum Neuen Testament aus Talmud und Midrasch* (6 vols.; Munich: Beck, 1922–1961).

remains available only in German. Other fine works, such as Gustaf Dalman's *The Words of Jesus*,[6] have been translated into English. In English, one of the most widely read books on this subject is Alfred Edersheim's *The Life and Times of Jesus the Messiah*.[7] These works, while still in use today, are out of date and full of incorrect views of Judaism.

Overcoming prejudice based upon misconception is a formidable task. Recognizing that some of our earlier teachings concerning Judaism and the Jewish people are not always accurate is a first step. Today, Christians are much more willing to study Jewish scholarship. The emergence of Israeli scholars as leading contributors to biblical research has generated a body of valuable academic literature in Modern Hebrew, much of which remains inaccessible to the English reader. We need more studies using comparative approaches between the New Testament and Talmudic literature to be written or translated into English. This type of work is long term and arduous, but the results illuminate the New Testament, especially the teachings of Jesus.

Christians should—everyone should—read Rabbi Joseph Telushkin's *Jewish Wisdom: Ethical, Spiritual, and Historical Lessons from the Great Works and Thinkers*.[8] All would also benefit from the writings of Abraham Joshua Heschel. His books, such as *God in Search of Man*,[9] offer fresh insight into the deeper meaning of the concept of God in the Bible. For Jewish thought, spirituality, literature, and mysticism, Heschel's book, *Heavenly Torah as Refracted through the Generations* is essential and enjoyable reading.[10] David Flusser of the Hebrew University has written a book on the life of Jesus that is a treasure store for anyone who really wants to understand the historical Jesus.[11] My own books, especially *Jesus the Jewish Theologian*,[12] place Jesus in his first-century setting and help Christian readers make practical applica-

---

[6] Gustaf Dalman, *The Words of Jesus Considered in the Light of Post-Biblical Jewish Writings and the Aramaic Language* (Authorized English version by D. M. Kay; Edinburgh: T&T Clark, 1909).

[7] Alfred Edersheim, *The Life and Times of Jesus the Messiah* (rev. ed.; Peabody, Mass.: Hendrickson, 1993).

[8] Joseph Telushkin, *Jewish Wisdom: Ethical, Spiritual, and Historical Lessons from the Great Works and Thinkers* (New York: Morrow, 1994).

[9] Abraham Joshua Heschel, *God in Search of Man: A Philosophy of Judaism* (Northvale, N.J.: Jason Aronson, 1987).

[10] Abraham Joshua Heschel, *Heavenly Torah as Refracted through the Generations* (Edited and translated by Gordon Tucker with Leonard Levin; 3 vols.; New York: Continuum, 2005).

[11] David Flusser, *Jesus* (Jerusalem: Magnes Press, 1997).

[12] Brad H. Young, *Jesus the Jewish Theologian* (Peabody, Mass.: Hendrickson, 1995).

tions today. In *The Parables: Jewish Tradition and Christian Interpretation*,[13] I compare the parabolic teachings of Jesus with rabbinic parables. Jesus tells story illustrations that are mirrored in the powerful sermons and Bible commentaries of ancient Jewish rabbis, scholars, and community leaders.

A more accurate understanding of Jewish teachings from the time of the ancient rabbis makes the message of the Gospels come alive with renewed vigor. One excellent place to start understanding Jewish thought is in the Prayer Book.[14] Many of us from a Christian background would develop a much different view of the Pharisees if we learned about their teachings from the prayers they prayed rather than from the sermons preached about them in our churches.

Most of us have heard the term *Pharisee* used in a derogatory manner. The *Oxford American Dictionary* even defines *Pharisee* as "a hypocritical self-righteous person." Such language should not surprise us, in fact there is good reason for it. Jesus did criticize harshly the hypocritical practices of some Pharisees—in much the same way that the Pharisees strongly condemned hypocrisy in themselves.

But Jesus also instructed his followers to do what the scribes and Pharisees taught, demonstrating that he saw their teachings as spiritually beneficial (Matt 23:1–2). Modern Christians, however, have been exposed to an environment, namely churches, where the Pharisees have been traditionally labeled as legalists of the worst order. In preaching and Sunday school lessons, the Pharisees play the lead antagonist to Jesus. I want to suggest that this characterization of the Pharisees is not only unfair, but also historically inaccurate.

Commonly the Pharisees are viewed as legalistic hypocrites. This view is seriously flawed. The best historical sources demonstrate that the Pharisees themselves condemned hypocrisy. As a matter of fact, the writers of the Dead Sea Scrolls who did not like the Pharisees because of their lenient rulings and desire to interpret the Written Torah through an oral interpretation that would make it easier to observe, loved to refer to the Pharisees as "those who seek after the smooth ways" *(doreshe halakhot)*[15] The "smooth

---

[13] Brad H. Young, *The Parables: Jewish Tradition and Christian Interpretation* (Peabody, Mass.: Hendrickson, 1998).

[14] I recommend the edition by Joseph H. Hertz, *The Authorized Daily Prayer Book* (New York: Bloch, 1985). The prayers not only deal with Sabbath worship, festivals, and life-cycle events, but also reveal a rich inner life on a personal level and also in the community of faith. This contemporary prayer book is a collection of ancient prayers, many of which would have been well known to Jesus and his disciples.

[15] See for instance the Pesher Nahum, 4Q169, Column 1. Compare Geza. Vermes, *The Complete Dead Sea Scrolls in English* (New York: Penguin Press, 2004), 62 and 474.

ways" seems to refer to their lenient rulings. These contemporaries of the
Pharisees from the Qumran community viewed them, as Bible teachers
who looked for an easier path. Later the rabbis who are the successors of
the Pharisees strongly criticized hypocrisy. Rabbi Eleazar declared, "Any
person in whom hypocrisy can be found, will bring down [divine] wrath
on the world . . ." (b. Sotah 41b). The Pharisees criticized hypocrisy within
their own ranks. They wanted genuine spiritual renewal. Perhaps it would
be more honest to view the criticism of Jesus in the same way. He had
hopes that his criticism would cause a revitalization spiritually of the Pharisaic movement. The fact that he singles out the Pharisees and calls upon
them specifically for a fresh spiritual awakening for holiness that flows
from the inside, as well as outwardly, must mean that Jesus was close to the
Pharisees in teaching and in practice. In truth, almost all religions have a
natural tendency to preach a high level of moral conduct, all the while,
some members of the faithful fail to reach the standard set in theory. With
all the criticism directed at the Pharisees among Christian teachers and educators, it is highly questionable whether church leaders always live out in
practice privately, what they preach and proclaim publically. A preacher,
minister or priest sometimes teaches the right way of living publically but
fails to meet the proper standard of behavior in his or her private life. Hypocrisy is a problem for all religious faith communities. At least the hypo-
crite knows what he or she should do. So the grotesque legalistic Pharisee
portrayed in Christian caricature is an unrealistic phantom. In fact Jesus
teaches his followers to do what the scribes and Pharisees teach (Matt 23:1–2).
He does indeed harshly critique some of the scribes and Pharisees as religious pretenders, but at the same time he accepts the content of their spiritual message. The harsh criticism was designed to reach the hearts of
spiritual leaders who could recognize their personal needs and shortcomings. This type of "within the family" criticism was never intended to fire
speeches of hatred against all the Jewish people until the end of time.

The Pharisees represented one of the most significant reform movements in Judaism at the close of the Second Temple period. We have formulated opinions about the Pharisees based upon a simple, uncritical reading of
the Gospels and on what we have heard preached from our pulpits. How
many of us really know what the Pharisees taught, or what the major thrust
of their movement was? Until we can answer these questions adequately, we
are not in a position to assess them fairly or responsibly.

The Sermon on the Mount explains how to pray, how to give money to
the needy in the community, and how to fast or repent. Jesus is concerned
with the proper way to pray. He does not request money for His ministry but
teaches how to give money directly to those in need. In fasting, He teaches a
heartfelt repentance between God and the individual. Surprising for most

of us from a Christian background, the Pharisees taught on these same themes. In fact, these concerns make up the foundation of rabbinic thought. By comparing the teachings of Jesus with common themes in rabbinic literature, we gain fresh insight into the deeper meaning of the conceptual world and environment that birthed this approach to loving God and demonstrating compassion to others.

THE SERMON ON THE MOUNT'S TEACHINGS ON PRAYER, CHARITY, AND FASTING

The Sermon on the Mount preserves the essence of Jesus' teachings concerning the kingdom of heaven and the life of discipleship. Sadly, few Christians have been willing to recognize the deep roots these teachings have in Pharisaic faith and practice. In the first centuries B.C.E. and C.E., as today, pious Jews lived life according to the proper interpretation of Torah; Jesus came to fulfill Torah by interpreting it properly for practical living. Christian New Testament scholar Hans Dieter Betz observes that, "As Jesus was a Jew, all the teachings of the Sermon on the Mount are Jewish in theology and cultural outlook."[16] The message of the sermon describes the spiritual life and moral conduct of the disciple who puts Jesus' teachings into practice. The themes are rooted in Jewish moral and ethical teachings.

CHARITY

In Matthew 6, Jesus opens his teachings with an emphasis on giving to people in need.

> Be careful not to do your "acts of righteousness" before men, to be seen by them. If you do, you will have no reward from your Father in heaven. So when you give to the needy, do not announce it with trumpets, as the hypocrites do in the synagogues and on the streets, to be honored by men. I tell you the truth, they have received their reward in full. But when you give to the needy, do not let your left hand know what your right hand is doing, so that your giving may be in secret. Then your Father, who sees what is done in secret, will reward you. (Matt 6:1–4 NIV)

Notice the word *righteousness* in the passage. Underneath the English is the Greek word *dikaiosynē*. Students of Koine Greek know that the basic meaning of *dikaiosynē* is "righteousness." But in this passage, "righteousness"

---

[16] Hans Betz, *The Sermon on the Mount* (Minneapolis: Fortress, 1995), 1.

does not seem to be the best translation. The reason for this deviation ultimately stems from the language in which Jesus was teaching.

A few New Testament scholars, such as Nigel Turner,[17] think that Jesus taught in Greek. Many scholars, such as Matthew Black or Joseph A. Fitzmyer,[18] think that Jesus taught in Aramaic. I am of the opinion that Jesus could carry on a simple conversation in Greek, and speak Aramaic, but when teaching he preferred Hebrew. Note that Hebrew and Aramaic are closely related languages, similar to the relationship of Dutch and German. The early rabbinic literature, written closest to the time of Jesus, is in Hebrew. All rabbinic parables are in Hebrew, and Jewish prayers are prayed in the Hebrew language. Ninety-five percent of the Dead Sea Scrolls are in Hebrew. Holy books, like the Torah and the Gospels, were generally written in Hebrew.[19]

In the Old Testament we often encounter the word *righteousness*. Underneath the English word stands the Hebrew *tsedakah*. Interestingly, in the ancient Greek translation of the Old Testament, called the Septuagint, *dikaiosynē* was used in a formulaic manner to translate *tsedakah*. In time, as the Hebrew language developed from biblical to post-biblical Hebrew, *tsedakah* assumed a range of meaning. In addition to meaning "righteousness," it could now mean "almsgiving" or "deeds of charity." In the translation above, the NIV renders it as "acts of righteousness." This shift in meaning is well documented in the academic literature. For example, in their chapter on languages of rabbinic literature, Hermann L. Strack and Günter Stemberger used *tsedakah* as the premiere example of how biblical Hebrew words assumed additional meanings in the post-biblical, Mishnaic period.[20]

In the time of Jesus, the Hebrew *tsedakah* could mean "charity," and when Hebrew influenced Greek, *dikaiosynē* could also assume the same meaning. That is the reason Matt 6:1 should be translated as, "Beware of doing your charitable deeds before people." The Greek of Matt 6:1 contains

---

[17] See Nigel Turner, *Grammatical Insights into the New Testament* (Reissued paperback ed.; Edinburgh: T&T Clark, 2004).

[18] See Matthew Black, *An Aramaic Approach to the Gospels and Acts* (3d ed.; Oxford: Clarendon, 1967; repr., Peabody, Mass.: Hendrickson, 1998); and Joseph A. Fitzmyer, *Essays on the Semitic Background of the New Testament* (Missoula, Mont.: Society of Biblical Literature, 1974).

[19] Randall Buth has called attention to Semitisms in the Gospels that could only come from Hebrew and not Aramaic, see his "Luke 19:31–34, Mishnaic Hebrew and Bible Translation," *JBL* 104 (1985): 680–85. Compare the excellent study of Jehoshua Grintz, "Hebrew as the Spoken and Written Language of the Second Temple," *JBL* 79 (1960): 32–49. See also my book, *Jesus and His Jewish Parables*, (Tulsa, Okla.: Gospel Research Foundation, 2000), 40–42, 51 n. 73.

[20] See Hermann L. Strack and Günter Stemberger, *Introduction to the Talmud and Midrash* (trans. M. Bockmuehl; Edinburgh: T&T Clark, 1991), 113.

a Hebraism,[21] and in order to capture the essence of the verse, we must look underneath the Greek text and recover the nuance of the Hebraism. The teaching in the Sermon on the Mount, like many rabbinic texts, deals with giving alms to the needy as acts of righteousness before God.

PRAYER

After opening with a teaching on almsgiving, Jesus then moves into a discourse on the meaning of prayer.

> And when you pray, do not be like the hypocrites, for they love to pray standing in the synagogues and on the street corners to be seen by men. I tell you the truth, they have received their reward in full. But when you pray, go into your room, close the door and pray to your Father, who is unseen. Then your Father, who sees what is done in secret, will reward you. And when you pray, do not keep on babbling like pagans, for they think they will be heard because of their many words. Do not be like them, for your Father knows what you need before you ask him. (Matt 6:5–8 NIV)

The hypocrites are pretenders who love to pray in order to appear holy, pious, and religiously proper to others in public. In reality, they are inwardly deficient in seeking a genuine and meaningful relationship with God through prayer. Sadly when we focus on the words, "standing in the synagogues," we seldom apply Jesus' teachings to our personal lives and may even entertain the thought that prayer in the synagogue is of little value.[22] But Jesus and His followers, themselves Jews, prayed in the synagogue.[23] They worshiped in the Temple. In fact, if Jesus were speaking to Christians of

---

[21] A Hebraism in the Gospels refers to a word or phrase in Greek which represents an authentic Hebrew saying of Jesus. The word or phrase is difficult to understand strictly from Greek. A Hebraism is awkward in Greek, but perfectly clear in Hebrew. One should remember that the early church leader Papias (130 C.E.) reported that Matthew wrote the sayings of Jesus in Hebrew (Eusebius, *Hist. eccl.*, 3, 39, 16).

[22] On first-century synagogues, see the important work of Donald D. Binder, *Into the Temple Courts: the Place of the Synagogue in the Second Temple Period* (Atlanta: Society of Biblical Literature, 1999). Compare just some of the texts from the New Testament that speak about the participation of Jesus and His followers in the synagogue study and Temple worship: Matt 4:23: 12:35; 13:54; Mark 1:21; 6:2; Luke 4:16; John 6:59; Acts 9:20; 13:5; and also Matt 21:12; Luke 2:22, 41; 22:53; John 7:14; Acts 3:1.

[23] The posture mentioned in the verse, "standing," has led some interpreters to conclude that this saying is directed against the Amidah prayer, the eighteen benedictions which were prayed while standing. Since Jesus entered fully into the life of His people, there is little doubt that He and His followers prayed some form of this prayer many times. The issue here is not the posture or the liturgy, but rather

today, He could say the same words about those who pray "in church," to be seen by others rather than seeking the face of God through inward struggle. Hypocrites are abundant in every creed and within all faith traditions. The Pharisees do not own the patent or possess the copyright on all hypocritical activity in the name of religious piety. Hypocrisy comes naturally for some Christians today, in much the same way as it came to some Pharisees in the Second Temple period. Today, however, it has become natural to use the Pharisees as a cover for our fraudulent spiritual life.

Like Jesus, who warns against making meaningless repetition in prayers mindlessly repeated over and over again, Rabbi Simeon declares, "do not allow your prayer to become a fixed mechanical task, but rather it must be an appeal for mercy and grace before the Omnipresent, as it said, *'For he is gracious and full of mercy, slow to anger, and abounding in loving kindness, and relenting of evil* (Joel 2:13)'" (*Avot* 2:18). Rabbi Simeon adds a very strongly worded warning about prayer, "Do not be wicked in your own heart" (Ibid.). Both for Jesus and the rabbis, the attitude of the heart is crucial for meaningful prayer. The fear of God must guide the heart into a deeper spiritual experience in prayer, and in how one lives out faith in an authentic walk of sincere obedience to God's commandments.

On the one hand, listening to Jesus and Rabbi Simeon might lead a listener to conclude that they oppose all liturgical prayers that are prayed by the community. But on the other hand, all evidence from the New Testament indicates that Jesus participates fully in the religious experience of His people. It was His custom to attend synagogue and to worship in the Temple. Moreover, His disciples continued this practice in the book of Acts. In addition, the beginning of the saying of Rabbi Simeon makes it clear that he does not oppose praying the set prayers established for the spiritual life of his people. He stresses, "Be careful to recite the Shema and to pray the Amidah. But when you pray, do not allow your prayer to become a fixed mechanical task" (*Avot* 2:18). When prayed with the proper attitude, the set prayers come alive with meaning.

Carmine Di Sante notes that there are many close connections between prayers prayed in the synagogue and early Christian liturgy. He wisely observes that Jesus' harsh attack against hypocritical prayer is not an attack against Jewish liturgy, but rather a call for each person to examine one's self motivation in prayer. He compares the hostile criticism opposing prayers offered in order to be seen by others, to the harsh words of the Hebrew prophets against the Temple worship (1 Sam 15:22–23; Isa 1:11–14; Jer

---

the attitude of the heart. Does one pray to be seen by others, or is the prayer flowing from heartfelt concern for a deeper relationship with God almighty?

7:21–23; Amos 5:21–23; Hos 6:6; Mic 6:6–9). The prophets were not opposed to the Temple worship. But they wanted the Temple service to be
conducted with full heartfelt participation. The people must obey God,
serve in action and not in word alone. The condition of their hearts is of
prime importance to God. They must worship in the Temple, but with an
authentic feeling flowing from an inner conviction demonstrating in action their full commitment to obey God's word. Di Sante writes that such
criticism of liturgy comes from "persons who know the liturgy of their
fathers 'from inside' and who, precisely because they know and love it, can
also be critical of it. And the purpose of their criticism is the same as the
purpose of the prophets: not to reject the liturgy but to rediscover it in all
its purity and authenticity."[24]

In the Sermon on the Mount, Jesus is not teaching against giving alms
to the poor. But He warns against the wrong motivation. He is not against
praying while standing in the synagogue. But prayer must flow from the
heart with the right attitude, desiring a deeper spiritual experience with
God, rather than to be seen as holy in the sight of others. The one giving
money to the needy or praying in a religious service should be intensely
concerned with how he or she appears in the sight of God, rather than in
the sight of other people. Yet much of the current teaching in the Christian
church about prayer centers on how to receive a positive answer for requests. Certainly Jesus taught His disciples to pray for their daily bread,
and by way of extension, all of their physical needs.[25] Prayer's most basic
meaning is communion with God. But prayer in the teachings of Jesus, as
well as in ancient Judaism, involved so much more than making requests or
spending time alone with God. As Shmuley Boteach notes, if your child
was extremely ill and in the hospital, you would probably not be praying
for a newer, bigger, more luxurious car. He observes, "The history of humankind is one of mistaken priorities and muddled values. Part of prayer's
supreme purpose is to recalibrate our desires. Prayer takes us away from the
strict confines of thinking of everything in terms of pure self-interest."[26]
Early Jewish and Christian prayer focused on life transformation. The person who prayed was changed and transformed by experiencing the divine
presence. In the modern period, rather than focusing on self-interest, more
attention in prayer must be devoted to avoiding distractions, meditating

---

[24] Carmine Di Sante, *Jewish Prayer the Origins of Christian Liturgy* (New York:
Paulist Press, 1985), 10.

[25] See my book, *The Jewish Background to the Lord's Prayer* (Tulsa, Okla.: Gospel
Research Foundation, 2000).

[26] Shumely Boteach, *Judaism for Everyone: Renewing your Life through the Vibrant Lesson of the Jewish Faith* (New York: Basic Books, 2002), 130.

upon Scripture, concentrating one's focus, directing one's heart to heaven, listening to the stillness of the divine presence, and hearing from God. In other words, prayer must be a recalibration of one's life energies toward the higher divine purpose, by discovering a meaningful spiritual walk in service to God's call and by helping others less fortunate in the community. Prayer is a call to action. A life of prayer is devoted to keeping the commandments of God. The fear of God guides meaningful prayer. Inner participation guides prayer.

Prayer is not a retreat from the world. Prayer helps each individual see the world from a different vantage point. Instead of viewing the world through the prism of self-interest, praying to God enables each person to see the world through the eyes of divine compassion. As Abraham Joshua Heschel observes, "The self is not the hub, but the spoke of the revolving wheel. In prayer we shift the center of living from self-consciousness to self-surrender."[27] In self-surrender, the individual helps others, and in so doing, assists in accomplishing God's will and purpose. Each person who prays participates in the redemptive plan. This is the call of Jesus to seek first the kingdom of heaven (Matt 6:33). Intimate communion with God in prayer will not allow personal self-interest and needs to become the center hub of the wheel. Heschel observes, "God is the center toward which all forces tend. He is the source."[28] The source and sustainer of all life requires our inner heartfelt participation in prayer. Jesus tells his followers to pray to God in personal devotion. The prayer flows from an inner life of constant devotion to God's will. Heschel challenges,

> Deeper forces and qualities of the soul must be mobilized before prayer can be accomplished. To pray is to pull ourselves together, to pour our perception, volition, memory, thought, hope, feeling, dreams, all that is moving in us, into one tone. Not the words we utter, the service of the lips, but the way in which the devotion of the heart corresponds to what the words contain, the consciousness of speaking under His eyes, is the pith of prayer.[29]

So it is not the words, the formula, or the liturgy that is of prime significance, but rather the inner participation of the individual's heart and soul. Jesus stressed that we must seek the divine presence in our prayers, being driven by the sublime purpose revealed by God's will rather than to be honored in the presence of other people who see us praying.

---

[27] Abraham Joshua Heschel, *Man's Quest for God: Studies in Prayer and Symbolism* (New York: Scribner, 1966), 7.
[28] Ibid.
[29] Ibid., 13.

FASTING

Jesus begins by teaching about almsgiving, moves to a discourse on prayer, and follows with this section on fasting:

> When you fast, do not look somber as the hypocrites do, for they disfigure their faces to show men they are fasting. I tell you the truth, they have received their reward in full. But when you fast, put oil on your head and wash your face, so that it will not be obvious to men that you are fasting, but only to your Father, who is unseen; and your Father, who sees what is done in secret, will reward you. (Matt 6:16–18 NIV)

Although Matthew combines his materials in a way that gives the impression Jesus sat down and gave a series of unrelated teachings in one class session, I am of the opinion that the Sermon on the Mount actually represents material that Jesus taught at different locations and times in his ministry. The three sub-units covering charity, prayer, and fasting, however, constitute an uninterrupted stretch of material that Jesus taught at one sitting. The reason for this assumption will become clearer as we move into the ancient Jewish sources.

In Jewish thought, fasting almost always involves abstinence from both eating food and drinking liquid. The person who fasts must wholly concentrate on God. The personal anguish of abstaining from satisfying the basic needs and wants of the body for food and water heighten the individual's spiritual awareness. The fast is often connected to repentance. Of course, the major fast in the Jewish sacred calendar each year is the Day of Atonement. In Matt 6:16, Jesus says, "When you fast . . ." These words would probably call to mind the fast for the Day of Atonement for most first-century Jewish listeners. This entire day is focused on personal inventory and repentance before God. In fact, it could be said that for the rabbis fasting is nearly synonymous with repentance. One returns home to God by denying oneself, subjugating the strong will for human self gratification, over to the divine will for holy living.

Nonetheless fasting is required on other days of the Jewish calendar. The ninth day of the Hebrew month, *Av* is the occasion which commemorates the time when the Temple was destroyed both by the Babylonians (586 B.C.E.) and the Romans (70 C.E.). It is a solemn fast day. In fact, in the preceding month, *Tamuz*, the time when the Romans first breached the walls of Jerusalem on the seventeenth day of the month is remembered as a national disaster. People fast from sunrise to sunset on the seventeenth of *Tamuz* and this is considered a minor fast. Other horrific events occurred on this day such as the worship of the golden calf in the wilderness and the cessation of the Temple sacrifices during the siege of Jerusalem. Another minor fast is associated with the assassination of Judea's final governor, Gedaliah (2 Kgs 25:25). Major fasts like the Day of Atonement require abstinence for a basic twenty-four hour period of time from sunset of the evening preceding the observance to sunset the next day. Most of the pious will start fasting early, an hour before sunset and then end it an hour or so after sunset the next day just to exercise caution. Fasts may be called for special prayer needs, such as a call to end a drought and to send rain. Like Christians during the Lenten season, often Jewish people take money that would have been used to buy food for themselves and give financial help to someone less fortunate. The words of the prophet Isaiah in chapter 58 are often quoted to describe the true purpose of fasting, "Is this not the fast which I choose . . . to let the oppressed go free, And break every yoke? Is it not to divide your bread with the hungry. . . . Then you will call, and the LORD will answer, You will cry, and He will say, 'Here I am'" (Isa 58:6–9 NASB).

Jesus is not opposed to the Jewish fasts of the sacred calendar of Israel. In strong loyalty to his people and their shared faith commitments, it seems clear that Jesus himself fasted on these days. The clear reference to set fast days of the calendar, "When you fast . . ." indicates that he participated fully in the liturgical yearly cycle of prayer and fasting followed by his people. Moreover, in the Sermon on the Mount, he teaches his followers how to fast. Much like his teaching on prayer, he supports the customs of ancient Israel but stresses the necessity for the right attitude of heart. Fasting is accompanied by heartfelt prayer. One should not pray for frivolous matters. The one who prays seeks to see the world from a divine perspective becoming more deeply aware of human need by seeing the world through God's eyes. Prayer should transform the one who prays. The worshiper must seek the face of God in genuine sincerity. Prayer and fasting require inner participation of the heart, soul and mind. Though he represents later Jewish thought, it is worth observing here that the great philosopher Maimonidies taught, "Each individual must free his or her heart from all other thoughts, and consider himself or herself as standing before the divine presence [*Shechinah*]" (*Mishnah Torah*, Prayer, 4:16). This means that inner participation of the heart is essential for meaningful prayer. Ritual and routine can never be a substitute for fasting and prayer that flows from a heart with a deep yearning for God. The ritual within the sacred calendar provides a context for increased awareness. But the individual must apply his or her heart with thoughtful interaction. So faith must guide the routine of daily prayer. Fasting must be accomplished with a pure purpose flowing from a determined faith. Heschel observed, "Faith is the beginning of intense craving to enter an active relationship with Him who is beyond the mystery, to bring together all the might that is within us with all that is spiritual beyond us."[30]

---

[30] Ibid., 109–10.

RABBINIC TEACHING ON CHARITY, PRAYER, AND FASTING

In Tobit, a pre-Christian apocryphal book, we read: "Prayer is good when accompanied by fasting, almsgiving, and righteousness" (Tob 12:8). Tobit is giving ethical instructions to his son Tobias. His instructions suggest that almsgiving, prayer, and fasting had already assumed a lead role in Jewish faith and piety in that period.

In a tractate on fasting in the Jerusalem Talmud, a legal codification that was edited and published early in the Byzantine period (324–610 C.E.), the trio—charity, prayer, and fasting—re-emerges in a discussion about what nullifies a harsh decree from heaven (y. Ta'anit 65b, ch. 2, Hal. 1).[31] According to Rabbi Leazar, a harsh decree may be averted through prayer, righteousness (almsgiving), and repentance (fasting). How did he conclude this? Because 2 Chr 7:14 says, "if my people, who are called by my name, will humble themselves and pray and seek my face and turn from their wicked ways, then will I hear from heaven and will forgive their sin and will heal their land" (NIV). We can easily see how he finds prayer and repentance in this verse, but to understand how he reads almsgiving into the text we must learn something about the manner in which ancient Jews interpreted their Bible.

RIGHTEOUSNESS IS CHARITY

The ancient rabbis and Jesus stress giving charity as well as the blessing of God that accompanies helping others in need.

> Do not store up for yourselves treasures on earth, where moth and rust destroy, and where thieves break in and steal. But store up for yourselves treasures in heaven, where moth and rust do not destroy, and where thieves do not break in and steal. For where your treasure is, there your heart will be also. The eye is the lamp of the body. If your eyes are good, your whole body will be full of light. But if your eyes are bad, your whole body will be full of darkness. If then the light within you is darkness, how great is that darkness! No one can serve two masters. Either he will hate the one and love the other, or he will be devoted to the one and despise the other. You cannot serve both God and Money. (Matt 6:19–24 NIV)

This passage represents a beautiful homily direct from the first century. In it Jesus exhorts his listeners to use their wealth wisely. Israel's sages also

---

[31] See *Genesis Rabbah* 44:12. Rabbi Leazar is Rabbi Eleazar ben Pedat (ca. 260 C.E.). See Wilhelm Bacher, *Die Agada der Palästinensischen Amoräer* (3 vols.; Strassburg: Truebner, 1892–1899), 2:13.

spoke of wealth management, and they recognized the foolishness of toiling to accumulate material gain. They too had heard and even repeated to their audiences the famous fable about the famished fox that slipped through a narrow opening into a vineyard. After feasting sumptuously, the fox tried to exit the same way but discovered he could not until he became lean again from hunger (*Ecclesiastes Rabbah* 5:14).[32] Moreover, the sages had learned from Scripture that everything in this world belongs to the Lord. This the psalmist proclaimed boldly: "The earth is the LORD's, and everything in it" (Ps 24:1 NIV). In light of the fact that a person enters and departs the world stripped of material possessions, while one walks upon this earth one merely functions as a steward and not the owner of one's property. Wisdom dictates then that we ought to manage our wealth in a way that pleases God.

Proverbs 19:17 also caught the attention of the sages: "He who is kind to the poor lends to the LORD, and he will reward him for what he has done." This verse contains the necessary ingredients for the concept of laying up treasures in heaven. Like Isa 57:15, 58:6–11, and Ps 34:18, this proverb establishes God's close identification with the poor. To be gracious to the poor is to lend to God. Will God repay the kindness? By all means! God will reward those who act mercifully and charitably to the poor. This, in essence, constitutes laying up treasures in heaven.

The concept of laying up treasures in heaven is expressed in pre-Christian literature. For example, Tob 4:8–9 reads: "If you have many possessions, make your gift from them in proportion; if a few, do not be afraid to give according to the little you have. So you will be laying up a good treasure for yourself against the day of necessity." Rabbinic literature contains a wonderful story about laying up treasures in heaven. In the first century C.E., Helena, Queen of Adiabene in northern Mesopotamia, and her son, Izates, converted to Judaism. At a time of famine in Judea, this royal family purchased grain from Alexandria and dried figs from Cyprus, and sent large sums of money to Jerusalem to relieve the poor. Apparently this is the famine that Luke mentions in Acts 11:27–30, that occurred during the reign of Claudius (41–54 C.E.). The famine devastated the entire country in 46 C.E. In the rabbinic version of the story Monobazus, King of Adiabene, the brother of Izates and son of Helena, is singled out as the hero. According to the rabbis, an argument ensued when relatives learned about the great sums of money the king had spent to feed the starving inhabitants of Jerusalem. His response to his charitably-

---

[32] Translated by Abraham Cohen, *Midrash Rabbah* (13 vols.; London: Soncino, 1939), 8:154.

challenged relatives was: "My fathers hoarded their treasures in store houses here on earth, but I am depositing them in store houses in heaven" (*t. Pe'ah* 4:18).[33] The fame of the royal family of Adiabene endures even in our day. In 1863 the French archaeologist F. de Saulcy excavated a majestic tomb in East Jerusalem. The tomb's grandeur suggested to him that it may have belonged to the kings of Judah, hence its name, Tomb of the Kings. Later investigation revealed, however, that this tomb belonged to Queen Helena, whose bones had been buried in Jerusalem (Josephus, *Ant.* 20:92–96).

In addition to the Hebraism in Matt 6:1, Jesus' message seems to contain a second one, namely the antithetical phrases "good eye" and "bad eye" in 6:22–23. The adjectives in Greek are *haplous* and *poneros* respectively. The meaning of *poneros* is "bad or evil," but *haplous* can mean, "sound, simple, single-minded, or sincere." In light of the context and the pairing with bad eye, I think that *haplous* should be translated dynamically as "good," as opposed to "sound, simple, single-minded, or sincere." Translating *ophthalmos haplous* as "good eye" yields a Hebrew idiom found in ancient literature, including the Bible. Proverbs 22:9 literally reads: "A good eye will be blessed, because it has given of its bread to the poor." Even today in Israel, when someone knocks on the door and solicits a donation for a charitable cause, the request is usually *ten be-ayin tovah,* which means, "give with a good eye." In a rabbinic saying from the Mishnah, describing the four types of people who give alms, the phrase "bad eye" describes two of the four types (*Avot* 5:16).[34]

In another way of speaking about almsgiving, Rabbi Leazar links Ps 17:15 to 2 Chr 7:14 because of the common word "face" in both verses. In the prayer of David we read, "As for me, I shall behold your face by righteousness" (Ps 17:15). Consider the following teaching.

> Rabbi Lazarus taught: "Three actions cancel out a harsh decree [of punishment from heaven.] These are, prayer, righteousness [i.e., charity or almsgiving] and repentance. All three are mentioned in one verse (2 Chr 7:14), 'if my people who are called by my name will humble themselves, and pray . . .' This refers to prayer! '. . . and seek my face,' This refers to righteousness [i.e., charity or almsgiving], which is further proven by Ps 17:15, where it is

---

[33] The rabbinic version is well attested in early Tannaitic sources.

[34] *Avot* is often referred to as the "Ethics of the Fathers." It is an important portion of the Mishnah and is found in its entirety and discussed in Chapter 7 below. In footnotes and bibliography it is the common practice to use the shorter, Hebrew name. It should not be confused with *Avot de Rabbi Nathan,* which is a longer work and part of a later corpus of works known as Midrash, which I discuss in Chapter 6 below.

said, 'As for me, I shall behold your face in righteousness [i.e., almsgiving].' Finally the words, '. . . and turn from their wicked ways,' refers to repentance [i.e., fasting]! If an individual will do all three, the promise in Scripture is, 'then I will hear from heaven, and will forgive their sin and heal their land' (2 Chr 7:14)."[35]

Because Rabbi Leazar understands righteousness as almsgiving, seeking the face of God is then accomplished by giving financial assistance to the needy. The Chronicler exhorts the people to seek God's face, whereas the psalmist informs them how they can behold God's face. In other words, Rabbi Leazar interprets Ps 17:15 as a clue to implementing the imperative to seek God's face. How does one seek God's face or behold his face? Through righteousness (*tzedakah*), or almsgiving!

PRAYER IN THE SERMON ON THE MOUNT

Let us return to Matt 6:5–8 to talk more about prayer in light of ancient Jewish sources. In verse 7, Jesus instructs his audience not to ramble on pointlessly when praying. Thinking that verbosity motivated the gods to act, pagans vainly repeated their petitions.[36] The substance and content of prayer is important. One must not pray for trifling concerns. Like Jesus, the apocryphal book of Sirach (Hebrew: *Ben Sira*), taught that one should pray a short prayer without vain repetitions.[37] Yigal Yadin, the famous Israeli archaeologist who excavated Masada and whose father played the key role in the acquisition of the Dead Sea Scrolls for the State of Israel, published a remarkable fragment from the Hebrew version of Ben Sira that was discovered at Masada. The discovery of the Hebrew text identifies the original language of Ben Sira as being Hebrew. I believe, along with a number of other scholars, that the gospels are derived from a source of Hebrew sayings of Jesus, therefore, the discovery of the Hebrew version of Ben Sira makes the parallel that much more meaningful. Like Ben Sira, Jesus taught his disciples not to be repetitive in prayer!

---

[35] See *y. Ta'anit* 65b, ch. 2, Hal. 1 and the parallel in *Genesis Rabbah* 44:12. Compare the comments of Chanoch Albeck, *Midrash Bereshit Rabbah* (3 vols.; Jerusalem: Wahrmann Books, 1965), 1:434 (Hebrew).

[36] For a fair assessment of pagan prayer, see M. Eugene Boring, Klaus Berger, and Carston Colpe, *Hellenistic Commentary to the New Testament* (Nashville: Abingdon, 1995), 61–62.

[37] Sirach (Ben Sira) 7:14: "Do not . . . repeat yourself in prayer." It is likely that Jesus would have known this work, written in Hebrew about 180 B.C.E. and translated into Greek in 132 B.C.E. Ben Sira is even quoted by the rabbis, and some of them may have considered the text inspired like Scripture.

In their commentaries on the Torah the rabbis also discuss the proper length of a prayer. In a rabbinic passage from an early commentary on Exodus, the discussion revolves around two cases of prayer of unusual duration, one brief and the other long.[38] It once happened that an advanced student stood up and read his prayers in an abbreviated form in the presence of Rabbi Eliezer. The student's peers complained to Rabbi Eliezer and nicknamed him *talmid hacham katsran hu,* which rhymes in Hebrew and means, "the advanced student who is a shortcutter." In defense of the shortcutter, Rabbi Eliezer pointed out that he did not make his prayer shorter than Moses' prayer, who prayed on behalf of Miriam, "Oh God, heal her!" (Num 12:13).

This incident repeated itself in nearly identical manner, except this time an advanced student read his prayers in a lengthened form before Rabbi Eliezer. His peers complained to Rabbi Eliezer and nicknamed him, *talmid hacham maarachan hu,* which rhymes in Hebrew and means, "the advanced student who is a lengthener." Once again, in defense of the student, Rabbi Eliezer appealed to the example of Moses when he fell down before the Lord for forty days (Deut 9:25), presumably in prayer. This story throws light on Rabbi Eliezer's instructive saying about prayer, "There is a time to be brief and a time to be lengthy!"

Early in the intertestamental period a group called the Hasidim emerged. The Hasidim were people of prayer. They prescribed directing the heart toward God not simply at the moment of prayer, but an hour before actually praying. While in prayer the Hasidim kept their hearts fixed on God. Nothing was allowed to interrupt this spiritual union. In fact, according to their teachings in the Mishnah, "Even if the king greets a man he may not return the greeting; and even if a snake were wrapped around his ankle, he may not interrupt his prayer" (*m. Berakhot* 5:1). Many insights into prayer can be gained by learning the life of piety lived by these Hasidim.

The Hasidim were very popular among the people and had a reputation for fantastic results when they prayed. For example, Rabbi Chanina ben Dosa would pray over the sick and say, "This one will live," or "This one will die." The people asked him how he knew. He replied, "If my prayer is fluent in my mouth, I know it has been accepted; and if not, I know it has been rejected." (*m. Berakhot* 5:5) Professor Shmuel Safrai has done pioneering scholarship and convincingly argues that of all the groups active in Israel at the close of the Second Temple Period, Jesus had more in

---

[38] See Jacob Lauterbach, trans., *Mekhilta Derabbi Ishmael* (3 vols.; Philadelphia: Jewish Publication Society, 1976), 2:91. This is probably Rabbi Eliezer ben Hyrcanus who is also called Rabbi Eliezer the Great (ca. 90 C.E.).

common with the Hasidim than any other.[39] They stood near the edge, but within the pale, of Pharisaism.[40]

From this brief survey of ancient sources, we can see that Jesus' teaching on prayer was in harmony with the teachings of other Jewish teachers of the period. Moreover, Jesus' teachings on this subject constitute only a tiny part of a larger discussion. In other words, viewed against the greater canvas of Jewish teachings on prayer, Jesus' teachings represent merely a glimpse of the overall picture.[41] As inspiring and powerful as Jesus' discourse is, it should not be considered in isolation from all other contemporary sources. His teaching must be integrated into the bigger picture in order for us to identify its more subtle aspects and appreciate where they converge with and diverge from principal streams of ancient Jewish thought on the subject.

FASTING IS REPENTANCE

Already we have seen that in Rabbi Leazar's interpretation of 2 Chr 7:14, repentance is a substitute for fasting. He states that prayer, righteousness (almsgiving), and repentance (fasting) can nullify a harsh decree from heaven. The close link between fasting and repentance finds expression in the book of Jonah, where fasting plays an important role in turning the Ninevites from their wicked ways (Jonah 3:5). Through fasting, or inflicting the body with hunger, people become acutely aware of their frailty. It produces an inner attitude of humility, which is pleasing to God, and which in the end should improve conduct (Jonah 3:10; cf. Isa 58).

Human nature, however, does not incline itself toward humility. It would rather exploit fasting as an opportunity to showcase piety. In Jesus' day this could be done because, when public fasts were called, certain aspects of daily grooming, such as bathing oneself and applying oil to the body, were neglected as an outward sign of repentance. Jesus seems to have held an opinion that contradicted another that became the prevailing view of the Mishnah. For Jesus, inner heart-felt contrition, which fasting helps

---

[39] Shmuel Safrai, "Teaching of Pietists in Mishnaic Literature," *JJS* 16 (1965): 15–33.

[40] The Hasidim were the forerunners of the Pharisees. The term *Hasidim* continued to be used even after the rise of the Pharisees. The deep spirituality of the Pharisees, who would be referred to as Hasidim in historical sources, can be seen in their acts of compassion and their prayers. See Adolf Büchler, *Types of Jewish-Palestinian Piety from 70 B.C.E. to 70 C.E.* (London: Jews' College, 1922).

[41] See my book, *Jewish Background*. On Jewish views of prayer, see Hayim Donin, *To Pray as a Jew: A Guide to the Prayer Book and the Synagogue Service* (New York: Basic Books, 1980).

accentuate, has little in common with attracting attention to oneself through external symbols of piety. Although symbols may prove helpful in some ways, they risk jeopardizing the true spiritual essence of fasting and repentance.

> When you fast, do not look somber as the hypocrites do, for they disfigure their faces to show men they are fasting. I tell you the truth, they have received their reward in full. But when you fast, put oil on your head and wash your face, so that it will not be obvious to men that you are fasting, but only to your Father, who is unseen; and your Father, who sees what is done in secret, will reward you. (Matt 6:16–18 NIV)

Much could be said about repentance in the faith and piety of early rabbinic Judaism that would provide a backdrop against which to view Jesus' teachings. Space will allow us to address only two dimensions of this fascinating subject: genuine repentance and divine compassion.

The rabbis never tire of acclaiming the power of repentance. Rabbi Simon states: "When a man shoots an arrow, how far will it travel? Over one or two fields. The power of repentance is so great, however, that it reaches the throne of glory!" In a similar vein, Rabbi Yose comments: "God has declared, 'Make for me an opening as an eye of a needle, and I will open it for you so wide, that armies of soldiers with heavy equipment can enter through it'" (*Pesik. Rab Kah.* 5:6; 24:12).[42] What these two rabbis have driven home is that repentance has an explosive impact upon God; God is highly sensitive to repentance. He responds vigorously to repentance even at the slightest hint of it, even if a person has committed terrible sins. For example, King Manasseh in the Bible is perhaps the most wicked man in the history of the Judean monarchy (2 Kgs 21:1–18), but God forgives him when he repents (2 Chr 33:10–17). In a delightful story from the Jerusalem Talmud, against the unanimous opinion of the ministering angels, who use their wiles to keep King Manasseh's cry of repentance out of the heavenly court, God rips a hole through the throne of glory in order to make a way for Manasseh's prayer to reach him (*y. Sanhedrin,* Chapter 10 Halakhah 2, 37b).[43] Jesus also captures God's merciful character in his parable of the Prodigal Son (Luke 15:11–32).[44] The moment the father sees his sorry son walking in the distance, he rushes to welcome him. If anything will move God to action, it is repentance; He just cannot resist it.

---

[42] William Braude and Israel Kapstein, trans., *Pesikta de-Rab Kahana* (Philadelphia: Jewish Publication Society, 1975), 98, 378. See Matt 19:24; Mark 10:25; Luke 18:25.

[43] See also *Pesik. Rab Kah.* 24:11, in Braude and Kapstein, *Pesikta,* 376.

[44] See Young, *The Parables,* 130–57.

ROSH HASHANAH AND THE THREE PILLARS

There is one other place in the literature, namely in discussions of Rosh Hashanah, where we find these three pillars of Jewish piety standing together. Rosh Hashanah is the Jewish New Year and marks the beginning of the Ten Days of Awe leading up to Yom Kippur, or the Day of Atonement. In preparation for Yom Kippur, when God opens the books of heaven and inscribes an official, annual account of each man's and woman's conduct, ten days are designated for reflection, soul-searching, and reconciliation with anyone a person has offended. Thus the Ten Days of Awe require careful introspection, personal inventory, and active efforts toward genuine reconciliation with others. The Almighty weighs each person's actions in the balance. One of the prayers of the liturgy on Rosh Hashanah states that almsgiving, prayer, and fasting are able to avert an evil decree (*Machazor Rinat Yisrael,* for Rosh Hashanah).[45]

FORGIVENESS AND RECONCILIATION IN RELATIONSHIPS

Another more, complex dimension of repentance involves restoring inter-personal relationships in the wake of some offense by one person against another. If a person has offended God, repentance and forgiveness can be achieved without undue complication. When one person has offended another person, however, rectifying the situation becomes more involved. Rabbi Leazar illustrates it in this manner:

> When a person insults his or her neighbor in public, and later seeks to apologize, the insulted one says, "You insulted me in public, but now you apologize in private! Go! Bring the very people before whom you insulted me, and I will accept your apology!" The Holy One blessed be he does not act in such a manner. When a man curses and reviles him in the market place, the Holy One says to the offender, "Repent in private, and I will accept your apology." (*Pesik. Rab Kah.* 24:12)[46]

Forgiving and seeking the forgiveness of one's neighbor play a crucial role in the process of repentance. This connection may be easily seen in Jewish teachings about the proper preparation of a person's heart in anticipation

---

[45] Shlomo Tal, ed., *Machazor Rinat Yisrael* (Jerusalem: Yad Shapira, 1984), 229. See also Ernst D. Goldschmidt, *Machazor Leyamim Noraim* (New York: Leo Baeck Institute, 1970), 171.

[46] See Braude and Kapstein, *Pesikta,* 378.

of Yom Kippur. During the ten days before the awe-inspiring Day of Atonement, pious Jews will seek out those whom they have wronged, and they also will be sought out by those who have wronged them. Without asking for and receiving forgiveness from one's neighbor, repentance remains incomplete. Expounding upon Lev 16:30, Rabbi Eleazar ben Azaryah makes this point: "For sins that are between a person and God, the Day of Atonement atones, but for sins that are between a person and another individual, the Day of Atonement atones only if the person has sought reconciliation with the other individual" (*m. Yoma* 8:9). The rabbis, just like Jesus, stress forgiveness and reconciliation for building meaningful relationships with God and with one another.

A story in the Babylonian Talmud echoes Rabbi Eleazar ben Azaryah's emphasis. Once Rabbi Eleazar came from the house of his teacher. Riding home on a donkey along the shore of the lake and feeling good about the fact that he had studied much Torah, he encountered a grotesque man. Rabbi Eleazar exclaimed, "How ugly you are! Is everyone in your town as ugly as you?" To that the man replied, "Go to the craftsman who made me and tell him how ugly is this vessel which you have made!" Realizing that he had sinned, he descended from the donkey, bowed low before the man, and begged his forgiveness. The man, however, insisted that Rabbi Eleazar tell his maker what he thought of his work. The man went his way with the rabbi following close behind. Upon entering the town, Rabbi Eleazar was greeted by the people with respect. Hearing these greetings, the man exclaimed, "May there never be more teachers like this one in Israel." Shocked, the people asked why, and the man explained what had happened. Finally, at the pleading of the townspeople, the man forgave Rabbi Eleazar. This story is instructive because in it Rabbi Eleazar recognized that he had sinned chiefly against the exceedingly ugly man. Accordingly, he sought forgiveness from the man and followed him until the man agreed to pardon him. Incidentally, after being forgiven, Rabbi Eleazar went to the House of Study (Hebrew: *Bet [Beit] Midrash*) and preached on the virtue of being able to yield like a reed (*b. Ta'anit* 20a–b; *Avot R. Nat.*, ver. A, ch. 41).[47]

Jesus also stresses the need for interpersonal reconciliation in his Sermon on the Mount and elsewhere. In Matt 5:23–24 we read: "If therefore you are presenting your offering at the altar, and there remember that your brother or sister has something against you, leave your offering there before the altar, and go your way; first be reconciled to your brother or sister, and then come and present your offering." Likewise, in the Lord's Prayer Jesus instructs the disciples to pray: "Forgive us our debts, as we also have forgiven our

---

[47] See also Young, *Jesus the Jewish Theologian*, 163–70.

debtors." The parable of the unforgiving servant (Matt 18:23–34) demonstrates the gravity of begging forgiveness for our enormous debt to God but
refusing to forgive fellow human beings their small debts. We want God to
be compassionate and forgiving to us, but we are reluctant to show the same
compassion toward others. Sadly, Christianity has often tamed the force of
Jesus' demands for reconciliation. The Sermon on the Mount teaches that
divine forgiveness will not be experienced *unless* reconciliation between individuals has been achieved.

Receiving the Kingdom of Heaven

Rabbi Joshua the son of Korcha asks, "Why does the *Shema* 'Hear, O Israel, the LORD our God is one' come before the recitation of 'If you shall diligently hearken to . . .' in the daily liturgy of prayer? First one must receive the kingdom of heaven and then one may receive the yoke of the commandments."

m. Berakhot 2:2

Rabbis Had No Need for Lexicons or Concordances

There is no evidence that the Rabbis prepared special lexica of the Bible;
they had no need of them. The entire rabbinic literature bears testimony to
the fact that the Rabbis knew the Bible by heart. Jerome testifies that the
Palestinian Jews of the fourth century were able to recite the Pentateuch
and the Prophets by heart. The Jewish sages could well manipulate their explanations without the help of special vocabularies of the Bible.

Saul Lieberman, *Hellenism in Jewish Palestine* (New York:
Jewish Theological Seminary, 1962), 52.

Master Teachers and Their Disciples

In first-century Jewish society, Torah shared center stage with Jerusalem. In the countryside, away from the activities of the Temple in Jerusalem, the synagogue and *bet midrash* ("house of study") emerged to play lead roles in the religious lives of the people. In the synagogue Torah was read and expounded, and in the *bet midrash* it was memorized and studied. These two institutions helped spawn a Torah-centric culture in first-century Israel.

Jesus taught his followers to "Go into all the world and make disciples" (Matt 28:19).[1] The teaching in the *Ethics of the Fathers* similarly gives top priority to the command to "raise up many disciples" (*Avot* 1:1). For disciples to be made, there is first a need for master teachers. Hillel (flourished from 20 B.C.E. to 10 C.E.) is said to have had seventy disciples. The least of them was Yochanan ben Zakhai (flourished from 50–80 C.E.), who raised up five main disciples. Rabbi Akiva (flourished from 100–130 C.E.) also raised up five disciples, but is described as having thousands who followed him to learn Torah. Jesus raised up twelve disciples and also had crowds of followers who listened to his words. Instead of writing a book he established his teachings in the Jewish oral method of preserving tradition. After all, the ancient rabbis of the Jewish community not only studied the Written Torah, but also utilized a memorized Torah which contained a commentary and explanation of the written word. This life application code of conduct was passed down by memory from master teacher to disciple, from one generation to the next, from Mount Sinai in the desert to the living room in the home.[2] Jesus developed a mentoring relationship with his disciples, who learned his teachings by heart and followed his example as apprentices. Jesus' teaching techniques have deep roots in the rich soils of Jewish education and Torah training.

---

[1] Note that the Great Commission focuses on obeying the commandments. Study the whole verse: "Therefore go and make disciples of all nations, baptizing them in the name of the Father and of the Son and of the Holy Spirit, and teaching them to obey everything I have commanded you. And surely I am with you always, to the very end of the age" (Matt 28:19–20 NIV).

[2] For more on the Oral Torah, see Chapter 6 below.

MENTORING WITH PURPOSE, LEARNING WITH THE HEART

The master-disciple model was extremely effective in late Second Temple and early rabbinic Judaism. The word for "disciple" in Hebrew is *talmid* (plural: *talmidim*). It really means "learner," one who is open to change and is actively seeking to learn how to live life to its fullest potential in the kingdom of heaven. In rabbinic literature we often see the phrase *talmid chakham,* referring to a "student or learner of the sage" (*chakham*).[3] In the Gospels, the Hebrew *talmid* is the equivalent of the Greek *mathētēs*. The base of this ancient Greek word can be seen in the English word "mathematics." To translate *mathētēs* into Latin, Jerome used *discipulus*. In Latin, *disco* means "to study," and from this root comes our English word "disciple."

When we read the word "disciple" in the Synoptic tradition—found in the first three gospels of the New Testament: Matthew, Mark, and Luke—we are dealing with the ancient world of late Second Temple period Judaism, and in that world *talmidim* clung to their teacher, whom they called "rabbi" (pronounced ra-beé), "my master teacher of great learning." The sage was known as one who could answer a question in any area because he had complete knowledge of the Bible, as well as the Oral Torah. The disciple was known as one who could answer any question relating to his specific area of study in the oral tradition: "a disciple is an individual who when asked a question of religious law related to his studies is able to answer it" (*b. Ta'anit* 10b). So while the sage had achieved a mastery understanding of all aspects of Jewish teachings, the disciple could interact with questions connected to his research.

The disciple is willing to endure hardship for his learning experience. Jesus' disciples speak about their commitment: they leave families and businesses in order to follow Jesus (Matt 19:27; Mark 10:28; Luke 18:28). In rabbinic literature the disciples of the sages neglect their business and sacrifice much to acquire Torah learning. The disciple is expected to serve his master teacher in caring for personal needs. By serving the master the disciple learns how to conduct his affairs in everyday life situations. He listens to his master's teaching while doing menial chores to assist his mentor. Because a disciple should have broad knowledge, he would usually study with one rabbi for a number of years and then go study under another sage. The master teacher was a mentor whose purpose was to raise up disciples who would not only memorize his teachings but also live out the teachings in

---

[3] This term *talmid chakham* is often misunderstood in Modern Hebrew, as a "wise disciple." Originally it referred to a learner of the sages or wise teachers.

practical ways. The halakhah describes how a disciple walks.[4] As we have seen, Torah learning is evidenced in behavior and a rich spiritual life. The disciple walks with God by living out in practice the teaching of his rabbi.

Jesus conducted his public ministry between approximately 27 and 30 C.E. At first, he centered his activities in the Galilee around Capernaum, and apparently moved around as a miracle worker and teacher, but without a following of disciples. At some point in time Jesus began inviting young people to become his disciples. Not all were able to make the sacrifice this decision required. For example, the rich young ruler could not give up his material wealth to join Jesus' core group of students (Luke 18:23). He seems to have affinities in thinking with the Babylonian Talmud, which warns that whoever engages in building becomes impoverished.[5] Or, cautions Luke, what king in his right mind would go out to battle with 10,000 soldiers against an opponent with 20,000 (Luke 14:31)? The decision to become a disciple of Jesus required sacrifice, hardship, and risk.

The Mishnah also illustrates the sacrifice required to be a disciple. The rabbis reason that although a man's father brings him into the world, his teacher who instructs him in God's wisdom from Torah brings him into the world to come. Therefore, the ties between a teacher and student assume precedence over the ties between a father and son (*m. Baba Metzi'a* 2:11). The language of the period also reflects these values. Disciples were called *banim,* "sons" or "children." For example, Jesus refers to disciples of the Pharisees as "children" in Luke 11:19. He also warns that a person cannot be his disciple without first hating his or her parents, spouse, children, and siblings (Luke 14:26). The manner in which "hating" is used in this verse represents a Hebrew idiom that does not mean literally "to hate" but employs comparative language. Disciples are to be so committed to learning from their masters that love of parents is like hatred. In the Matthean parallel (Matt 10:37), the evangelist renders the idiom more dynamically as "love less." This saying of Jesus shares the same hierarchy of values as the mishnaic passage: family relationships take a secondary role to the relationship between a teacher and his disciple. In rabbinic literature the disciple is obligated to honor his master-teacher above his own father, even though the Ten Commandments teach honor of parents.[6] Perhaps considered dysfunctional by twenty-first-century standards, this sort of thinking prevailed in Jesus' day. To become a disciple of a respected teacher represented

---

[4] The root meaning of the word halakhah is the verb, *halakh,* which means "to walk." Halakhah refers to rules of conduct that guide a person's life. How can one obey the will of God in daily living?

[5] Compare *b. Yebamot* 63b and *b. Sotah* 11a.

[6] See *m. Keritot* 6:9 and *m. Baba Metzi'a* 2:11.

a great honor, so the family and community rallied to help a young man realize his aspiration.

THE ANCIENT CLASSROOM

Rabbinic literature records that rabbis taught while seated, and their
classrooms often were an orchard, vineyard, or portico of the Temple.[7] These
open-air classrooms provided subject material and excellent illustrations for
the lessons. For instance, Jesus' parable of the Net (Matt 13:47–50) may well
have been told along the shores of the Sea of Galilee while fishermen emp-
tied their nets. The parable of the Sower (Matt 13:3–9) may have been told
while a farmer was sowing seed. The illustration of the Tares among the
Wheat (Matt 13:24–30) may have been given while the farmers were burning the chaff. The intense heat of the fire under the sun in the Middle East
would drive home the point of Jesus' message. Luke 5:3 notes that Jesus sits
down in a boat to teach the people who assembled by the water's edge. In the
Sermon on the Mount, Jesus tells his audience to look at the birds of the air
and consider the lilies of the field (Matt 6:25–34). I suspect both were
readily visible when he made these remarks.

The process of asking and answering questions represents a basic way of
learning in ancient Judaism. A teaching session was not so tightly planned as a
modern university lecture. Instead, the master skillfully guided the direction of
the teaching by asking and answering questions. For example, Rabbi Eliezer
once remarked, "Repent one day before your death!" To which his disciples replied, "What man knows when he will die?" "All the more," Rabbi Eliezer declared, "let him repent today lest he die tomorrow, let him repent tomorrow
lest he die the day after, and so all of his days should be spent in repentance"
(*Avot R. Nat.*, vers. A, ch. 15).[8] The impression is that Rabbi Eliezer knew the
direction in which he was headed from the start of the lesson.

We have glimpses of this manner of interaction in the Gospels. For example, at the age of twelve Jesus strolls into the Temple precincts. When his
parents find him, he is "sitting in the midst of the teachers, both listening to
them, and asking them questions" (Luke 2:46). The next verse says that, "All
who heard him were amazed at his understanding and his answers," suggesting
that Jesus' questions are actually answers in the context of the conversation.
Toward the end of his life, while being interrogated by the chief priests, Jesus

---

[7] Compare the sitting posture of Jesus when he teaches (Matt 5:1; 26:55;
Luke 5:3).

[8] Also see parallels in *Avot R. Nat.*, vers. B, ch. 29; *Avot* 2:15; *b. Shabbat* 153a,
and *Ecclesiastes Rabbah* 9:8.

Circumcision of Jesus, Luke 2:21
(Wood engraving by Bernard A. Solomon)

answers, "If I tell you, you will not believe; and if I ask a question, you will not answer" (Luke 22:67–68). In other words, the priests are not willing to engage Jesus in a fair, even-handed professional conversation, so Jesus says very little.

TEACHING IN PARABLES

Parables are another feature the Synoptic tradition and rabbinic literature share. In Jewish thought, parables belong to a style of teaching known as *agadah*. Parables represent an agadic, or story-like, approach to theology. Because people enjoy the art of storytelling, parables are a highly effective tool for communicating subtle aspects of the biblical text or profound theological concepts.

The classical form of the parable, involving the king, father, landowner, tenant farmer, son, and/or servant, is found in only two bodies of writings: rabbinic literature and the New Testament.[9] The classical form of the parable does not appear in the texts recovered at Qumran. Moreover, parables do not appear in every part of the New Testament, but only in the first three Gospels. Because of the continuity between certain features of Pharisaic and rabbinic traditions, and the fact that the rabbis and Jesus regularly taught in parables, I think Jesus was not far removed from the overall movement of Pharisaism.

---

[9] See Young, *The Parables*, 3–38.

THE PHARISEES RECONCEIVED

Despite some of the harsh-sounding remarks Jesus directed at the Pharisees in the Gospels, his approach to Torah and their approach belonged to the same stream of Judaism. The Pharisees believed in angels, the resurrection of the dead, and the final great judgment of all humankind. Jesus affirmed these same three beliefs and, like the Pharisees, he adhered to the Oral Torah. Jesus' conduct never violated the Oral Torah as he interpreted it, and ample evidence from rabbinic literature indicates that many rabbis would support Jesus' approach, which stressed a foundation of loving God first and loving one's neighbor as oneself.

It is helpful to note something about the manner in which the word *Pharisee* appears in ancient literature. In rabbinic literature the term can merely designate a certain sect vis-à-vis another. In other words, the Pharisees may be mentioned in contrast to the Sadducees. The term may be used in a pejorative manner to connote moral shortcomings among the ranks of Jews in a given community. In the Mishnah the *makkot perushin*, or "blows of the Pharisees," are listed among the things that destroy the world (*m. Sotah* 3:4). This refers to the damage done by those who are corrupt but outwardly appear pious. These types are hypocrites, teaching the truth but living a lie. In the Babylonian Talmud, the Jewish King Alexander Yanai actually fights the Pharisees and brutally represses them. But when he is near death he offers this advice to his wife, "Do not fear those who are Pharisees, and those who are not Pharisees, but fear the hypocrites who pretend to be like Pharisees" (*b. Sotah* 22b). He esteems the true Pharisees, who live their lives according to the best of their teachings. When Pharisees, or those who identify with them, refer to themselves as Pharisees, their intention usually is to offer a critical self-examination. Outside of the Gospels and the writings of the Jewish historian, Josephus (37–ca. 100 C.E.), the word carries a neutral connotation. If anything, in these texts, the Pharisees are spiritual leaders, and possess outstanding character.

In the Gospels the picture becomes more complicated because the writing and editing process involved several stages or layers. Over time, the readers of the Gospels changed, and a change in audience impacts interpretation. In the first level of development, Jesus criticizes the hypocritical practices of some spiritual leaders with whom he identifies. "Do what they teach," Jesus declares (Matt 23:1–2). In the final stage, however, Christian readers view the text from outside the Jewish community of the first century: Jesus is leading the Christian community in a debate against his enemies, the Pharisees, who represent the Jewish community. Jesus is no longer an insider seeking reform, but the leader of a new, separate religion. In the Synoptic Gospels, where Jesus criticizes the Pharisees, we must be careful not to make the mistake of seeing

Jesus as an outsider. Rather, he offers heart-felt criticism of a movement with which he identifies. Like the passage from the Mishnah, Jesus' critique of the Pharisees reflects the self-critical tendencies of the Pharisaic movement itself.

Modern Christians selectively read the Gospels from the perspective of traditional church teachings. Seldom does anyone observe that some Pharisees warn Jesus of a death plot to save his life (Luke 13:31). Few recognize that the leader of the Pharisees, Gamaliel, argues the apostles' case against the Sadducean priests led by Caiaphas (Acts 5:34–39). Rabban Gamaliel saves the leaders of the church in these court proceedings. In fact, Acts 5:26 records that when the soldiers attempt to arrest the apostles, they are warned not to use force because the people, many of whom are Pharisees, will stone the soldiers for apprehending the apostles.

Such examples demonstrate that the Pharisees are not always portrayed in a negative manner in the New Testament. Matthew's gospel depicts Jesus teaching followers to live by the spiritual message of the Pharisees (Matt 23:1–2). This text has far-reaching implications. Jesus did not teach this about any other group of spiritual leaders, at least no evidence suggests that he supported the spiritual teachings of other groups as he did the scribes and Pharisees who sat on Moses' seat. However, not all the Pharisees lived up to their teachings, so while one may observe and practice what they teach, one should not follow the example of those who fail to practice what they preach.

The painful historical rift that the church and synagogue underwent in the first century has impacted the way Christians read the Gospels and the way they relate to the Jewish people. This is problematic because later Christians stood as outsiders, whereas Jesus was an insider. A Roman Catholic bishop may reprove priests in his order—this is constructive criticism—but a leader of a Protestant denomination who attacks those priests quickly develops into religious bigotry. I, as a Christian, should offer constructive criticism of my church, but if I criticize the local synagogue, that represents an entirely different and unacceptable situation. Jesus was a Jewish leader, addressing a Jewish audience, seeking reform and spiritual revitalization of Judaism. The change of audience over time was decisive. The church has at times read the Gospels as if Jesus were a Christian pastor attacking the leaders of the synagogue.

WHAT JESUS THOUGHT OF THE PHARISEES

Jesus says, "The scribes and the Pharisees sit on Moses' seat; therefore all that they say to you, do and obey, but do not do according to their actions; for they say, and do not do" (Matt 23:2–3). Moses' seats actually existed in Jesus' day. They could be found in synagogues, and apparently were reserved for a distinguished scholar who read and expounded Scripture before a congregation. From the ruins of a late third-century synagogue in Chorazin, archaeologists recovered a *cathedra de-Moshe,* as the name appears in rabbinic literature. It is quite significant that Jesus recognizes the authority of the Pharisees to teach Torah, and teaches his own disciples to "do and obey" all that the Pharisees teach.

Jesus' remark about the Pharisees illustrates that the problem is not with their teaching or approach to Torah, but with their ability to practice what they preach. His mention of what they teach surely must include their Oral Tradition. Ben Azzai, who lived about a century after Jesus, faced the same challenge. A bachelor himself, he once declared regarding any man who does not marry, "It is as if he has shed blood and diminished the Divine Presence!" Of course, his audience did not allow him to get away with that. They immediately spoke up, "Some preach well and put their message into good practice. Others put their message into good practice, but preach poorly. But you! You preach well, but put your message into poor practice!" (*b. Yebamot* 63b).[10] Ben Azzai's dilemma helps us put Matt 23 into perspective. Although we cannot know the tone of Jesus' voice and the expression of his face when he criticized the Pharisees, I suspect that those in the audience, including Pharisees, heard some irony and hyperbole in his words. Perhaps they even chuckled. They were being challenged by an insider to pursue needed reforms.

Later in Matt 23, a list of criticisms appears, in particular seven "woes" directed against the Pharisees. As I have suggested, these criticisms represent an ongoing in-house discussion. In the Jerusalem Talmud, the rabbis enumerate seven types of Pharisees (*y. Berakhot,* Chapter 9, Halakhah 5, 60a).[11] Of the seven, only one type serves as a positive role model. The remaining six serve as negative examples, the type of people the rabbis sought to pressure into striving for a higher standard of piety. The positive type of Pharisee is described as a Pharisee of love. Like Abraham (Gen 15:6; Jas 2:23), the Pharisee of love is beloved as a friend of God.

SIMILARITIES BETWEEN THE RABBIS' AND JESUS' DISCIPLES

Much insight can be gained by studying the master-disciple relationship in both the Gospels and rabbinic literature. As previously mentioned, the

---

[10] See parallels in *t. Yebamot* 8:4 and *Genesis Rabbah* 34:14. Compare also Strack and Billerbeck, *Kommentar zum Neuen Testament,* 1:910–11.

[11] Though most Christians never consider the background of the Apostle Paul, in many ways he is a Pharisee of love. See my book, *Paul the Jewish Theologian* (Peabody, Mass.: Hendrickson, 1997), 106–13.

rabbis were the spiritual heirs of the Pharisees. At least six similarities can be seen in the way rabbis mentored their disciples and Jesus taught his core group. First, Jesus gave a radical call to the mentoring relationship for select disciples. He summoned them by saying, "Come follow me" (Matt 4:19; 8:22; Mark 1:17; 2:4; Luke 5:27; etc.) Second, he demanded that they must conduct themselves like a disciple who "hears these words of mine and does them" (see Matt 7:24; Luke 6:47). which probably referred to memorizing his teachings by heart. Jesus' teachings were structured to encourage memorization. For instance, memory aids can be detected in the Lord's Prayer (Matt 6:9–15; Luke 11:2–4), the Beatitudes (Matt 5:2b–12; Luke 6:20b–26), and many parables. Third, the disciples learned by observation. They followed the example of Jesus and were expected to conduct themselves like their master (Matt 16:24–28; Mark 8:34–9:1; Luke 9:23–27). Fourth, they learned by working alongside Jesus, serving in an apprenticeship for active ministry that required them to "hear and obey" (see Matt 10:1–4; Mark 3:13–19). Fifth, the disciples of Jesus were sent on an assignment where they worked alone and reported back to Jesus what they had done (Matt 10:5–25; Luke 10:1–20). Sixth, they were accountable to their master's supervision. Jesus evaluated their work and encouraged them to achieve a more meaningful inner spiritual life by seeking first the kingdom of heaven (Matt 6:33).

Torah Learning Is Required for All

Every person in Israel is obligated to be engaged in Torah learning, whether one is poor or wealthy, whether one is whole in body or afflicted with suffering, whether one is young or one is old and feeble, even a poor person who is supported by charity and goes from door to door seeking benevolence, even the man supporting his wife and children—everyone is required to find a set time during the day and the night to study Torah, as it was said, "you shall go over it, again and again, day and night" (Joshua 1:8).

Moses Maimonides, *Mishnah Torah, Hilkot Talmud Torah* 1:8

The Essence of Judaism

Two thousand years ago, when a non-Jew asked Hillel, the leading Rabbi of his age, to define Judaism's essence, the sage could have responded with a long oration on Jewish thought and law, and an insistence that it would be blasphemous to reduce so profound a system to a brief essence. Indeed, his contemporary, Shammai, furiously drove away the questioner with a builder's rod. Hillel, however, responded to the man's challenge: "What is hateful to you, do not do to your neighbor: this is the whole Torah. The rest is commentary; now go and study"—a model statement that has defined Judaism's essence ever since.

> Rabbi Joseph Telushkin, *Jewish Wisdom: Ethical, Spiritual, and Historical Lessons from the Great Works and Thinkers* (New York: William Morrow and Company, Inc., 1994), xix–xx.

CHAPTER 3

Torah Is More Than Law

Almost all English translations of the Bible translate the Hebrew word *torah* as "law." Modern Western Christians often have, as a result, received a distorted perspective of Torah from uninformed preaching and Sunday school teachings. It is indeed a legal code with strict requirements, and in its most narrow sense, sometimes Torah can mean law. But "law" can also be a very misleading translation. To understand Torah strictly as law would be like translating the word *parent* as "disciplinarian." Such a translation produces an unfair characterization of what a parent truly is. Describing Torah only as law is similarly lacking.

The verb *yarah,* from which the noun *torah* comes, means "to shoot at a target with force and accuracy." It also means "revelation," and first and foremost refers to a revelation of the nature and character of God, and how to live life to its fullest measure in a way that is pleasing to God. It means to shoot and hit the target accurately based upon the revelation of God. That is the root meaning of the word, and it should not be forgotten when surveying the various nuances of Torah in Judaism. It is not a useless legal code by which no one could ever be expected to live. On the contrary, its teachings give greater meaning to every dimension of a person's life.

The five books of Moses may be called Torah. In Jewish thinking these five books hold a place of distinction in the canon because in them God communicates His tremendous revelation to Moses on Mount Sinai face to face (Exod 33:11; Deut 34:10). In Judaic thought, Moses receives not only the Written Torah but also its oral interpretation, or Oral Torah.[1] The prophets after Moses receive the word of the Lord in visions and dreams, but they do not speak to God face to face. Moreover, the subsequent writings of the canon can be viewed as layers of commentary on these five books of the Torah. Accordingly, in Jesus' day, the Jewish people paid special attention to

---

[1] For more on the Oral Torah, see Chapter 2 above. In Jesus' day it was forbidden to write the Oral Torah. After being preserved in an oral history in Jewish thought from the time of Moses on Mount Sinai, it was compiled in a book in about 200 C.E. called the Mishnah. See more on the Mishnah in Chapter 6 below.

memorizing, studying, explaining, and applying the Torah, because it revealed the true understanding of God and His character.

THE TORAH IS LIFE—HALAKHAH

Like the sages, Jesus faced the challenge of making the Written Torah
understandable, relevant, and doable through the Oral Torah. In some cases,
obscure or seemingly outdated aspects of the commandments given at
Mount Sinai were illuminated and explained through intense scrutiny of the
text itself (i.e., midrash). In other cases the commandments were made relevant by means of oral traditions handed down from one generation of sages
to another (i.e., mishnah; see above).[2] Typically, a combination of both approaches enabled the community to preserve, maintain, and practice the revealed will of God in Torah. All of this activity belonged to the realm of Oral
Torah.

Jesus teaches in the Sermon on the Mount, "It was said, 'Whoever divorces his wife, let him give her a certificate of dismissal,' but I say to you
that everyone who divorces his wife, except for the cause of unchastity"
(Matt 5:31–32). His remarks here represent an excellent example of halakhah. Jesus' comment on divorce belongs to a controversy that raged in the
first century. The controversy arose out of an ambiguous phrase found in
Deut 24:1: *ervat davar*. *The Brown-Driver-Briggs-Gesenius Hebrew and English Lexicon* translates this phrase as "*nakedness of a thing,* i.e., prob. *indecency, improper behavior.*"

Ancient Jewish scholars struggled with the precise meaning of *ervat
davar,* as modern Christian scholars do today. The KJV of Deut 24:1 reads:
"When a man hath taken a wife, and married her, and it come to pass that
she find no favour in his eyes, because he hath found some uncleanness
[*ervat davar*] in her: then let him write her a bill of divorcement, and give it
in her hand, and send her out of his house." The NIV reads essentially same,
except for its translation of *ervat davar,* which is rendered as "something
indecent."

The opinions of the Schools of Shammai (ca. 50 B.C.E.–30 C.E.) and
Hillel (active ca. 20 B.C.E.–10 C.E.) on the matter appear in the Mishnah
(*Gittin* 9:10). Shammai takes the more conservative position with marriage,
but embraces a more flexible position with the text. He reads *ervat davar* as if

---

[2] See Jonathan Schofer, *The Making of a Sage* (Madison: University of Wisconsin Press, 2005), 68, where Schofer observes, "This process of transmission is to
be replicated in every exchange of traditional learning—students receive from their
elders, and in their maturity they pass on what they know to new generations."

it were *devar ervah*, which suggests something unchaste about the woman. Hillel takes the more liberal position with marriage but embraces a more rigid reading of the text. For him, *ervat davar* means just what it says, something unseemly. Hillel's interpretation of Deut 24:1 treats ruining a meal as unseemly behavior and, therefore, recognizes poor cooking skills as possible grounds for divorce. In reality, he claims that incompatibility is sufficient cause for divorce, which is the approach taken in modern jurisprudence. Rabbi Akiva, who lived about a century after Hillel and Shammai, takes a position more liberal than Hillel's. Underscoring the wording, "When a man hath taken a wife . . . and it come to pass that she find no favour in his eyes," Rabbi Akiva accepts a husband finding a more attractive woman as grounds for divorce.[3]

Jesus' words in Matt 5:32 reflect the opinion of the School of Shammai. By saying, "except for the cause of unchastity," Jesus informs those listening to his teaching that he interprets *ervat davar* as some sort of unchaste act between a married woman and another man. In the heated discussion about Deut 24:1 and divorce in the first century, Jesus stands alongside Shammai at the more conservative end of the spectrum.

The rabbis tended to be realists, and chartered a humane and practical theological course. While they recognize incompatibility as a potential threat to the long-term happiness of a marriage, they champion marriage and the establishment of a family and a nurturing environment in the home. They take seriously the admonition of Gen 2:18, "It is not good for man to be alone." A man without a wife is half a man, who lives without joy, goodness, or blessing in his life (*b. Yebamot* 62b). The following delightful story reflects their values on the subject of marriage and family.

> A woman in Sidon had been married to her husband for ten years without giving birth for him a child. They came to Rabbi Simeon bar Yochai and requested to be divorced from one another.[4] He said to them, "I request from you, just as you have always shared a festive life together, so do not part from each other without some festivity." They took his advice. They celebrated a holiday, made

---

[3] Sometimes these teachings are interpreted to mean that Judaism, by allowing divorce, does not maintain family values. However, unlike modern pastors, the ancient rabbis had to serve as judges in divorce cases. On Jesus' teachings about divorce and remarriage, see Young, *Jesus the Jewish Theologian,* 113–17, and the excellent article by David Bivin, "'And' or 'in order to' Remarry," *Jerusalem Perspective* 50 (1996): 10–17. When translated correctly, Luke 16:18 does not make remarriage after divorce adultery. Jesus certainly would reject Rabbi Akiva's view; divorcing in order to marry another was an unacceptable use of the divorce and remarriage law.

[4] If a marriage did not produce children in ten years, it was customary for the couple to part, remarry someone else, and seek to raise children (*b. Yebamot* 64a).

a great feast and drank very freely. Feeling then in a good humor he said to her: "My daughter, pick out any article you want in my house and take it with you to your father's house." What did she do? When he was asleep [from drinking so much wine] she gave an order to her servants and handmaids to lift him up on the bed and take and carry him to her father's house. At midnight he awoke from his sleep, and when the effects of the wine passed from him he said: "My daughter, where am I?" She replied: "Did you not say to me last night, 'Take any article you like from my house and go to your father's house?' There is nothing in the world I care for more than you." They again went to Rabbi Simeon bar Yochai and he and prayed for them, and they became fertile. (*Song of Songs Rabbah* 1.4.2)[5]

JESUS' LOVE FOR TORAH

A passage from the Sermon on the Mount that has spawned considerable misunderstanding in Christian thinking through sermons and Bible lessons is Matt 5:17–19. The passage reads:

Do not think that I came to abolish the Law or the Prophets; I did not come to abolish, but to fulfill. For truly I say to you, until heaven and earth pass away, not the smallest letter or stroke shall pass away from the Law, until all is accomplished. Whoever then annuls one of the least of these commandments, and so teaches others, shall be called least in the kingdom of heaven; but whoever keeps and teaches them, he shall be called great in the kingdom of heaven. (NASB)[6]

I have heard this passage preached in sermons numerous times. Sadly, the thrust of these sermons too often has headed in directions far afield from Jesus' original aim. The explanation usually goes something like this: Jesus came to fulfill or satisfy the demands of the Law, and by doing so rendered it obsolete for those who profess faith in Christ. In other words, by fulfilling the Law, Jesus canceled it. This train of reasoning has always eluded me, and I suspect that, if I were to question those who hold this view, they too would flounder in their explanations. After all, in fulfilling the law and the prophets, Jesus could not also cancel them.

This approach finds favor because of a tendency in Christian theology throughout history to view everything negative as being authentically Jewish and opposed to true Christianity. In Christian theology the Law has often been viewed negatively and, therefore, as belonging to Judaism, whereas

---

[5] See Harry Freedman and Maurice Simon, eds., *Midrash Rabbah* (9 vols.; London: Soncino, 1951), 9:48–49.

[6] I have written about this passage in *Jesus the Jewish Theologian*, 264–69.

grace, something positive, belongs exclusively to Christianity. This simplistic paradigm can serve to make Christians feel good at the expense of Judaism, and represents a gross distortion of the truth. Both Torah and grace are good, both come from the God of Israel, and both stood firmly at the forefront of Jewish theology prior to flowing into and enriching Christian theology. There is grace in Law and Law in grace.

Jesus does not say that he intends to render the Law obsolete. Rather he seeks to strengthen it through proper interpretation and application. Professor David Flusser has pointed out that Paul makes a similar remark in Rom 3:31: "Do we then 'nullify' the Law through faith? . . . On the contrary, we 'establish' the Law." Jesus states, "Think not that I have come to abolish the law and the prophets; I have come . . . to fulfill them" (Matt 5:17). The Greek verbs *katargeō*, "cause to stand," and *histēmi*, "establish," which Paul uses here in Rom 3:31, are not the same Greek verbs used to translate what Jesus said originally in Hebrew in Matt 5:17. In the latter passage the two Greek verbs are *kataluō*, "cancel," and *plēroō*, "fulfill." I suspect that Christian commentators and preachers have not traditionally recognized that Jesus and Paul said very similar things because of the different wording of the Greek. In Hebrew, however, the words are the same. "To fulfill" the law means to interpret the message accurately and to live out the meaning of the text in practice.

In rabbinic literature we find similar language to express the same idea. For example, *Avot* 4:11 says, "Each individual who fulfills the Torah in the midst of poverty, shall in the end fulfill it in the midst of wealth. But each individual who cancels the Torah in the midst of wealth shall in the end cancel it in the midst of poverty." Here the word for "fulfill" is *kiyem,* and the word for "cancel" is *betel.* Only Mishnaic Hebrew, not biblical Hebrew, uses these verbs in this manner. Hence, what we have in Matt 5:17 and Rom 3:31 seems to reflect Hebrew as a living language of the first century.

In Matt 5:18–19 Jesus continues his discourse concerning his high view of Torah and his intention to safeguard its integrity through sound teaching. Here Jesus states that not one *yod* or *kotz* shall pass away from the Law. Being the smallest letter of the Hebrew alphabet, the *yod* resembles the dot of an English "i," and a *kotz* is a tiny ornamental stroke with which scribes adorn letters. In English, Jesus might have said that not one dot of an "i" will be taken from the Torah and the prophets.[7]

---

[7] After writing this, I discovered that Edgar J. Goodspeed translated Matt 5:18 with an English dynamic equivalent phrase, ". . . not one dotting of an *i* or the crossing of a *t* will be dropped from the Law. . . ." See *The Complete Bible: An American Translation* (Chicago: University of Chicago Press, 1951), 4.

Rabbinic literature includes a delightful story about a *yod* from the Law that was uprooted by King Solomon. Like all powerful kings in the ancient Middle East, he amassed horses, soldiers, gold, silver, and wives (1 Kgs 4:20–28; 9:15–28; 11:1–8). His efforts were simply an attempt to strengthen his country's military and economy. The numerous wives were a form of foreign policy. By marrying into the royal families of other kingdoms, Solomon was able to secure strategic alliances, both economic and defensive. As pragmatic as this may have been, Solomon's behavior did not impress the rabbis. They were embarrassed to read in the Bible that, conducting himself like a Gentile king, Solomon had completely ignored Deut 16:16–17, which specifically warns the king against such activity. Thus they told the following agadic story:

> Even if all the nations of the world gather together to uproot one word of the Torah, they would be powerless to accomplish it. How do we learn this? From Solomon because of his attempt at uprooting one letter of the Torah the accusation was brought against him. Who presented the accusation against him? . . . The letter yod of the word *yarbeh,* "he multiplied." Rabbi Simeon [ben Yochai] taught: The Book of Deuteronomy ascended and prostrated itself before the Holy One, blessed be He, saying to Him, "King of the Universe, Solomon has uprooted me and made of me an invalid document. After all, since a document out of which two or three letters are void is entirely invalid. King Solomon sought to uproot the letter yod out of me. It is written, 'He should not multiply (*lo yarbeh*) horses to himself' (Deut. 17:16), but he has multiplied horses to himself. It is written, 'Neither shall he multiply wives to himself' (Deut. 17:17), but he has multiplied wives to himself. It is written, 'Neither shall he greatly multiply to himself silver and gold' (Deut. 17:17), but he has multiplied silver and gold to himself." The Holy One, blessed be He, answered, "Go! Solomon will be canceled and a hundred like him, but not even a single yod that is in you shall ever be canceled (*Leviticus Rabbah* 19:2)."[8]

As in Jesus' declaration, no one should cancel even the smallest letter of the Torah, but should take care to interpret it properly. Matthew 5:18 further underscores the commitment Jesus had to teaching Scripture. Proper interpretation of the Torah is required to obey its teachings. After declaring that not even a *yod* or *kotz* will pass away from the Torah, Jesus warns,

---

[8] See Freedman and Simon, eds., *Midrash Rabbah,* 4:238–39, *Exodus Rabbah* 6:1, *Song of Songs Rabbah* 5:11, and *y. Sanhedrin,* ch. 2, Hal. 6, 10a. Compare the excellent critical edition, Mordecai Margulies, ed., *Midrash Vayikra Rabbah* (5 vols.; Jerusalem: Wahrmann, 1979), 2:220–21 (Hebrew). The Tanna Rabbi Simeon bar Yochai (ca. 115 C.E.) is named in the Jerusalem Talmud and the best texts of *Leviticus Rabbah.* On this rabbinic leader, see Elie Wiesel, *Sages and Dreamers: Biblical, Talmudic, and Hasidic Portraits and Legends* (New York: Summit Books, 1991), 299–311.

"Whoever then annuls one of the least of these commandments, and so teaches others, shall be called least in the kingdom of heaven; but whoever keeps and teaches them, he shall be called great in the kingdom of heaven" (Matt 5:19). The issue is the proper interpretation and implementation of Torah. In his Great Commission (Matt 28:19), Jesus not only raises up disciples but also teaches them to observe his commandments. In other words, this passage emphasizes the importance of the proper interpretation of Torah, as Jesus placed the teachings of Scripture on a firmer footing.

EXAMPLE FROM THE SERMON ON THE MOUNT: LIGHT AND HEAVY COMMANDMENTS

In Matt 5:19 Jesus makes a sophisticated allusion to a juxtaposition of two verses from the Torah, Deut 5:16 and 22:6–7. A similar sort of allusion is found in the Mishnah (*Avot* 2:1): "Be as meticulous in fulfilling a light commandment as a heavy commandment, because you do not know what type of reward will be given for which commandment." The sages categorize Deut 5:16, "Honor your father and mother," as a major, or heavy, commandment, whereas Deut 22:6–7, which allows taking offspring or eggs from a bird's nest but prohibits the taking of the mother bird, they classify as a minor, or light, commandment. Jesus most probably was familiar with this type of classification between the light and heavy commandments. The terminology of the "least" commandments (Matt 5:19) or the "weightier matters of the law" (Matt 23:23) are essentially the same terms used by the rabbis. Obviously, dishonoring one's father and mother represents a more serious offense than taking captive a mother bird along with her eggs or offspring. One may remove the eggs or take the young chicks but the mother must not see and feel anguish over the loss of her offspring. Nevertheless, through reading their biblical text midrashically, Jesus and the sages conclude that the minor commandment is as significant as the major commandment: Do not be least in the kingdom by canceling even the least of the commandments.

The reward promised in Deuteronomy for honoring one's father and mother is prolonged days and well being; the reward promised for releasing the mother bird is prolonged days and well being. According to the principles of midrash, the repeated promise of reward for both commandments indicates that the minor or lesser commandment is as significant as the major or heavy commandment. Hence the warning in the Mishnah, "Be as meticulous in fulfilling a light commandment as a heavy commandment," because both carry the same reward (*Avot* 4:1).

Tapping into this same complex of ideas, Jesus makes his point by means of a play on the Hebrew expression *mitzvah kalah*, "minor or light commandment." Whoever neglects a light commandment and teaches others to do so will be a lightweight in the redemptive movement Jesus is leading, but whoever carries out the light commandments and teaches others to do so, will be called a heavyweight in the kingdom of heaven. No one among the disciples of Jesus should even try to remove the dot of an "i" from the Torah, but should instead urge proper interpretation and application.

ANOTHER EXAMPLE: THOU SHALL NOT KILL

In Matt 5:21–22 we catch a glimpse of Jesus bending and stretching the biblical text according to principles of midrash, to teach his distinct approach to Torah. Another example of a major commandment, "You shall not kill," is listed as one of the Ten Commandments found in Exod 20:12. The phrase "Whoever kills shall be liable to judgment" stems from an ancient Jewish interpretation of Gen 9:6, where the first prohibition against murder is found in the Bible. In the ancient Aramaic translation of the Torah known as Targum Onkelos, Gen 9:6 reads: "Whoever sheds the blood of man—and this is confirmed by witnesses—is deemed guilty by the judges." In other words, whoever sheds blood shall be liable to judgment. Jesus sharpens the plain, literal meaning of Exod 20:12 by saying, "But I say to you that everyone who is angry with his brother shall be liable to judgment." As he did in Matt 5:19, Jesus compares murder (a major commandment) with anger at one's brother (a minor commandment). His linking together murder and anger stems from Deut 19:11 and midrashic comments upon that verse. For example, Rabbi Eleazar states, "He who hates his neighbor is considered a murderer, for it is said, 'But if any man hates his neighbor and lies in wait for him and attacks him and mortally wounds him so that he dies'" (Deut 19:11).[9] Rabbi Eleazar and Jesus understand this verse to suggest a sequence of escalating stages that culminate with murder. Hate leads to lying in wait, lying in wait leads to attacking, and attacking leads to mortally wounding.

Jesus approaches Torah in such a way that minor commandments are given the same attention as major commandments. He allows for no part of the Torah to be neglected in his distinct approach to interpreting it. He is an organic part of his Jewish socio-historical context.[10] We too often view Jesus in a historical vacuum with the result that we transpose our twenty-first-century Western values and concerns onto him. We tend to make him into a good Methodist, Catholic, Baptist, Anglican, Pentecostal, or whatever denominational orientation we may be. The historical Jesus remains a Jew. His

---

[9] Michael Higger, *Massekhtot Derekh Eretz* (2 vols.; New York: Moinester, 1935), 2:313; ET 2:117.

[10] See especially David Flusser, *Judaism and the Origins of Christianity* (Jerusalem: Magnes, 1988), 494–508.

faith and obedience to his Father in heaven had at its center the precious gift given at Mount Sinai: Torah.

TORAH IS MORE THAN LAW

In the Sermon on the Mount we can see Jesus working the Torah and interacting with his audiences as he teaches them his distinct approach for implementing the ancient precepts for living that God gave to Moses on Mount Sinai. It is an approach that inclines toward a strict interpretation of Torah, sometimes going beyond the plain reading of the text in order to reach for the highest essence of the divine revelation. It is also an approach that places a premium on even the smallest details of Torah, neglecting neither *yod* nor *kotz*. Jesus does not miss the dot of an "i."

Jesus' teachings were not contrary to the spirit of Judaism of his day. His message, spiritual concerns, moral values, and prophetic warnings were in line with the best trends and theological achievements of the Jewish people during the Second Temple period. When reading the rabbinic literature, which received much inspiration from the first-century Pharisaic movement, one discovers a remarkable continuity with Jesus' own teachings, both in thought and in the handling of the biblical text. The Pharisees, Jesus, and the rabbis of the Talmudic literature share many common thoughts, values, and principles of scriptural interpretation, which stream from earlier sources rooted in Second Temple period Judaism, in all its rich diversity and cultural expression. Therefore, interactive comparative study is essential for modern learners who seek a true understanding of the rabbinic literature and Gospel teachings.

Repairing the World

The world is torn by conflicts, by folly, by hatred. Our task is to cleanse, to illumine, to repair. Every deed is either a clash or an aid in the effort of redemption. Man is not one with God, not even with his true self. Our task is to bring eternity into time, to clear in the wilderness a way, to make plain in the desert a highway for God. "Happy is the man in whose heart are the highways" (Psalm 84:6).

Abraham Joshua Heschel, *God in Search of Man* (New York: Farrar, Strauss and Giroux, 1993), 357.

A Terrorist Court

A Sanhedrin court which condemns one person to death in a seven-year period is considered to be terrorist. Rabbi Eleazar the son of Azaryah said, "Even one person in seventy years." Rabbi Tarfon and Rabbi Akiva said, "If we had been sitting on the court, no one would ever be put to death."

m. Makkot 1.10

CHAPTER   4

The Great Sanhedrin

After the Romans burned the Temple in 70 C.E., the Sanhedrin emerged from the ashes as a guiding force for the Jewish community. It provided a forum for leadership during the formative period of the Second Temple up to the fifth century C.E. The Sanhedrin underwent significance changes during its long and illustrious history. It evolved and developed as it was impacted by major historical events, such as the Maccabean Revolt (166–60 B.C.E.), the destruction of the Temple (70 C.E.), the Bar Kokhba revolt (132–135 C.E.), and the work of Rabbi Judah the Prince in Sepphoris (ca. late second century C.E.). As a result of this complex history, scholars debate many issues concerning the multifaceted functions and basic make-up of the Sanhedrin. The debate among the best of scholars is intense, and without agreement on some key issues. Here we will lay a foundational understanding of the institution of the Sanhedrin.

TORAH SCHOLARSHIP—TORAH LEADERSHIP

Some scholars narrowly define the Sanhedrin as a judicial court in the legal system, judging cases like a modern court of law. Others have given the Sanhedrin a much more extensive role in Jewish society, almost like the three branches of the American government, with legislative powers to make laws, judicial authority to pass judgment in criminal cases and interpret the religious legal code of ethics, and executive functions to preside over discussions and enforce decisions.[1] Almost all agree that the Sanhedrin established the calendar for religious observance, which greatly influenced not only the Temple worship, but also impacted the large Jewish communities living outside the land of Israel in the Diaspora. The Sanhedrin calculated the leap years, established the new moons, and set the dates for the appointed festivals of the sacred calendar.[2]

---

[1] See Yeshayahu Gafni and Yaron Tsur, with English editor Isaac Gottlieb, *Jerusalem to Jabneh: The Period of the Mishnah and Its Literature* (Ramat-Aviv, Israel: Everyman's University, 1980), unit 3, 23–33.
[2] See Hugo Mantel, *Studies in the History of the Sanhedrin* (Cambridge, Mass.: Harvard University Press, 1965), 188–95.

Certainly the Sanhedrin had greater authority during some periods of its history than others. For instance, the Gospel of John, as well as the Jerusalem Talmud, teaches that the authority to try capital cases and give the death penalty was removed from the Sanhedrin's jurisdiction forty years before the destruction of the Temple (i.e., ca. 30 C.E.; John 18:31; *y. Sanhedrin,* Chapter 1, Halakhah 1, 18a). Generally speaking, Greek historical sources tend to describe the Sanhedrin more as a court of law, while Hebrew references provide evidence for a wider scope of influence. All the sources should be studied for a comprehensive understanding of the composition and the function of the Sanhedrin.

Focusing on the primary sources, eminent scholar Sidney H. Hoenig studied all references to the Great Sanhedrin in the Greek texts as well as the rabbinic literature. He sought to define the nature of the Great Sanhedrin, not accepting the prevailing view that it was only a court of law. Hoenig claimed, "The Great Sanhedrin was a religious body devoted to the interpretation of the biblical and traditional law, the Halakah."[3] Some of the evidence suggests that they were ordained with the laying on of hands much like the elders of Israel appointed to assist Moses (Exod 18:13–27).[4] Hoenig also observed, "The study of rabbinic sources reveals that the Great Sanhedrin as a tribunal of religious law and justice was composed of men learned in the law."[5] So the members of the Sanhedrin were spiritual leaders who had attained a high level of Torah learning.

THE SANHEDRIN AND THE NEW TESTAMENT

The Sanhedrin is portrayed in the New Testament; Joseph of Arimathea is mentioned as one of its members (Luke 23:50). However, we should not assume that every court session or council gathering described in the New Testament is the Great Sanhedrin of seventy-one.[6] For instance, Josephus tells us that Gabinius (consul of Rome in 58 B.C.E.) divided the land of Israel into five district courts called *synedria* (Josephus, *Ant.* 14.91; *Jewish War* 1.170)[7] These courts were local courts that dealt with civil matters and

[3] Sidney H. Hoenig, *The Great Sanhedrin* (New York: Yeshiva University Press, 1953), 12.
[4] See Emil Schürer, *The History of the Jewish People in the Time of Jesus Christ,* (rev. ed.; 3 vols.; Edinburgh: T&T Clark), 2:211.
[5] See Hoenig, *The Great Sanhedrin,* xiii.
[6] On the number seventy-one, see Num 11:16; Luke 10:1–20; *m. Sanhedrin* 1.5–6.
[7] See Hugo Mantel, "Sanhedrin," *Encyclopaedia Judaica* (ed. Cecil Roth; 17 vols.; Jerusalem: Keter, 1972) 14:836–39.

Jesus Teaching in the Temple, Luke 2:46
(Wood Engraving by Bernard A. Solomon)

Roman law. They left the religious questions of Torah alone. These local courts should never be confused with the Great Sanhedrin.

The book of Acts relates how Caiaphas, the high priest and leader of the Sadducees, caused a major argument with Rabban Gamaliel the Elder, the leader of the Pharisees (Acts 5:17–42). This discussion may well have taken place in the *Lishkat Hagazit,* the "Chamber of Hewn Stone" or the *Chanut,* the "Trade Halls," both of which were located in the Temple complex and are described as meeting places for sessions of the Great Sanhedrin.[8] Nearly all the priests were Sadducees. Their leader, Caiaphas, had the apostles arrested and brought before the Sanhedrin (Acts 5:17–21). He wanted to punish them severely, but Rabban Gamaliel the Elder, who represented the Pharisees, argued convincingly in favor of the apostles. He noted that the Romans had suppressed many messianic movements that soon grew weak and disappeared. If this new movement was from God, he argued, they should not fight it. Rather they should wait and see if God blessed it. He warned, "Who are we to fight against God?" (Acts 5:39). The council agreed with Rabban Gamaliel and released the apostles.

---

[8] See *b. Shabbat* 15a on the meeting places of the Sanhedrin.

The Trial of Jesus

Some scholars believe that the whole Sanhedrin met together to decide the fate of Jesus in a night trial before sending him to Pontius Pilate, the Roman Governor. This view is certainly incorrect: the Sanhedrin did not meet at night, they did not meet in the residence of the high priest, and forty years before the destruction of Jerusalem they could not consider capital cases. Luke's version of the trial makes it clear that Caiaphas, who co-operated with the Roman authorities, convened "their" council. The pronoun "their" must refer to a meeting of Sadducees and not to the Great Sanhedrin, as this nighttime assembly does not fit what we know of the latter group (Luke 22:66). This meeting included elders and scribes of the Sadducees. It may have been a representative conference of the *Bet Din Hakohenim,* the "House of Law [Court] of the Priests," but it was their council and not the Sanhedrin.

The confusion is in part due to the Greek word for "conference, council, committee," which is *synedrion.* This is the origin of the term *Sanhedrin.* The Greek word, however, may simply refer to a committee meeting or a council, as well as a court session. The context of a word determines its meaning. Here it cannot refer to the Great Sanhedrin of seventy-one, even though this is the linguistic background for the name Sanhedrin. The context in which this group goes about its business is not the context in which the Sanhedrin operated. Hebrew sources usually refer to it as *Bet Din,* "House of Law," or *Bet Din Hagadol,* "the Great House of Law," rather than use the term *Sanhedrin.*

Scholars who argue that Jesus appeared before the Great Sanhedrin during an illegal night session point to the Gospel of Mark's descriptive term, the "whole" council (Mark 14:55). The Greek word, *holos,* meaning "whole," should be understood in light of the Lukan parallel (Luke 22:66–71). This is the whole council of the chief priests who convene the session at night during the Passover, so that the ones who are sympathetic with Jesus will not be informed about the meeting. We do not hear of any one else present, like Rabban Gamaliel. Rather, the high priest and his supporters are the ones who are shown questioning Jesus. Others, especially the Pharisees would have been involved with the Passover celebration. It is even possible that the Sadducees observed Passover at a different time according to their own calendar, which was different from the Pharisees' calendar.[9]

---

[9] Compare the treatment of Daniel A. Chwolson, *Das letzte Passamahl Christi und der Tag seines Todes* (Leipzig: H. Haessel, 1908) who noted the disagreements over the time to celebrate the Passover in rabbinic sources. Some of these issues have been discussed by Annie Jaubert, *The Date of the Last Supper* (Staten Island, N.Y.: Alba House, 1965) who concluded that Jesus observed the Passover according to the Essene calendar. Her conclusion cannot be accepted. Nonetheless it is quite possible that some groups disagreed on the time for observance of the Passover meal. The

It seems to have been the Sadducees' intention to arrest Jesus while the common people and the Pharisees celebrated Passover. They viewed Jesus' movement as a threat to political stability: a messianic movement would jeopardize the already unsteady relationship between the Jewish people and the imperial power of Rome. The high priest was appointed by Roman decree, and functioned in the Temple as a liaison between Rome and the common people. Caiaphas wanted to tell Pilate that Jesus claimed to be the Messiah, a political charge against the Roman empire. They could not, however, arrest Jesus on the Temple Mount because he was surrounded by crowds of people who largely supported him (Matt 21:46; 26:55; Mark 12:12; 14:49; Luke 20:19; 22:53).[10] Support for Jesus aside, the Sadducees were despised by the Pharisees and many others in Jewish society. It seems clear, then, that the trial of Jesus was not a meeting of the Great Sanhedrin.

THE TRIAL OF PAUL

However, it does seem likely that the Apostle Paul was brought before the Great Sanhedrin (Acts 23:1–10). The apostle notes that the governing body was representative of the different power factions in Jerusalem, being composed of both Sadducees and Pharisees. The Apostle Paul boldly proclaims to the council that he is a Pharisee. He claims that he was brought before them because of his belief in the resurrection. The doctrine of the resurrection is rooted in the oral traditions of the Pharisees, and so the Sadducees rejected it. The colorful description in Acts portrays a loud clamor erupting as the Sadducees and Pharisees debate the doctrine of the resurrection. It is noteworthy that it is the Pharisees who say of Paul, "We find nothing wrong with this man" (Acts 23:9).[11]

Sadly, New Testament scholars have been slow to recognize how the Pharisees at times supported the community of believers against the persecution of the Sadducees. The Great Sanhedrin was by no means a kangaroo court that obeyed the dictates of a single individual or group. Rather, the Sanhedrin appears in the literature as a representative body of different factions, in which the rich diversity of views held by the common people

---

Sadducees may have used a different calendar. Jesus most probably obseerved Passover according to the dominant view among the Pharisees.

[10] In Luke 22:6, Judas agrees to betray Jesus in the absence of the multitudes of people because most of the Jews supported or sympathized with Jesus whether or not they became active disciples.

[11] See Simon Kistemaker, *Exposition of the Acts* (New Testament Commentary 17; Grand Rapids: Baker, 1990), 816. He correctly observes that "The Pharisees claim Paul as their protegé because he and they believe the same doctrinal tenets."

received a voice that could be heard in the deliberations of the great council meetings. A majority vote could determine action on a particular issue.

THE SANHEDRIN'S LEADERSHIP AND PURPOSE

The purpose of the Great Sanhedrin was to elucidate the deeper meaning of Torah in practical terms, so that the people could have confidence that their lives were guided by authentic interpretation of the divine revelation in their sacred traditions. The greatest minds of the spiritual leadership were summoned into service in order to fulfill this high purpose. The Hebrew sources indicate that the Sanhedrin exercised power in the legislative and executive sphere of influence, and did not function merely as a court system. The presiding leader, or *Nasi,* served alongside the chief magistrate, the *Av Bet Din,* and also with a sage, the *Chakham,* who was an expert in the Bible. The sage provided knowledgeable scholarship for intense study of issues under consideration. These three individuals fulfilled an executive role in the functions of the Great Sanhedrin. The other sixty-nine members may well have been divided into three groups of twenty three representing regional and community interests of the entire country.[12] These sixty-nine council members, together with the presiding leader and the chief magistrate of the executive branch, made up the seventy-one voting members. The selection of an odd-number of members would prevent a stalemate tie in a close vote on a controversial issue that might split the Sanhedrin. The evidence for reconstructing the functions and the composition of the Sanhedrin is inconclusive, however, so caution must be exercised in drawing conclusions about the body.

The Talmud describes the entrance of the three executive officers (the *Nasi*) during the Yavneh period, which spanned from the destruction of the Jerusalem Temple in 70 C.E. until the beginning of the Bar Kokhba Revolt in 132 C.E. The period's name comes from the site of a decisive council meeting at the village of Yavneh, a city on the Mediterranean coast, west of Jerusalem (see map below).

> Our Rabbis teach: When the presiding leader [*Nasi*] comes in, everyone stands to his feet, and they do not sit back down until he instructs them, "Be seated." When the chief magistrate [*Av Bet Din*] comes in, one row stands up on one side and the other row on the other stands up and they remain standing until he sits down. When the sage [*Chakham*] comes in, everyone stands up as he walks

---

[12] The notion that there were subgroups of the Great Sanhedrin is based on conjecture.

by, and then sits down [as he passes by them] until he sits down in his position. (*b. Horayot* 13b)

Certainly it would not be accurate to ascribe this custom to the entire history of the Great Sanhedrin. This is one of the main problems of research; since the council enjoyed a long history, it is difficult, if not impossible, to know for certain if a custom described was practiced throughout its history, or even how the composition and function of the Sanhedrin changed from one period of time to another. Sometimes the rabbinic sources described the way the Sanhedrin should function, rather than the way it actually operated. In any case, the honor given to the Nasi at Yavneh demonstrates his authority.

HAVE TORAH WILL TRAVEL

The Sanhedrin moved from place to place, according to historical circumstances. Clearly the mobility of the Great Sanhedrin helped the foundation of Jewish community to survive overwhelming catastrophes such as the destruction of the Temple. When Yochanan ben Zakhai led the way for Bible scholars to go to Yavneh, the seat of the Sanhedrin was moved from Jerusalem to the new center of Jewish learning and community life. The transference of the Sanhedrin's power and authority from Jerusalem to Yavneh was a major achievement for Rabban Yochanan ben Zakhai's leadership, and paved the way for the continuation of Jewish life after the Temple. The Jewish Diaspora recognized this change in authority and accepted the rulings of the transferred Sanhedrin in establishing the sacred calendar. Some monies collected for the Temple from the Diaspora were sent to Yavneh.

At Yavneh, Bible scholarship became an even more important part of carrying out the legislative activities of the Sanhedrin. The community had to learn how to live without the Temple. Everyone who had learned Torah before the destruction of the Temple came to Yavneh to teach Torah. The new situation made it imperative for Torah scholarship to face the tragedy of national suffering and interpret the message of the Bible for their new circumstances. The heartfelt prayers of the people would be the substitute for blood sacrifices; the fruit of their lips pure sacrifices. After all, God longed for the hearts of his people, not the blood of animals, as the Hebrew prophets of old had proclaimed (see my discussion of prophetic criticism of Temple worship in Chapter One, pp. 12–13).

A mobile Sanhedrin that could move from one seat of influence to another enabled the leadership to respond effectively to new needs. The Talmud explains how the great council moved from one city to another:

"The Sanhedrin moved . . . from Jerusalem to Yavneh, from Yavneh to Usha . . . and from Usha to Shefaram and from Shefaram to Bet Shearim, and from Bet Shearim to Sepphoris, and from Sepphoris to Tiberias" (*b. Rosh HaShanah* 31a–b).

So the activities of the Sanhedrin were not stifled during national emergencies. The biblical tradition of a mobile ark and a Tent of Meeting, which were the constant traveling companions and treasured possessions of a group of wandering tribes in desert regions (Exod 25:13; Num 10:17–21, 33), made transitioning the Sanhedrin from the Temple precincts to Yavneh seem natural. The needs of the community were perhaps even greater in their new circumstances, and the Torah had to be applied in its new setting. In addition, the Jewish people living in the dispersion needed the deliberations of the Sanhedrin to establish their sacred calendar and to solve questions relating to religious law and observance. In this, and subsequent generations, the Torah is given to the community of faith to interpret.

Tragedy forced the Jewish people to endure war, famine, and exile (see especially 2 Kgs 17:5–41; 24:1–25:30). The resilience of the people was discovered in their ability to take the Torah with them wherever they traveled. Scholars who were forced to leave one city, would establish a center of Torah learning in another village. For a number of years Rabbi Simeon bar Yochai lived, studied, and taught Torah while hiding in a cave. Though the Temple was destroyed, the Jewish people preserved the institutions of their community life and their faith experience because the Sanhedrin could be moved. Torah learning and faithful observance of the tradition were the life of the people. Even in modern times, during the Nazi reign of terror, schools and synagogues were established in ghettos and concentration camps under the most unimaginable circumstances.

FOLLOW THE TEACHERS OF TORAH

During the Yavneh period, the Torah teaching—"Follow justice and justice alone, so that you may live and possess the land the LORD your God is giving you" (Deut 16:20, NIV)—was interpreted to mean that everyone should follow the scholars of learning to the places where Torah is taught. The Hebrew wording of this text is very strong. The word for "justice" is *tzedek,* which is also translated as "righteousness," and the term parallels the concept of salvation. The word for "follow," *radaf,* is often translated as "to pursue or seek diligently." So if the people of Israel are to possess the land of promise and fulfill their purpose, they must pursue righteousness, justice, and salvation. Raising up disciples to learn and disseminate Torah learning, then, is paramount.

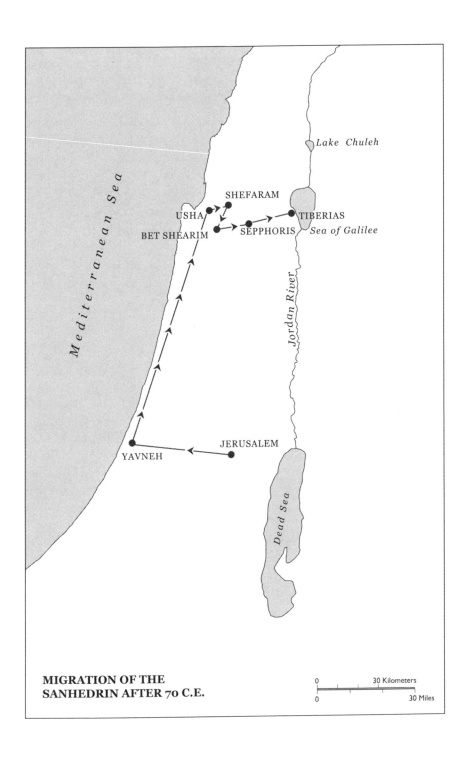

Lake Chuleh

Mediterranean Sea

SHEFARAM

USHA

BET SHEARIM

SEPPHORIS

TIBERIAS

Sea of Galilee

Jordan River

JERUSALEM

YAVNEH

Dead Sea

**MIGRATION OF THE
SANHEDRIN AFTER 70 C.E.**

0   30 Kilometers

0   30 Miles

"Justice and only Justice shall you follow" (Deut 16:20). You shall follow the sages to their academies of learning: Follow Rabbi Eliezer to Lydda, Rabban Yochanan ben Zakhai to Beror Chayil, Rabbi Joshua to Pekiin, Rabban Gamaliel to Yavneh, Rabbi Akiva to Bene Berak, Rabbi Chananiah ben Teradyon to Sikhnin [in Galilee], Rabbi Yose to Sepphoris. (*b. Sanhedrin* 32b)

Torah scholarship never resided exclusively in Jerusalem. Galilee, too, was a place of great learning, where synagogues and academies were integral to community life. While the New Testament does give witness to the fact that there was regional rivalry between Judea and the Galilee area, there is abundant evidence of rich culture and religious piety in Galilee.[13] For instance, the zealot movement had its roots in the conservative religious mind set of Galilee. The people were devout. They studied the Torah. The holy family worshiped in the local synagogue, and like other pious Jews in Galilee, they made pilgrimage to the Temple in Jerusalem. Academies of learning supported the religious needs of the community.[14] Rabbinic literature mentions great scholars from the Galilee region.

When persecution became strong in Jerusalem, such as the siege and destruction in 70 C.E. or the attacks on Jewish people and prohibitions against religious observance during the time of Hadrian, the centers of learning in other areas of the country were strengthened and intensified with a greater force for teaching Torah. Leading scholars changed addresses but continued the pursuit of their careers. The very nature of the oral tradition, explicating and bringing out the true meaning of the written code, fostered the establishment of centers where Torah could be memorized and passed on from one generation to the next. They sought to raise up disciples, who would be walking Bibles, teaching and fulfilling the commandments of God by proper interpretation. The master-disciple model was the chosen method for preserving the tradition and making it come alive in future generations. "Follow justice" in Deut 16:20 means to follow the masters of Torah to their centers of activity, where the teachings of Scripture and correct interpretation can be learned and practiced.

The foundation for mobile Torah learning developed largely from the message of the Hebrew prophets. The prophet Amos makes it clear how the people could move from the Temple to Yavneh. The seat of the Sanhedrin could be moved. Scholars could travel to new locations where they would foster Torah learning. God did not desire all the ceremonies, festivals, and

---

[13] See Mark A. Chancey, *The Myth of a Gentile Galilee* (Cambridge: Cambridge University Press, 2002.

[14] This is supported by archaeological evidence that has emerged from excavations of cities such as Gamla in the Galilee. See Chancey, *Myth of a Gentile Galilee,* 129–32.

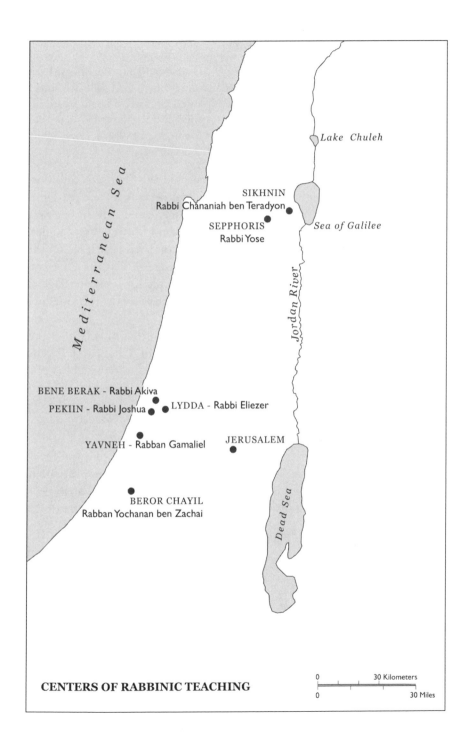

Lake Chuleh

Mediterranean Sea

SIKHNIN
Rabbi Chananiah ben Teradyon

SEPPHORIS
Rabbi Yose

Sea of Galilee

Jordan River

BENE BERAK - Rabbi Akiva
PEKIIN - Rabbi Joshua   LYDDA - Rabbi Eliezer

YAVNEH - Rabban Gamaliel   JERUSALEM

BEROR CHAYIL
Rabban Yochanan ben Zachai

Dead Sea

CENTERS OF RABBINIC TEACHING

0   30 Kilometers
0   30 Miles

offerings of the Temple. God longed for true worshippers who pursued justice, which emerges from Torah learning.

> I hate, I despise your religious feasts; I cannot stand your assemblies. Even though you bring me burnt offerings and grain offerings, I will not accept them. Though you bring choice fellowship offerings, I will have no regard for them. Away with the noise of your songs! I will not listen to the music of your harps. But let justice roll on like a river, righteousness like a never-failing stream! (Amos 5:21–24, NIV)[15]

I hope from the prior discussion of Jesus and the Pharisees, and now the Torah, that we see Jesus and his professional peers in a different light. The Pharisees constituted a significant reform movement within late Second Temple period Judaism. Laboring faithfully and fruitfully for decades, they had done considerable groundwork before the arrival of Jesus on the religious horizon. I would even go so far as to suggest that the Pharisees played an indispensable role in preparing the people for Jesus' message of radical obedience to God's redemptive agenda—the gospel of the kingdom of heaven.

As a final thought on this subject, keep in mind that only two groups survived with their leadership intact after the demise of Jerusalem in 70 C.E. Those two groups were the Pharisees, who soon evolved into the rabbis, and the early Christian community. Roman military might erased the Essenes and Sadducees from the ledger of history. The survival of the Pharisees in the face of a terrible national disaster, and their successful transformation of late Second Temple period Judaism into rabbinic Judaism, is a sign of their inner strength, personal fortitude, focused concentration on Torah education, organizational resiliency, ability to connect with the spiritual life of the common people—and beyond the scope of pure scholarly analysis—divine favor.[16] Moreover, consider our tremendous loss had not the Phari-

---

[15] Compare also Isa 1:11–17. The prophet decried the sacrifices and Temple service, calling upon the people to, "Learn to do good; seek justice, reprove the ruthless, defend the orphan, plead for the widow" (NASB). Certainly a distinction should be made between the historical setting of Amos and Isaiah and the interpretation of their words in the Yavneh period. The Hebrew prophets were not opposed to worship in the Temple nor did they long for its destruction. They called for needed reforms and a pure worship flowing from sincere motives of the heart. Their teachings, however, made the elimination of the Temple a positive development where prayer in the local synagogue become more pertinent.

[16] Probably the political connection between Sadducees and the Romans and their pervasive influences cause the demise of this group which was closely linked to the now-destroyed Temple. The religious separatism of the Essenes caused a religious disconnect from the common people. See also, E. P. Sanders, *Judaism Practice and Belief 63 B.C.E. to 66 C.E.* (London: SCM, 1992), 942–94.

sees passed on their traditions, interpretations, and religious values to rabbinic Judaism. Without the assistance of rabbinic texts we would know far less about the conceptual, textual world of early Christianity, as well as Judaism.

The Sinfulness of Humanity

A curious explanation is given why the whole human race originated from one man: "Because of the righteous and the wicked, that the righteous should not say, 'We are the descendants of a righteous ancestor,' and the wicked say, 'We are the descendants of a wicked ancestor'" (Sanh. 38a). The moral is that neither can plead hereditary influence as the deciding factor in their character.

God does, however, intervene to this extent, that after a man has made his choice, whether good or bad, opportunity is granted to him to persevere in the course he has taken. The good man is encouraged to be good, and the bad to remain bad. "In the way in which a man wishes to walk he is guided" (b. Makkot 10b). "If one goes to defile himself, openings are made for him; and he who goes to purify himself, help is afforded him" (b. Shabbat 104a).

> Cohen, *Everyman's Talmud: The Major Teachings of the Sages* (New York: E.P. Dutton, 1949), 94.

The Greatness of Jesus

The greatness of Jesus lay in that he lent new grandeur to humility, in that he broke down the barriers of the school and brought the wisdom of life from the learned home to the lowliest, thus striking the keynote of humanity. He actually became the redeemer of the poor, the friend of the cheerless, the comforter of the woe-stricken. He lent, both through his life and through his death as the Man of Sorrow, a deeper meaning, a more solemn pathos to suffering, sickness and sin. Life received from him a new holiness, a greater inspiration.

Kaufman Kohler, *Hebrew Union College and other Addresses* (Ark Publishing: Cincinnati, 1916), 225–26.

CHAPTER 5

Parallel Rabbinic and New Testament Texts

In this chapter we bring together a selection of Jewish teachings that are parallel in theme, thought, and application to the Gospels. Some of these parallels date before the time of Jesus, like the teachings of Hillel, but most of them date later. The point is not to argue who influenced whom, whether the rabbis plagiarized the Gospels or Jesus robbed from the rabbis. Moreover, trying to assess inferiority or superiority of one ethical message over the other is meaningless. A more meaningful and fruitful study of these texts recognizes the facts that connect these teachings together. First and foremost, the Gospels and the rabbis are connected to each other through a common Jewish heritage. The real question is how to discover the rich sources that formed a foundation, or database, for both the Gospels and the rabbinic literature. Jesus used this database in different ways than the rabbis did. The powerful originality of Jesus is discovered in the incredible combination of teachings he puts together, to demonstrate what it looks like for people to love God with all their hearts and to love their neighbors as themselves.[1] In his message, the kingdom of heaven is described as an ever-increasing force for good that transforms people and impacts circumstances in a way that brings healing and wholeness to a hurting world.[2]

Here it is argued that texts must be used to interpret texts: the rabbinic texts illuminate the Gospel texts, and the Gospel texts provide insight into the original meaning and authentic setting of the rabbinic texts. Pinchas Lapide notes that one could put together a "Jewish Sermon on the Mount" without "using a single word from Jesus" because there are so many clear and

---

[1] In a Sunday evening seminar that met in Prof. Flusser's home, a religious Jewish student seemed offended by the esteem Prof. Flusser gave to the teachings of Jesus. The student remarked that there was nothing new in the teachings of Jesus, and that he could write a Gospel based upon the Talmud. Prof. Flusser answered, "Yes. You could do that now, but only after Jesus, in his wisdom, had already done it for you."

[2] See Young, *Jesus the Jewish Theologian*, 49–74.

compelling parallels between rabbinic literature and the Gospels. He is quick, however, to qualify such a notion:

> Such a paraphrase is possible only because we do possess Jesus' Sermon on the Mount. For the fact that the plaster, the cement, and all the building stones come from the Jewish quarries in no way diminishes the greatness of the architect who has used these raw materials to design and erect his own moral code. After all, Beethoven did not invent a single new note to compose the Ninth Symphony, his immortal masterpiece.[3]

The originality of Jesus must be seen not only in the combination of ethical teachings and their synthesis into a whole way of life, but also in his emphasis on the kingdom of heaven, which takes on a greater dynamic force in his teaching. More than keeping commandments, the kingdom is the power of God operating in the individual's life to bring healing and salvation.[4]

MULTIPLE CONNECTIONS

Scholars do not doubt that there is an historical connection between Judaism and Christianity. The survival of Judaism following the destruction of the Temple in 70 C.E., and the spiritual awakening that flourished during the period of renewal at Yavneh parallels Jesus' disciples preserving his teachings and formulating communities of believers in diverse cultures and regions. Oral tradition is behind the rabbinic literature and the Gospels. Common sources from the Second Temple period, some oral and others written, in intermediate stages of development, impacted the compilation of the Gospels and the rabbinic literature.

There also is a linguistic connection between these texts. The Gospels reveal a Hebrew background that is seen in the language of the Gospels and in the tradition of the church.[5] The rabbinic texts preserve a rich Mishnaic Hebrew that is very close to the spoken language of the Jewish people in the Second Temple period and certainly shows the language of literary sources near to the time. There is a thematic connection. The rabbinic texts and the Sermon on the Mount reveal concerns for similar themes. This is no small point. What is the ultimate concern of these Jewish teachings and the Ser-

---

[3] Lapide, Pinchas, *The Sermon on the Mount* (New York: Orbis, 1986), 10.

[4] See Young, *Jesus the Jewish Theologian*, 49–83.

[5] See my discussion of the Hebrew origins of Jesus' teachings in Chapter One as well as the similarities between the rabbinic texts and the Sermon on the Mount throughout Chapters One through Three in this book. See also Young, *Jesus and His Jewish Parables*, 40–42, 51–54.

mon on the Mount? They both seek to interpret biblical revelation and apply it in practical ways. There is a theological connection. The Gospel and rabbinic texts begin with an understanding of the character of God and the need for every human being to pursue a course of life that will please Him, being rightly related, one to the other, in the bond of community and faith.

Hans Windisch was one of the great Bible interpreters from a previous generation of scholars who has made enduring contributions to academic research and analysis. In his striking work entitled, *The Meaning of the Sermon on the Mount,* published in 1950, he bases his exegesis on a careful study of the Greek text of the Gospels, but he also recognizes the value of comparative study between the rabbinic literature and the teachings of Jesus.[6] When commenting on what it means to be "perfect" as one's Father in heaven is perfect, Windisch turns to the rabbinic literature. He advises serious comparative study.

> The saying about perfection in ch. 5:48 is therefore a general or regulative principle that allows for still other applications than those to the treatment of our enemies. It is not to be interpreted in the sense of the Greek (and of the "theological") concept of perfection, but recalls the 'mighty works' of God toward men, familiar from God's concrete revelation of himself in Scripture, history, and nature, which know no limits in their bestowal of all that is good. The best commentators on this saying of Jesus are not the Christian theologians, who transform it into an exorbitant, rigorous, and impossible demand, but the Rabbis.[7]

Windisch recalls the teachings of Rabbi Meir, who calls on each individual to be merciful and forgiving like God. But it is remarkable that Windisch here claims that the rabbis teach more meaningful truth as commentators on the sayings of Jesus than the Christian theologians.

TEXTS THAT INTERPRET TEXTS

In this chapter, selected texts are provided for comparative study and reflection. These texts are, of course, only a small sample of source materials. As one reads these texts one must ask oneself questions about the issues presented. Below are some suggested interpretive questions that will help with one's exploration.

---

[6] Hans Windisch, *The Meaning of the Sermon on the Mount* (Philadelphia: Westminster, 1950).

[7] Windisch, *The Meaning,* 84. Windisch probably penned these words in Leiden around 1928. Certainly Windisch believed in historical exegesis and valued the commentary of Christian theologians.

1. How, if at all, are these texts related to one another?

2. Do they use similar words or phrases?

3. Do they express similar ethical principles?

4. What do they reveal about God's character?

5. What do they demand in human behavior?

6. What type of environment would give birth to these teachings?

7. What common sources in the Jewish heritage could have influenced the development of these teachings?

8. What role did the Hebrew Bible play in teaching divine revelation to the community of faith?

9. How would these teachings be passed down in the oral tradition from Master to disciple, from one generation to another?

10. How do these parallel texts help us understand the issues confronting people of faith?

11. What practical wisdom can be learned from these teachings which can be applied in everyday life?

12. How do these parallel texts reveal similarities in thought patterns and conceptual worldviews? How are they different?

The hard question is this: how are the Gospels and the rabbinic literature connected to the tree of ancient Judaism, with its deep roots in biblical faith and true life experience from the land of Israel during the Second Temple period?

THE ATTRIBUTES OF DISCIPLES

Great is the peace which is given to those who study Torah, as was said, "All your children shall be taught by the LORD, and great shall be the peace of your children" (Isa. 54:13).

Great is the peace which is given to the meek, as was said, "But the meek shall inherit the earth and delight themselves in the abundance of peace" (Ps. 37:11).

Blessed are the poor in spirit, for from them is the kingdom of heaven.

Blessed are those who mourn, for they will be comforted.

Blessed are the meek, for they will inherit the earth.

Blessed are those who hunger and thirst for righteousness, for they will be filled.

Great is the peace which is given to those who work righteousness, as was said, "And the work of righteousness will be peace" (Isa 32:17). (*Sifre Numbers* 42)[8]

Blessed are the merciful, for they shall receive mercy.

Blessed are the pure in heart for they shall see God.

Blessed are the peacemakers, for they shall be called the children of God.

Blessed are those who are persecuted because of righteousness, for from them is the kingdom of heaven. (Matt 5:3–7)

LIGHT ON A LAMP STAND

To what may Moses be compared at that time? To a light which is set upon a lamp stand from which many lights are ignited. Nothing is lacking from this light, in the same way that nothing is lacking from the light of Moses. (*Sifre Numbers* 93)[9]

You are the light of the world. A city set on a hill cannot be hidden. Neither do people light a lamp and put it under a basket. Instead they put it on a lamp stand, and it gives light to everyone in the house. (Matt 5:14–15)

GOOD WORKS GLORIFY GOD

Rabbi Simeon son of Eleazar taught, "When the people of Israel do the will of their Father in heaven, then His name is magnified in the world." (*Mekhilta deRabbi Ishmael,* on Exodus 15:2)[10]

In the same way, let your light so shine before people that they may see your good works and glorify your Father who is in heaven. (Matt 5:16)

TORAH RIGHTLY INTERPRETED

. . . if the Torah is abolished in part, it is abolished completely. [The Torah said], "But Solomon has desired to abolish a yod [which is the smallest letter of the alphabet] from me!" The Holy One Blessed be He responded, "Behold Solomon and a thousand like him will be abolished but not one letter

Do not think that I have come to destroy the Torah and the prophets; I have not come to abolish them but to fulfill them. (Matt 5:17)

---

[8] Hayyim S. Horovitz, ed., *Sifre al Bemidbar Vesifre Zuta* (Jerusalem: Wahrmann, 1966), 47.

[9] Horovitz, *Sifre,* 94.

[10] Lauterbach, *Mekhilta Derabbi Ishmael,* 2:28.

from you [the Torah] will ever be abolished." (*y. Sanhedrin* 20c; Ch. 2 Halakhah 6)

ANGER AND MURDER

"If any person hates his or her neighbor, and lies in wait for him and attacks him [and wounds him mortally so that he dies]" (Deut. 19:11). From this verse it was understood: if a person has transgressed a light commandment, he or she will finally transgress a weighty commandment. If one will transgress [the commandment]: "You shall love your neighbor as yourself" (Lev. 19:18), that one will finally be led to transgress [the commandment]: "You shall not take vengeance or bear any grudge" (Lev. 19:18), and the commandment: "You shall not hate your brother or sister" (Lev. 19:17), and [the commandment], "That your brother or sister may live beside you" (Lev. 25:36)—until that person will finally be led to commit murder. Therefore it is said: "If any person hates his or her neighbor and lies in wait for him and attacks him." (*Sifre Deuteronomy* on 22:13)[11]

Rabbi Eleazar taught, "The one who hates his or her neighbor is considered a murderer, because it was said, 'But if any one hates his or her neighbor and lies in wait, and rises up to attack, and then strikes that one so that he or she dies' (Deut. 19:11)." (M. Higger, *Massekhtot Derekh Erez*, vol. 2, 312.)

You have heard that it was said to the people long ago, "Do not murder" and anyone who murders will be subject to the judgment. But I tell you that anyone who is angry with his brother or sister will be subject to judgment. (Matt 5:21–22)

---

[11] Louis Finkelstein, ed., *Sifre Devarim* (New York: Jewish Theological Seminary, 1969), 267. See the English translation by Reuven Hammer, *Sifre: a Tannaitic Commentary on the Book of Deuteronomy* (New Haven, Conn.: Yale University Press, 1986), 243–44.

LUSTFUL THOUGHTS AND ADULTERY

In regards to the commandment, "Do not commit adultery," it has been taught, explained Rabbi Simeon son of Lakish, that any one who commits adultery physically with his body shall be called an adulterer, but we say to you, that anyone who commits adultery with his eye shall be called an adulterer. (*Pesikta Rabbati* 24)

You have heard that it was said, "Do not commit adultery." But I tell you that anyone who looks lustfully at a woman has already committed adultery with her in his heart. (Matt 5:27–28)

RETALIATION

Our Rabbis taught: Those who are insulted but do not insult, hear themselves reviled without answering, act through love and rejoice in suffering, of them the Scripture teaches, "But they who love him are as the sun when he goes forth in his might" (Judges 5:31). (*b. Shabbat* 88b)

You have heard that it was said, "An eye for an eye, and a tooth for a tooth." But I tell you, Do not compete with one who is evil. If someone slaps you on your right cheek, turn to him the other as well. (Matt 5:38–39)

Rabbi Chama ben Chanina taught, "Even if [your enemy] rises early to kill you, and comes to your house hungry and thirsty, you should give him food and drink. Why? [Because it is written,] 'If your enemy is hungry, give him or her bread to eat. If your enemy is thirsty, give him or her water to drink. By doing so, you will heap coals of fire upon his or her head, and the LORD will make your enemy to be at peace with you' (Proverbs 25:21–22). Hence you should not read and interpret the verse to mean, 'the LORD will reward [*yishalem*] you.' Rather you must read and interpret the verse to mean, 'the LORD will make your enemy to be at peace with you [*yashlimenu*].'" (*Midrash on Proverbs* 25)[12]

---

[12] Burton Visotzky, *The Midrash on Proverbs* (New Haven: Yale University Press, 1992), 168, (Hebrew edition), *Yalkut Hamachiri*, on Proverbs 25:21–22,

CHARITY, PRAYER, AND FASTING

Rabbi Leazar taught: "Three actions cancel out a harsh decree [of punishment from Heaven.] These are prayer, righteousness [i.e., giving charity or almsgiving], and repentance. All three are mentioned in one verse (2 Chron. 7:14), 'if my people who are called by my name will humble themselves, and pray . . .' This refers to prayer! '. . . and seek my face,' This refers to righteousness, which is further proven by Psalm 17:15, where it is said, 'As for me, I shall behold your face in righteousness." Finally the words, '. . . and turn from their wicked ways,' refers to repentance [i.e., fasting]! If an individual will do all three, the promise in Scripture is, 'then I will hear from heaven, and will forgive their sin and heal their land' (2 Chron. 7:14)." (*y. Ta'anit* 65b ch. 2, hal. 1)[13]

Beware of practicing your righteousness [i.e., giving charity or almsgiving] in front of other people in order to be seen by them; for then you will have no reward from your Father who is in heaven. (Matt 6:1)

And when you pray, you must not be like the pretenders who love to stand and pray in the synagogues and at the street corners, in order that they may be seen by other people. Truly, I say to you, they have received their reward. (Matt 6:5)

And when you fast, do not look dismal, like the pretenders who disfigure their faces in order that other people will know that they are fasting. Truly, I say to you, they have received their reward. (Matt 6:16)

THE DISCIPLES' PRAYER

May His great name be magnified and celebrated as holy, in the world which He created according to His will. May He cause His Kingdom to reign in your lives, during your days and in the lives of all the house of Israel, in this world and in the time that is near to come. Let all the people say, Amen. (Kaddish, Daily Prayer Book)

58b; cf. *b. Megillah* 15b, quoted by Israel Abrahams, *Studies in Pharisaism and the Gospels* (Series 1; New York: KTAV, 1967), 165.

[13] See *Genesis Rabbah* 44:12.

Rabbi Eleazar taught to pray these words, "Do Your will in Heaven above. Grant contentment of spirit to those who fear You upon the earth, and accomplish what is good in Your sight. Blessed is the One who hears and answers prayer." (*t. Berakhot* 3:7, *b. Berakhot* 16b)

Pray then like this: "Our Father who is in heaven, may your name be celebrated as holy. May your continue to establish your kingdom. May your will be done on earth as it is in heaven. Give us this day our necessary bread. Forgive us our sins as we also have forgiven those who have sinned against us. Lead us not into the grasp of temptation, but deliver us from the evil one." (Matt 6:9–13)

May it be Your will, O Lord our God, and God of our ancestors, to train us in Your Torah and to make us cling to Your commandments. Do not lead us into the grasp of sin, and not into the grasp of trespass and iniquity. Do not lead us into the grasp of temptation or disgrace. Do not let the evil inclination rule over us, but remove us far away from an evil person or an evil companion. (See Hertz, *Daily Prayer Book*, 24–25)

FORGIVENESS

Everyone who is merciful to others, will receive mercy from Heaven. Everyone, however, who does not show mercy to others, will not receive mercy from Heaven. (*b. Shabbat* 151b)

For if you will forgive others their trespasses, so also will your heavenly Father forgive you. But if you will not forgive others their trespasses, neither will your Father forgive your trespasses. (Matt 6:14–15)

Abba Shaul taught, "O be like Him! In the same way that He is gracious and merciful to forgive, you must be gracious and merciful as well." (*Mekhilta deRabbi Ishmael* on Exodus 15:2)[14]

---

[14] Lauterbach, *Mekhilta Derabbi Ishmael*, 2:25.

Storing Up Treasures

Monobaz the King (of Adiabene) arose and dispersed all his accumulated assets to the poor [during the time of famine, about 46 C.E.]. His relatives sent a message to him, saying, "Your ancestors stored up treasures, and increased the wealth of their ancestors. But you have freely given away your [treasures] and those of your ancestors." He answered by saying, "My ancestors accumulated wealth for the world below, but I have stored up treasures for the world above; they stored up treasures in a place over which the hand of the thief can break in, but I have stored up treasures in a place where a thief's hand can never break in. My ancestors stored up treasures which bear no fruit (where interest does not accumulate). I have stored up treasure where interest accumulates and bears much fruit. My ancestors stored up treasures of money but I have stored up treasures in souls, which is taught in Scripture, "The fruit of the righteous [i.e., charitable acts] is a tree of life" (Prov. 11:30)

. . . My ancestors stored up treasures for this world, but I have stored up treasures for myself in heaven, in the world to come, as is proved by Scripture, "Righteousness [i.e., charitable acts] saves from death" (Prov. 10:2) . . . Almsgiving and deeds of loving kindness outweigh all the other commandments in the Torah. Righteousness [i.e., almsgiving] benefits others living in this life. Deeds of loving kindness, however, can benefit others both those living in this life and those who have already died. Almsgiving provides only for the benefit of poor people, but acts of loving-kindness can benefit both the poor and the rich. Almsgiving only

Do not store up for yourselves treasures on earth, where moth and rust consume and where thieves break in and steal, but store up for yourselves treasures in heaven, where neither moth nor rust consumes and where thieves do not break in and steal. For where your treasure is, there will your heart be also. (Matt 6:19–21)

provides support for a poor person's financial needs, but deeds of loving-kindness can provide help not only for a poor person's finances, but for all his or her physical needs as well. (*y. Pe'ah* 15b, bottom, Ch. 1 Halakhah 1 *t. Pe'ah* 4:18)

FAITH AND ANXIETY

Rabbi Simeon ben Eleazar asked, "Have you ever seen a wild animal or a bird practicing a profession? Yet they have their sustenance provided for without anxiety and were they not created to serve me? But I was created to serve my Maker. How much more then, should I have my sustenance provided for without anxiety. But I have done wrong and so I have given up my right to sustenance without worry." (*m. Kiddushin* 4:14)

Do not worry about your life, what you will eat or drink; or about your body, what you will wear. Is not life more important than food, and the body more important than clothes? Look at the birds of the air; they do not sow or reap or store away in barns, and yet your heavenly Father feeds them? How much more valuable are you than they?

Rabbi Eliezer the Great taught, "Whoever has a piece of bread in his basket today, and questions in his heart, 'What shall I eat tomorrow?' is of little faith." (*b. Sotah* 48b)

Who of you by worrying, will add length to his height? Why do you worry about clothes? See how the flowers of the field grow. They do not work or spin yarn. Yet I tell you that not even Solomon in all his splendor was dressed as well as one of these. If that is how God clothes the grass of the field, which is here today and tomorrow is thrown into the fire, how much more will he clothe you! O you of little faith! (Matt 6:25–30)

WORRY

"Do not worry about tomorrow's trouble. You do not know what a new day will bring forth" (Prov. 27:1). After all, tomorrow may come and you will be no more. Then you will have suffered trouble over a world which is not your own. (*b. Yebamot* 63b)

Do not worry about tomorrow, for tomorrow will have enough worry in its time. Let the day's own trouble be sufficient for that day. (Matt 6:34)

"I am that I am" (Exodus 3:14). The Holy One blessed be He, is saying to Moses, "Go and tell Israel that I was with you in this slavery and I will be with you when you are in bondage to other kingdoms in the future." He replied to Him, "Lord of the Universe! Sufficient is the evil in the time in which it is suffered!" (*b. Berakhot* 9b)

JUDGING OTHERS

Hillel said, "Do not judge your neighbor, until you put yourself in his or her place." (*m. Avot* 2:5)

Do not judge, or you too will be judged. (Matt 7:1 [NIV])

With the measure that a person measures, it will be measured back to him or her again . . . Just as Samson sinned with his eyes [looking at the Philistine woman] so also the Philistines put out his eyes [making him blind] . . . (*m. Sotah* 1:7–8)

For with the judgment that you judge another, you will be judged. With the measure you measure, it will be measured back to you. (Matt 7:2)

THE SPLINTER AND THE LOG

Rabbi Yochanan explained what is the meaning of the words, "And it came to pass, in the days when the judges judged . . . " (Ruth 1:1). It means that this was a generation in which the judges passed judgment upon each other. If the judge said to a person, "Take the splinter from between your teeth," that person would respond, by saying, "Take the log out of your eye." (*b. Baba Batra* 15 b)

Why do you see the splinter that is in your friend's eye, but do not notice the log that is in your own eye? Or how can you say to your friend, "Let me take the splinter out of your eye," when there is a log in your own eye? You pretender! First take the log out of your own eye, and then you will see clearly to take the splinter out of your friend's eye. (Matt 7:3–5)

Rabbi Tarfon asked, "I wonder if there is anyone in this generation who can accept correction? If someone says, 'Take the splinter out of your eye,' the other responds, by saying, 'Take the log out of your own eye.' " (*b. Arakhin* 16b)

What Is Holy?

In the same way that a treasure must not be revealed to everyone, so also with the precious words of Torah. One must not go into the deeper meaning of them, except in the presence of those individuals who are suitably trained [and worthy]. (y. Avodah Zarah 41d, ch. 2, Hal 8)[15]

All that is consecrated holy [i.e., kodashim, "animal offerings"] and yet has become rendered ritually unclean [i.e., terefah], cannot be redeemed and then fed to the dogs. [Feeding such meat to the dogs would be disrespectful to holy things.] (m. Temurah 6:5)

Do not give what is holy to the dogs. Do not throw your pearls before swine because they will probably trample them under foot and turn to attack you. (Matt 7:6)

The Golden Rule

On one occasion, a person came up to Rabbi Akiva and asked him, "My Teacher, teach me the entire Torah as one." He answered him, "If Moses our Teacher was on Mount Sinai for forty days and nights and was still learning Torah, after all that time, how can you have the audacity to ask me to teach you the entire Torah as one!"

Rabbi Akiva, however, continued, "But my friend, there is one principle which sums up and contains the entire Torah as one, it is the teaching, 'What is hateful to you, do not do to another.'" (Avot R. Nat., vers. B, ch. 26)

In everything, do to others what you would have them do to you, for this sums up the Torah and the prophets. (Matt 7:12)

Hillel taught . . . "What you do not want someone to do to you, do not do to them. This sums up the Torah and the rest is commentary. Now you must go learn it!" (b. Shabbat 31a)

[15] See also Jacob N. Epstein and Ezra Z. Melamed, *Mekhilta Derabbi Shimeon* (Jerusalem: Hillel, 1980), 158 (Hebrew).

"You shall love your neighbor as yourself" (Lev. 19:18), Rabbi Akiva taught, "This is the great, all-inclusive, fundamental principle that sums up the Torah." (*Sifra* on Leviticus 19:18)

THE TWO WAYS

"Behold I set before you this day a blessing and a curse" (Deut. 11:26). Why is this said? Because it says, "I have set before you life and death, blessing and curse" (Deut. 11:26). Lest Israel should say, "Since the Omnipresent has set before us two ways, a way of life and a way of death, we may walk in which ever we choose." The Scripture teaches: "And you shall choose life" (Deut 30:19).

A Parable. It may be compared to one who sat at the crossroads. Two paths were before him, one which was smooth at its beginning, but its end was thorny, and the other which was thorny at its beginning, but its end was smooth. He would tell those who were coming and going, "You see this path which is smooth at its beginning? For two or three steps you walk in its smoothness but it ends up in thorns. You see this other path which is thorny at its beginning? For two or three steps you walk in thorns, but it ends up in smoothness." Thus Moses spoke to Israel: You see the wicked who are prosperous in this world? For two or three days they prosper, but they end up being confounded afterwards, as it is said, "for the evil man has no future" (Proverbs 24:20). It says, "And behold the tears of the oppressed" (Ecclesiastes 4:1) and "The fool folds his hands" (Ecclesiastes 4:5). Further it says, "The way of the wicked is deep darkness" (Proverbs 4:19). You see the righteous

Enter through the narrow gate. For wide is the gate and broad is the road that leads to destruction, and many enter through it. But small is the gate and narrow is the way that leads to life, and only a few find it. (Matt 7:13–14)

who are afflicted in this world? For two or three days they are afflicted, but they end up rejoicing afterwards. Thus it says: "[that he might humble you and test you,] to do good to you in the end" (Deut. 8:16). It says, "Better is the end of the thing than its beginning" (Ecclesiastes 7:8). It says, "For I know the plans I have for you [says the LORD, plans for good and not for evil]" (Jeremiah 29:11). It says, "The path of the righteous is like the light of dawn" (Proverbs 4:18). (*Sifre Deuteronomy* 53)[16]

Rabbi Akiva taught . . . "It only teaches that the Omnipresent placed before him two ways, the way of life and the way of death." (*Mekhilta of Rabbi Ishmael* on Exodus 14:29)[17]

THE TWO BUILDERS

Rabbi Elisha the son of Avuyah told this parable, "A person who has done good works and has also learned much Torah, to what is this individual like?

To one who builds a house by laying a foundation with large stones below and then builds with bricks above, in order that no matter how much water may flood against its foundation, the house will not wash away. But the person who has not done good works even though he or she has learned much Torah, to what is this individual like? To one who builds a house by laying a foundation with bricks below and then stones above, so that even if a little water flows against the foundation, it will at once destroy the house." (*Avot R. Nat.,* vers. A, ch. 24)

Therefore everyone who hears these words of mine and puts them into practice, is like a wise person who built his house upon the rock. The rain came down, the flood waters rose, the winds blew, and beat against that house. It did not fall, because it was built upon the rock. Everyone who hears these words of mine, however, and does not put them into practice, is like a foolish person who built his house upon the sand. The rain came down, the flood waters rose, the wind blew, and beat against that house. It fell down and great was its crash. (Matt 7:24–27)

---

[16] Finkelstein, *Sifre Devarim,* 120–21 (Hebrew). See Hammer, *Sifre,* 110–11 (English translation).
[17] Lauterbach, *Mekhilta Derabbi Ishmael,* 1:249.

Tikun Olam—"Mending a Broken World"

A "mending" takes place . . .

"The vessels are broken." "The Shekhina is in exile." God Himself is in a state of Tzimtzum—"retreat from the world"—without which the very being of the world would be impossible . . .

Even so, the radical problematic in the logic of Tikkun comes clearly to light. The "exile of Shekhina" and the "fracture of the vessels" refers to cosmic, as well as historical realities: it is that rupture that our Tikkun is to mend.

But how is this possible when we ourselves share in the cosmic condition of brokenness? Yet just in response to this problematic the kabbalistic Tikkun shows its profoundest energy.

It is precisely if the rupture, or the threat of it, is total, that all powers must be summoned for a mending. If the threat is to man, there is need to invoke divine as well as human power.

If the threat is to God—the "exile" is "an element in God Himself"—then human power must aid the divine.

> Emil Fackenheim, *To Mend the World: Foundation of Post-Holocaust Jewish Thought* (New York: Schocken Books, 1989), 253.

PART II

Introduction to Rabbinic Literature

After considering the conceptual world of the rabbis in the stream of ancient Jewish thought, it is time to turn to the rabbinic literature and consider each text. The Bible is the spring of living water that nourished the thought process and the development of written sources. As can be seen from the preceding section on texts that interpret texts, the rabbinic literature contains incredible parallels to the teachings of Jesus. But these parallels must be studied within their historical context. One must ask, Who said this? Where was this written? What is known about the written sources? Just as the student of the New Testament discovers that scholars disagree on the date and place of the twenty-seven documents of the Christian canon, so also we will discover that scholars hold different views concerning the composition of rabbinic literature. The Torah and Oral Torah have been given for study. Today, it is exciting to learn of current research, scholarly debate, fresh analysis, and practical application of this rich heritage that has so much to offer, not just for the Jewish community, but also to Christians and all others who desire to learn.

Life's Full-Energy Activities

Our Rabbis teach, "Four activities must be accomplished with full energy: Immersion in the study of Torah, actions done to help others, praying to God and an individual's life's work."

How do we learn about the "immersion in the study of Torah and actions done to help others"?

Because it is written, "Only be strong and very courageous to observe and to do, according to all the Torah which Moses My servant commanded you" (Joshua 1:7).

Hence the words, "Only be strong" refer to immersing oneself in the study of Torah, and the words to be, "very courageous" refer to actions which are accomplished to help others. How do we learn about "praying to God"?

Because it is written, "Wait with hope for the LORD, be strong, and allow your heart to take courage" (Psalm 27:14). How do we learn about "an individual's life's work"?

Because it is written, "Be strong, and let us prove ourselves courageous for our people" (2 Samuel 2:12).

   b. Berakhot 32b

CHAPTER 6

Introduction to Early Jewish Writings

Having explained the Sermon on the Mount within the context of ancient Jewish thought and tradition, we will now examine the specific literary works that belong to the rabbinic literature—Mishnah, Talmud, and Midrash—as well as some of the outstanding personalities mentioned in them who played a part in their formation. According to Jewish tradition, Moses received more than the five books of the Torah at Mount Sinai. The rabbis found support for this idea in Lev 26:46: "These are the statutes and the ordinances and the *torot* ["laws"] which the LORD established between himself and the children of Israel by the hand of Moses at Mount Sinai." They interpreted the plural *torot* to mean that God gave two Laws at Mount Sinai—one in writing and one by word of mouth. As we have seen, the aim of the Oral Torah is to interpret and help implement the Written Torah.

MISHNAH

In Jewish tradition, the Bible is called *Mikra,* meaning "that which is read." In order for something to be read, it must be in written form, so calling the Bible *Mikra* underscores that it is a written text. In addition to the written books of the Bible—the five books of Moses, or Torah, and the remaining sections of the Bible, or *Mikra*—there exists another tradition of oral teachings referred to as the Mishnah. *Mishnah* means "that which is repeated." The Mishnah was memorized and repeated in antiquity because the sages transmitted it orally from one generation to the next. Jewish tradition discouraged the writing down of the oral law in order to maintain a distinction between *Mikra* and Mishnah.

The oral law helped preserve the relevance and application of the Written Law. For example, in 1 Macc 2 we read that, at the start of the revolt against the Greeks, a group of pious men refuse to defend themselves on the Sabbath. As a result, the Greeks easily slaughter them and their wives and children (1 Macc 2:29–38). In the wake of this tragedy, Jewish legal opinion embraced the attitude that an observant Jew must defend him or herself on the Sabbath. The Torah was given so that you might live by it (Lev 18:5), not die by it, so the Torah principle of preserving life overrides the law of observing the Sabbath. Thus the oral interpretation clarifies issues that are not explained in the written text.

In Jesus' day, both oral and written laws were viewed as Torah. In an early rabbinic commentary on Leviticus we find this comment:

> "These are the rules [*chukim*] and judgments [*mishpatim*] and laws [*torot*, that is, 'revelations'] which the LORD established between Himself and the children of Israel through Moses on Mount Sinai" (Lev 26:46). The "rules" [*chukim*] refer to interpretations of the text [midrash], "judgments" refer to the principles of jurisprudence, and "laws" [*torot*, plural], teach that two laws were given to Israel on Mount Sinai: one written, and the other one was given orally. (*Sifra Torat Kohanim,* Behukotai Parashta 2, Perek 8)[1]

This comment demonstrates the inclusive nature of Torah, both Written and Oral. Torah constitutes more than the physical, written revelation given at Mount Sinai through Moses to Israel. The midrashic process of textual interpretation and its results were also understood to have been given at Mount Sinai. Moreover, Torah encompasses a whole, unique, pious approach to life that centers around faith in God, study of his Word, and obedience to his will. In reality, this is the meaning of Jesus' Sermon on the Mount, his approach to God's revelation on Mount Sinai. Jesus does not destroy Torah for Christians, he gives Torah fresh meaning through practical application in everyday life.

We may talk about Mishnah in a broad or narrow sense. In a broad sense, Mishnah may refer to everything Moses received from God at Mount Sinai that was not in written form. This would include the material preserved in the *midrashim* (the commentaries on the biblical text), which we will discuss below. In a narrow sense Mishnah refers to a specific canon or collection of legal opinions compiled under the direction of Rabbi Judah HaNasi, who is often called simply "Rabbi" in rabbinic literature.

RABBI JUDAH HANASI

A descendent of the family line of the great sage Hillel, Rabbi Judah flourished at the end of the second and beginning of the third centuries C.E. During the latter years of his life, he relocated himself and his col-

---

[1] Rabbenu Hillel, ed., *Sifra Debe Rav Hu Sefer Torat Kohanim* (Jerusalem: Schachne Koleditzky, 1971), 183.

leagues and disciples from Bet Shearim in the southern foothills of the Lower Galilee, to the city of Tzipori (or Sepphoris), in the Lower Galilee, three miles north and slightly west of the town of Nazareth. Rabbi Judah's work on the Mishnah is primarily associated with his residency in Tzipori. As a descendant of Hillel, he benefited from a prestigious family lineage going all the way back to King David. He was extremely well educated in Jewish tradition, as well as pious, humble, wealthy, and respected by the Romans, including the emperor himself. In essence, he embodied the most admirable qualities a sage could have. As a result of his learning, character, wealth and pedigree, Rabbi Judah became the spiritual leader of the Jewish people, hence the title Rabbi Judah HaNasi, or Rabbi Judah the Prince or Presiding Leader.

Rabbi Judah lived in the wake of the second failed Jewish revolt against Rome (Bar Kokhba Revolt) in 132–135 C.E. and the harsh ban which the Roman emperor Hadrian (76–138 C.E.) enacted against the study of Torah and practice of Judaism. Hadrian's banning of Judaism, which threatened any who violated it with death, was repealed by his successor, Antoninus Pius, sometime after 138 C.E. During this period of rebuilding, Rabbi Judah labored to strengthen his coreligionists and encourage the study and practice of Torah. With these goals in mind, Rabbi Judah undertook a massive project to collect, edit, and format a large corpus of legal opinions, both from his day and earlier generations, in order to establish a standard canon that would serve as the basis for legal discussions of future generations. Thus what had been preserved in the collective memory of disciples who were living books needed to be written.

The Mishnah that Rabbi Judah complied and edited contains the opinions and sayings of sages and rabbis from about 300 B.C.E. to 220 C.E. Nearly all of the Mishnah is written in Hebrew, which offers us a clue as to what languages were spoken in Israel in the first and second centuries C.E. Rabbi Judah collected opinions and sayings of earlier generations that had been preserved and transmitted in Hebrew. This suggests that during the time prior to Rabbi Judah's work, Hebrew was among the living, spoken languages of the Jewish people in Israel.

Today one may find easily an English translation of Rabbi Judah's Mishnah. For example, Herbert Danby, an Anglican scholar, translated the Mishnah in Jerusalem while at St. George's Cathedral. He completed the translation in 1933, and it was published by Oxford University Press. Reprinted numerous times in hardcover, Danby's translation of the text runs 789 pages in length. In 1964 a Jewish scholar, Philip Blackman, prepared a multi-volume edition of the Mishnah with English translation, Hebrew text, and commentary published by Judaica Press, Ltd. in New York City.

MISHNAH'S SIX ORDERS AND TRACTATES

The Mishnah is subdivided into six "orders or divisions," called *sedarim.* These six orders are further subdivided into *massekhtot,* or "tractates." The first order is *Zera'im,* or "Seeds," and mainly deals with agricultural laws. *Zera'im* has eleven tractates, the first of which is *Berachot,* or "Blessings," which opens with a discussion about prayer and giving thanks to God. From its very beginning, the Mishnah focuses on prayer.

The second order is *Mo'ed,* or "Appointed Time," and it deals with the Jewish holidays such as the Sabbath and Yom Kippur, otherwise known as the Day of Atonement. *Mo'ed* has twelve tractates.

The third order is *Nashim,* or "Women." It has seven tractates and mainly deals with laws and concerns relevant to women. For example, one of its tractates is called *Kiddushin,* or "Holiness," and addresses the proper procedure for a man to betroth a woman. The name of this tractate indicates the sanctity of home and family in Jewish thought.

The fourth order is *Nezikin,* or "Damages." *Nezikin* mainly deals with torts and casuistry and is a guide for public life. One must remember that the old rabbis, unlike today's pastors, by necessity were required to deal with civil law. *Nezikin* has ten tractates, one of which is the *Ethics of the Fathers.* A very old collection of ethical maxims and teachings of wisdom, the *Ethics of the Fathers* stands as the most celebrated tractate of the Mishnah, which is why its translation is provided in this book.[2]

Kodashin, or "Holy Things," is the fifth order of the Mishnah. Subdivided into eleven tractates, it addresses concerns centering around Temple worship. For example, *Tamid,* one of the oldest tractates of the Mishnah, deals with the proper procedures for offering the daily whole offering. In *Kodashin* one can find eye-witness accounts of the Temple and its worship in operation.

The sixth, last, and longest order of the Mishnah is *Toharot,* or "Purities." It discusses topics of ritual purity and is divided into twelve tractates. For example, from the tractate *Mikva'ot* 5:4 we learn that a person may ritually immerse for baptism in sea or ocean water. In the New Testament, after Philip had explained Isaiah 53 to the Ethiopian eunuch, the eunuch requested baptism (Acts 8:36), probably in the surf of the Mediterranean Sea, in accordance with the general guidelines found in *Mikva'ot* (which means "Ritual Immersion Baths").

---

[2] The translation in this book is my own. This text was essential study material for all Jewish learning. In many ways, it is the best introduction for early Jewish thought and literature.

READING A MISHNAIC CITATION

A tractate may be further subdivided into *perakim,* or "chapters," which may in turn be divided into *mishnayot,* or "mishnah verses." So here we encounter a third usage of the word *mishnah.* As the smallest subdivision of the Mishnah, a mishnah refers to a section of the text, often about twice the length of a Bible verse. So, if we encounter the Mishnaic citation *Avot* 3:1, (i.e., *The Ethics of the Fathers,* 3:1) to look up this reference we would turn to the fourth order of the Mishnah, which is *Nezikin* (we would need to know that *Avot* belongs to *Nezikin,* or to look it up in the table of contents, because no information about the order is included in a mishnaic citation), then turn to *Avot,* to the third chapter and the first mishnah.

TRACTATES OF THE MISHNAH

FIRST DIVISION—*ZERA'IM* ("SEEDS")

1. *Berakhot* ("Prayers and Blessings")
2. *Pe'ah* ("Gleanings")
3. *Demai* ("Produce not certainly tithed")
4. *Kil'ayim* ("Diverse Kinds")
5. *Shevi'it* ("The Seventh Year")
6. *Terumot* ("Heave-offerings")
7. *Ma'aserot* ("Tithes")
8. *Ma'aser Sheni* ("Second Tithe")
9. *Challah* ("Dough-offering")
10. *Orlah* ("The Fruit of Young Trees")
11. *Bikkurim* ("First-fruits")

SECOND DIVISION—*MO'ED* ("APPOINTED TIME")

12. *Shabbat* ("The Sabbath Rest and Worship")
13. *Eruvin* ("The Fusion of Sabbath Limits")
14. *Pesachim* ("Feast of Passover")
15. *Shekalim* ("The Shekel Dues")
16. *Yoma* ("The Day of Atonement")
17. *Sukkah* ("The Feast of Tabernacles")
18. *Yom Tov* or *Betzah* ("Festival days")
19. *Rosh haShanah* ("Feast of the New Year")
20. *Ta'anit* ("Days of Fasting")
21. *Megillah* ("The Scroll of Esther")
22. *Mo'ed Katan* ("Mid-Festival Days")
23. *Chagigah* ("The Festal Offering")

THIRD DIVISION—*NASHIM* ("WOMEN")

24. *Yevamot* ("Sisters-in-law")
25. *Ketubot* ("Marriage Deeds")
26. *Nedarim* ("Vows")
27. *Nazir* ("The Nazirite-vow")
28. *Sotah* ("The Suspected Adulteress")
29. *Gittin* ("Bills of Divorce")
30. *Kiddushin* ("Betrothals")

FOURTH DIVISION—*NEZIKIN* ("DAMAGES")

31. *Baba Kamma* ("The First Gate")
32. *Baba Metzi'a* ("The Middle Gate")
33. *Baba Batra* ("The Last Gate")
34. *Sanhedrin* ("The Sanhedrin")
35. *Makkot* ("Stripes")
36. *Shevu'ot* ("Oaths")
37. *Eduyyot* ("Testimonies")
38. *Avodah Zarah* ("Idolatry")
39. *Avot* ("Ethics of the Fathers")
40. *Horayot* ("Instructions")

FIFTH DIVISION—*KODASHIM* ("HOLY THINGS")

41. *Zevachim* ("Animal offerings")
42. *Menachot* ("Meal offerings")
43. *Chullin* ("Animals killed for food")
44. *Bekhorot* ("Firstlings")
45. *Arakhin* ("Vows of Valuation")
46. *Temurah* ("The Substituted Offering")
47. *Keritot* ("Extirpation")
48. *Me'ilah* ("Sacrilege")
49. *Tamid* ("The Daily Whole Offering")
50. *Middot* ("Measurements")
51. *Kinnim* ("The Bird-offerings")

SIXTH DIVISION—*TOHOROT* ("PURITIES")

52. *Kelim* ("Vessels")
53. *Ohalot* ("Tents")
54. *Nega'im* ("Leprosy signs")
55. *Parah* ("The Red Heifer")
56. *Tohorot* ("Cleannesses")
57. *Mikva'ot* ("Immersion pools")
58. *Niddah* ("The Menstruant")
59. *Makhshirin* ("Predisposers ")
60. *Zavim* ("They that suffer a flux")
61. *Tevul Yom* ("He that immersed himself that day")
62. *Yadayim* ("Hands")
63. *Uktzin* ("Stalks")

THE TALMUD

After having been compiled, edited, and formatted by Rabbi Judah and his colleagues, the Mishnah became the foundation for the next layer of Jewish legal scholarly activity, which developed into the Talmud. The word *talmud* literally means "that which is studied." The Talmud follows the Mishnah and quotes it directly. A component of the Talmud, in which study of the Mishnah is undertaken and commentary that seeks to explain all possible interpretations is produced, is called the *Gemara.*

Since the time of Ezra and Nehemiah (ca. 458–424 B.C.E.), a large and vigorous Jewish community had been residing in what was once Babylonia, but which in 539 B.C.E. became the empire of Persia. After the two failed revolts against Rome (the first in 66–70 C.E., and the second in 132–135 C.E.) and the harsh decrees of Hadrian (76–138 C.E.) that banned Judaism, the glory of the scholarly Jewish community in Israel began to fade in the emerging light of the Babylonian academies. Located in Persia, the Babylonian Jewish community had the advantage of living in the shadow of a government more sympathetic to it than Rome had been. Moreover, a surge of Christian activity in Israel, which included the building of numerous churches at the advent of the Byzantine era, also created an environment less conducive to Jewish scholarly activity. In Persia, Christianity had made only modest inroads, whereas in the West it had become the official religion of the Roman Empire.

JERUSALEM TALMUD AND BABYLONIAN TALMUD

In Israel the Jewish community produced the *Yerushalmi,* or "Jerusalem Talmud."[3] In Babylonia the Jewish community produced the *Bavli,* or "Babylonian Talmud." The *Yerushalmi* was compiled, edited, and formatted sometime about 350 C.E., although a complete compilation of the materials that could have been included in the *Yerushalmi* was never fully realized. The most influential editor and compiler of the Jerusalem Talmud was Rabbi Yochanan ben Napcha (ca. 180–279 C.E.) who opened an academy of Torah learning in Tiberias, which attracted some of the greatest scholars of the time. Rabbi Yochanan's father died before he was born and his mother died at childbirth. He was raised by his grandfather. In his youth, he studied for a short time with Rabbi Judah Ha-Nasi who saw greatness in him. His extensive knowledge and influence in Tiberias at his academy of learning impacted significantly the compilation of the Jerusalem Talmud. Shorter in length and less polished than the *Bavli,* the *Yerushalmi* has characteristics that reflect the historical situation of the Jewish communities in Israel. Waning in vigor, these communities were unable to supply the resources and scholars necessary to have seen this task to completion.

As a result the Babylonian Talmud eclipsed the Jerusalem Talmud and emerged as the great literary work of rabbinic Judaism. Tradition credits the monumental task of compiling, editing, and formatting the Babylonian Talmud to Rav Ashi. He lived from 335 to 428 C.E. and served as the head of the celebrated academy at Sura, in modern Iraq. There, surrounded by zealous students and seasoned scholars, he spearheaded the effort that eventually culminated after his lifetime in a second canon of Jewish legal material.

THE BABYLONIAN TALMUD

FIRST DIVISION—*ZERA'IM* ("SEEDS")

1. *Berakhot* ("Prayers and Blessings")

SECOND DIVISION—*MO'ED* ("APPOINTED TIME")

2. *Shabbat* ("The Sabbath Day Rest and Worship")	5. *Yoma* ("The Day of Atonement")
3. *Eruvin* ("The Fusion of Sabbath Limits")	6. *Sukkah* ("The Feast of Tabernacles")
4. *Pesachim* ("Feast of Passover")	7. *Yom Tov* or *Betzah* ("Festival-days")

---

[3] The complete English translation of the Jerusalem Talmud is called *The Talmud of the Land of Israel.* Sometimes it is called the *Talmud of Jerusalem* or the *Palestinian Talmud.*

8. *Rosh haShanah* ("Feast of the New Year")

9. *Ta'anit* ("Days of Fasting")

10. *Megillah* ("The Scroll of Esther")

11. *Mo'ed Katan* ("Mid-Festival Days")

12. *Chagigah* ("The Festal Offering")

THIRD DIVISION—*NASHIM* ("WOMEN")

13. *Yevamot* ("Sisters-in-law")

14. *Ketubot* ("Marriage Deeds")

15. *Nedarim* ("Vows")

16. *Nazir* ("The Nazirite-vow")

17. *Sotah* ("The Suspected Adulteress")

18. *Gittin* ("Bills of Divorce")

19. *Kiddushin* ("Betrothals")

FOURTH DIVISION—*NEZIKIN* ("DAMAGES")

20. *Baba Kamma* ("The First Gate")

21. *Baba Metzi'a* ("The Middle Gate")

22. *Baba Batra* ("The Last Gate")

23. *Sanhedrin* ("The Sanhedrin")

24. *Makkot* ("Stripes")

25. *Shevu'ot* ("Oaths")

26. *Abodah Zarah* ("Idolatry")

27. *Horayot* ("Instructions")

FIFTH DIVISION—*KODASHIM* ("HOLY THINGS")

28. *Zevachim* ("Animal offerings")

29. *Menachot* ("Meal offerings")

30. *Chullin* ("Animals killed for food")

31. *Bekhorot* ("Firstlings")

32. *Arakhin* ("Vows of Valuation")

33. *Temurah* ("The Substituted Offering")

34. *Keritot* ("Extirpation")

35. *Me'ilah* ("Sacrilege")

36. *Tamid* ("The Daily Whole offering")

SIXTH DIVISION—*TOHOROT* ("PURITIES")

37. *Niddah* ("The Menstruant")

THE JERUSALEM TALMUD

FIRST DIVISION—*ZERA'IM* ("SEEDS")

1. *Berakhot* ("Prayers and Blessings")

2. *Pe'ah* ("Gleanings")

3. *Demai* ("Produce not certainly tithed")

4. *Kil'ayim* ("Diverse Kinds")

5. *Shevi'it* ("The Seventh Year")

6. *Terumot* ("Heave-offerings")

7. *Ma'aserot* ("Tithes")

8. *Ma'aser Sheni* ("Second Tithe")

9. *Challah* ("Dough-offering")

10. *Orlah* ("The Fruit of Young Trees")

11. *Bikkurim* ("First-fruits")

SECOND DIVISION—*MO'ED* ("APPOINTED TIME")

12. *Shabbat* ("The Sabbath Rest and Worship")

13. *Eruvin* ("The Fusion of Sabbath Limits")

14. *Pesachim* ("Feast of Passover")

15. *Shekalim* ("The Shekel Dues")

16. *Yoma* ("The Day of Atonement")

17. *Sukkah* ("The Feast of Tabernacles")

18. *Yom Tov* or *Betzah* ("Festival days")
19. *Rosh haShanah* ("Feast of the New Year")
20. *Ta'anit* ("Days of Fasting")
21. *Megillah* ("The Scroll of Esther")
22. *Mo'ed Katan* ("Mid-Festival Days")
23. *Chagigah* ("The Festal Offering")

THIRD DIVISION—*NASHIM* ("WOMEN")

24. *Yevamot* ("Sisters-in-law")
25. *Ketubot* ("Marriage Deeds")
26. *Nedarim* ("Vows")
27. *Nazir* ("The Nazirite vow")
28. *Sotah* ("The Suspected Adulteress")
29. *Gittin* ("Bills of Divorce")
30. *Kiddushin* ("Betrothals")

FOURTH DIVISION—*NEZIKIN* ("DAMAGES")

31. *Baba Kamma* ("The First Gate")
32. *Baba Metzi'a* ("The Middle Gate")
33. *Baba Batra* ("The Last Gate")
34. *Sanhedrin* ("The Sanhedrin")
35. *Makkot* ("Stripes")
36. *Shevu'ot* ("Oaths")
37. *Avodah Zarah* ("Idolatry")
38. *Horayot* ("Instructions")

FIFTH DIVISION—*KODASHIM* ("HOLY THINGS")

SIXTH DIVISON—*TOHOROT* ("PURITIES")

39. *Niddah* ("The Menstruant")

THE MINOR TRACTATES

The Minor Tractates of the Talmud, usually numbering fifteen books, are added to the published Hebrew editions of the Talmud after the fourth division called *Nezikin,* which deals with damages.[4] Scholars debate the origin and background of these sources. In general, they teach a high ethical lifestyle and intensely spiritual way of looking at the world. They treat circumstances surrounding life events, such as marriage, comforting those who mourn, writing a Torah scroll, converting to Judaism, manners and customs in studying Torah, and, in general, how one conducts daily affairs. Daily actions like wearing the *tefillin,* or phylacteries, leather objects worn on the arm and forehead during Jewish prayers, the meaning of the *tzitzit,* tassels worn by Jews as part of their religious observance, and laws regulating the *mezuzah,* a small box on the door post of the home that contains the words found in Deut 6:4–9 and 11:13–21, all are discussed (see further descriptions of tefillin, tzitzit, and the mezuzah below).

---

[4] See M. Lerner's overview of the Minor Tractates, "The External Tractates," in *The Literature of the Sages* (ed. Shmuel Safrai; Philadelphia: Fortress, 1987), 367–409.

Some of the teachings in the Minor Tractates of the Talmud are only found in their texts, without other parallel sayings elsewhere in rabbinic literature. The longest of the tractates, *Avot of Rabbi Nathan,* which is forty-one chapters, is a running commentary on the *Ethics of the Fathers.* The text used for the *Ethics of the Fathers* demonstrates that the commentary is based upon early source materials.[5] Other tractates are short, like the chapter on peace, *Perek Hashalom,* which is just one chapter; sometimes it is added to the preceding text as a conclusion joining them together, making the total number of Minor Tractates in this collection fourteen instead of fifteen. The foundational core of the teaching materials in these tractates is very early and reveals much about the customs and faith traditions in ancient Judaism.

Though some scholars date the Minor Tractates of the Talmud to the Gaonic period, from the ninth to the twelfth centuries C.E., or even later, the scholar who has probably done the most intensive research and best textual study, Michael Higger, views these texts as coming from the Tannaitic period (20 B.C.E.–220 C.E.).[6] In his view, they were written in the land of Israel but edited in Babylon, and are based upon very early sources which were rejected by Rabbi Judah when he compiled the Mishnah. They became like an apocrypha, "outside writings" of the Mishnah. Because of the acceptance of the Mishnah's authority, they became less significant and were considered "minor tractates." Later compilers and editors influenced the texts at some points, but the core material remained rooted in the teachings of the Tannaim. So the texts were first compiled after the Mishnah and before the Talmud, though based upon earlier oral traditions. Of course, each individual text has a history of its own and must be studied separately. They all contain fundamental teaching materials on everyday conduct and teach a high moral and spiritual way of living.

The most complete English edition is found in the Soncino Talmud collection and it contains fifteen books, each with a different historical background and content.[7] Higger also made English translations of some of these

---

[5] Compare, for instance, Louis Finkelstein, "Introductory Study to Pirke Abot" *JBL* 58 (1938): 13–50; and his Hebrew work, *Mevo Lemasekhtot Avot Veavot Derabbi Natan* (New York: Jewish Theological Seminary, 1950).

[6] Michael Higger, *Seven Minor Tractates* (New York: Bloch, 1930), 5. He observes that "Nearly all the passages found in these seven tractates go back to Tannaitic sources. The compiler was a Palestinian and lived before the completion of the Babylonian Talmud. He utilized Tannaitic and other early sources. A number of statements found in these treatises are not found anywhere else." Regarding the other tractates in this collection, see Higger's other published works.

[7] Abraham Cohen and Israel Brodie, eds., *The Minor Tractates of the Talmud* (2 vols.; London: Soncino Press, 1971), xi.

books: *Derekh Eretz, Derekh Eretz Zuta,* and the last seven tractates.[8] Judah Goldin worked with *Avot of Rabbi Nathan* and made an excellent English translation of this text with an engaging introduction.[9] There are two versions of *Avot of Rabbi Nathan.* In 1887, Rabbi Solomon Schechter made a critical edition of these texts in Hebrew, which looks similar to a harmony of the Gospels or a Synopsis to New Testament, used to compare the similar and different wordings of individual story units in Matthew, Mark, and Luke. Scholars can compare the two Hebrew versions and gain insight from Schechter's annotations. In English, version B to *Avot of Rabbi Nathan* has been translated by Anthony Saldarini.[10]

The Minor Tractates, therefore, may be considered external teachings from the time of the compilation of the Mishnah, which were considered to be non-canonical and therefore placed outside the collection of Rabbi Judah the Prince. In published editions of the Hebrew Talmud, they are printed after the order of *Nezikin.* In the Soncino English Talmud collection they are published in a separate two-volume set. The texts were edited by Abraham Cohen, and represent ancient collections of *baraitot* edited in later times.[11] The themes of these writings focus on religious life in the community of faith. While it seems that they were originally written in Israel, they were edited and sometimes modified with later interpolations in Babylon. By reading and studying these ancient rabbinic writings one can feel the spiritual inner life of the Jewish people living in community.

1. *Avot of Rabbi Nathan* ("The Fathers according to Rabbi Nathan") contains forty-one chapters. This text gives commentary and explanation for the *Ethics of the Fathers.* It contains legal discussions, stories of Jewish theology in Agadah, and much ethical and moral teaching. Some scholars believe that the text was compiled by Rabbi Nathan, the second-century

---

[8] See Michael Higger, *The Treatises Derek Erez* (Brooklyn: Moinester, 1935), where he worked on a critical text and included a fine English translation and introduction to the texts. See also Higger, *Seven Minor Tractates.*

[9] Judah Goldin, *The Fathers according to Rabbi Nathan* (New Haven: Yale University Press, 1955).

[10] Anthony J. Saldarini, *The Fathers According to Rabbi Nathan* (Leiden: Brill, 1975). For the best Hebrew edition, see Solomon Schechter, *Avot Derabbi Natan* (Vienna: Lippe, 1887). A new introduction with brief textual notes has been prepared by Menahem Kister, *Avot de-Rabbi Nathan* (Jerusalem: Jewish Theological Seminary, 2005).

[11] The word *baraita* (sing.), *baraitot* (pl.) refers to an "outside" teaching coming from early Tannaitic sources which Rabbi Judah did not include in the Mishnah he compiled. These earlier teachings appear frequently in the rabbinic literature from later times. An excellent study and collection of these teachings was done in a ten volume work by Michael Higger, *Otzar Habaraitot* (10 vol.; New York: Shulsinger, 1938).

Tanna and son of a Babylonian exilarch, who went to the land of Israel to learn and to teach Torah.

2. *Soferim* ("On Scribes and their Work") contains twenty-one chapters.[12] The scribes were a caste of pious workers who were entrusted with the most sacred duty of preserving the divine word. This text describes the laws pertaining to handling and copying sacred scrolls, the materials suitable for the task, prayers and preparations that had to be made, as well as the public reading of Scriptures and liturgy for Sabbaths, holy days, and fasts. The teaching of *Soferim* lays down the rules governing the custom of reading the Psalms for daily worship and for the festivals.

3. *Semachot* ("On Joys," also called *Evel Rabbati,* "Great Mourning") contains fourteen chapters. This text deals with funeral arrangements, comforting the bereaved, and much more relating to grief and recovery.[13] The text contains parables, halakhah, agadah, and much useful information about caring for families suffering grief. Burial customs, such as gathering the bones for secondary burial, are discussed.

4. *Kallah* ("On the Bride") contains one chapter. As the name implies, this text deals with the subject of marriage. Betrothal, wedding, chastity, and sexual purity are treated in this important work.

5. *Kallah Rabbati* ("On the Bride," Greater Version) contains ten chapters. This text explores marriage and family concerns.[14] Expanding upon the purity of mind and body discussed in *Kallah,* the teachings of this tractate deal with proper personal behavior and moral conduct in daily affairs. The text is rich in stories and folklore traditions.

6. *Derekh Eretz Rabbah* ("On the Great Way for Living Life") contains eleven chapters. Like Paul's teachings on the fruit of the Spirit (Gal 5:22) or the message of the Dead Sea Scrolls on humility (1QS II, 24–25; III, 6–12; V, 4, 24; etc.), this text explores the life of discipleship. For acquisition of Torah learning, what is required of the disciple? Good manners and proper etiquette, and a life of humility and service for others is needed to obtain the wisdom of Torah.

7. *Derekh Eretz Zuta* ("On the Lesser Version for the Way of Living Life") contains ten chapters. Similar to the previous text, the lesser version gives moral and ethical teachings on humility and the proper way to live a

---

[12] See Michael Higger, *Masekhet Sofrim* (Jerusalem: Makor, 1970).

[13] The best edition is the one in Hebrew by Michael Higger, *Treatise Semahot* (New York: Bloch, 1931). David Flusser made extensive use of this text in his study of parables, *Yahadut Umekorot Hanatzrut* (Tel Aviv: Sifriyat Poalim, 1979), 150–209. The best English edition and translation is Dov Zlotnick, *The Tractate Mourning* (New Haven: Yale University Press, 1966).

[14] See Michael Higger, *Masekhtot Kallah* (Jerusalem: Makor, 1970).

meaningful life as a Torah learner. The difference between this and the previous tractate is its orientation; *Derekh Eretz Zuta* is concerned more with Torah scholars. One will discover rich proverbs and wisdom sayings similar to the *Ethics of the Fathers*.[15]

8. *Perek Hashalom* ("On Peace") contains one chapter. Sometimes viewed as the conclusion of the previous text, in truth it is a separate document. The echoes of Messianic teachings are seen in this text. Society will be in a state of decline and moral decay, in a spiral of indecency that will lead to the coming of the Messiah. This text speaks about the force of shalom in the world and how lives can be changed through improved peaceful relations.

9. *Gerim* ("On Converts") contains four chapters. This chapter deals with the treatment of converts in the Jewish community. Genuine proselytes must be received fully into the Israelite covenant of faith. The process of circumcision, baptism, and sacrifice is discussed. They must be given favor for they are like Abraham the Patriarch, who showed the example of faith.

10. *Kutim* ("On Samaritans," foreigners) contains two chapters. This text discusses the Samaritans and their intermingling of traditional Jewish customs with pagan beliefs and influences (see 2 Kgs 17:24–41). The question of whether Samaritans should be treated as wayward Jews or as Gentiles seems to be an open issue in this text, which indicates its early provenance. The text looks to a time when the Samaritans may be received back into the fold of the Jewish community, when they renounce Mount Gerizim as a holy rival to Jerusalem and affirm belief in the resurrection of the dead.

11. *Avadim* ("On Slaves," Hebrew servants) contains three chapters. This text deals with the laws concerning Hebrew servants and their release. (Even at its best, slavery was a horrific and reprehensible institution. Nonetheless slavery was practiced in the ancient Near Eastern cultures of the Hebrew Bible and made up a significant segment of the economy in the Greco-Roman world.) Scriptural teachings on the dignity of each human being laid down regulations for the humane treatment of slaves. These teachings became the basis of this text, which describes the redemption of slaves and the process of how the Hebrew slave could be released from servitude.

---

[15] Some of the *Derekh Eretz* and *Derekh Eretz Zuta* materials contain sayings attributed to Tannaim, but many of the teachings are unattributed. Could this literature preserve some of the early teachings of the *hasidim,* or pious ones, such as Chanina ben Dosa, Chanan Hanechba, or even Choni the Circle Drawer? Although their teachings are hardly recorded in rabbinic literature, it is possible that some of these high moral and ethical traditions were originally formulated orally in these pious circles and later preserved anonymously in the external tractates, outside the more authoritative Mishnah.

Jesus and the Woman at the Well, John 4:7–16
(Wood Engraving by Bernard A. Solomon)

12. *Sefer Torah* ("On the Book of the Torah") contains five chapters. This text deals with the Torah and how it is preserved in the community of faith. It has a strong similarity with the first five chapters of *Soferim,* which also discusses the proper materials and techniques used to copy a Torah scroll. Additionally, this tractate gives a list of the divine names that may not be erased. It reveals a great reverence for the holy names of God and prohibits profane usage of any of the sacred names.

13. *Tefillin* ("On Phylacteries") contains one chapter. This text discusses the laws relating to praying while wearing tefillin (see description above). Wearing tefillin fulfills the Scripture, "You shall bind them as a sign on your hand and they shall be as frontlets on your forehead" (Deut 6:8). In the Torah, this sign is connected to God's redemptive power: "It shall serve as a sign to you on your hand, and as a reminder on your forehead, that the Torah of the LORD may be in your mouth because it was with a powerful hand that the LORD brought you out of Egypt" (Exod 13:9). The

prevalence of this practice is demonstrated by the discovery at Qumran of tefillin.[16] While in Matt 23:5 Jesus warns his disciples against making an ostentatious display of religiosity by enlarging the tefillin or lengthening the tzitzit (see description above and below) to draw attention to one's devotion, he most certainly put on tefillin and wore tzitzit. Jesus emphatically declares, "these you ought to have done" (Matt 23:23); that is to say, these commandments must be fulfilled, but with the right attitude of the heart. Like Jesus, the rabbinic literature warns against the ostentatious display of tefillin.[17]

14. *Tzitzit* ("On Prayer Shawl Fringe") contains one chapter. This text discusses traditions and laws relating to the prayer shawl fringe (see description above). The tzitzit fulfills the commandment of Scripture, "Speak to the children of Israel that they shall make for themselves tassels [prayer shawl type fringes] on the corners of their garments throughout their generations. They shall weave a blue cord into the fringe of each corner. This fringe shall cause you to look at and remember all the commandments of the LORD, so as to do them" (Num 15:38–39; see also Deut 22:12). The wearing of the tzitzit reminds the individual of the commandments of God and how to live a meaningful life of spirituality. This tractate answers questions like: When the prayer shawl is used as a burial shroud, for instance, should the fringe or tassel be tied according to proper ritual or should it be untied because it is touching a dead body for burial? This fringe is most definitely the "hem of the garment" from the clothing of Jesus that the woman sick with the flow of blood touched in order to be healed (Matt 9:20; Luke 8:44).[18]

15. *Mezuzah* ("On the Doorpost Box Container,") contains two chapters. This text discusses the importance of the mezuzah (see description above), and the laws that regulate how it is attached to the doorpost of the home as a sign of God's covenant with Israel. The hanging up of a mezuzah fulfills the commandment, "You must write them on the doorposts of your house and upon your gates" (Deut 6:9).

---

[16] See Yigal Yadin, *Tefillin from Qumran* (Jerusalem: Israel Exploration Society, 1969).

[17] See, for instance, Rabbi Judah ben Batira's warning in *Sifra* 86a (Isaac H. Weiss, ed., *Sifra*, [Vienna: Salsberg, 1862]) against enlarging the prayer shawl fringe; also cf. *b. Baba Batra* 98a, where there is a warning against becoming boastful with the prayer shawl. Here in the Minor Tractate, *Tefillin* 1:13, there is a warning against overlaying the box with gold. Jesus and the rabbis stressed having the correct attitude of the heart.

[18] The Greek word *kraspedon* is the term used to describe this prayer shawl fringe. See BDAG, 564. See also Matt 14:36 and Mark 6:56, where the sick come to touch the prayer shawl fringe and are healed. The RSV translates the word as "fringe."

Title Page from the Talmud (Tractate Sanhedrin)

Page from the Talmud (Tractate Sanhedrin)

READING TALMUD CITATIONS

Both Talmuds reflect the structural arrangement set by the Mishnah. The Mishnah contains sixty-six tractates; the Jerusalem Talmud comments on thirty-nine of the tractates, and the Babylonian Talmud discusses thirty-seven of them. In other words, the structure of the Mishnah provided the framework around which later Jewish scholars built the Talmud. A traditional citation for the Talmud is given in the form of "*b. Ta'anit* 3a." The "*b.*" stands for the Babylonian Talmud, distinguishing references to the Babylonian Talmud from the Jerusalem Talmud, which is usually indicated by the abbreviation "*y.*" The name *Ta'anit* is a tractate of the Mishnah which belongs to the Order of *Mo'ed,* the "3" refers to the page, and the "a" indicates the front side of the page (the back side is "b"). So in the English translation of the Talmud, pages 5 and 6 of *Ta'anit* are also labeled with the traditional notation according to the Hebrew edition with 3a–b. Usually three or four pages of English text are needed to translate one page of a Hebrew and Aramaic Talmudic passage.

On a representative page of Talmud one sees a rectangular portion of text centered and surrounded by a border of additional texts. The central text is the Talmud proper. It consists of a series of alternating sections of Mishnah text and related Gemara.

The sections of Mishnah tend to be short, and begin with the Hebrew abbreviation for Mishnah in bold letters. The Gemara sections are longer and begin with the Hebrew abbreviation for Gemara in bold print. Gemara is an Aramaic noun that is related to the verb *gemar,* meaning "to learn by memorization." To say that the Gemara functions as a commentary on the Mishnah represents only part of the story. The Gemara comments on *and* supplements the Mishnah. It also uses the Mishnah as a springboard for launching into all sorts of discussions that can deviate substantially from the original content of the Mishnaic quotation.

RASHI—RABBI SHLOMO BEN YITZAK

Bordering the centered chunk of Mishnah and Gemara are later commentaries. Rabbi Shlomo ben Yitzak, otherwise known by the abbreviation "Rashi," wrote the essential commentary on the Talmud.[19] He also wrote important commentaries on most books of the Bible. Virtually every Talmud, except for specialized modern editions, has been printed with Rashi's commentary running along the outside border of the Mishnah and Gemara. In

---

[19] See Chaim Pearl, *Rashi* (New York: Grove Press, 1988).

reality, Rashi's commentary was composed by more than one Rashi, since his son also worked on the explanation.

Rashi was born in Troyes, France in 1040 C.E., and worked prolifically as a biblical commentator until his death in 1105. Toward the end of his life he witnessed the tragedy inflicted upon the French Jewish communities by the unruly hoards participating in the first Crusade of 1095. He lost family and friends as the Crusaders marched through France.

One remarkable feature of a page of Talmud is the geographic and temporal distances that it spans. The Mishnah represents Jewish thought up to approximately 220 C.E. The Gemara represents a later layer of learning originating mainly in the great Babylonian academies during the Byzantine period (135–638 C.E.). Rashi's commentary offers a sample of the achievements of the French academies in the Middle Ages. So on a page of Talmud, from Rabbi Judah's Mishnah to Rashi's commentary, 800 years of Jewish learning, from Israel to Babylonia, from Babylonia to Europe, offers itself to be examined, studied, argued, and supplemented by Jewish scholars of today. The Talmud is as awe-inspiring a monument to the legacy of Jewish biblical scholarship as the pyramids in Egypt are to the splendor of the Pharaohs.

MIDRASH

We now direct our attention toward the midrashic literature, especially toward the midrashic commentaries committed to writing at about the same time as the Mishnah. When talking about interpreting the five books of Moses, we have entered the world of midrash. A good way to make the transition in our discussion from Mishnah to midrash is by taking an actual example where the two function in tandem to reinforce each other on a point of *halakhah,* or "rabbinic law."

In *Nega'im* 2:5 of the Mishnah we read: "A man may examine any leprosy-signs excepting his own leprosy-signs. Rabbi Meir says: 'Excepting also those in his near of kin.'" In typical Mishnaic fashion, *Nega'im* 2:5 makes no appeal to Scripture, it merely states an anonymous opinion followed by the opinion of Rabbi Meir. In other words, there is no proof text from the Bible to buttress Rabbi Meir's opinion, which offers further qualification of the anonymous opinion.

In a midrash called *Sifre al Bemidbar* we find a comment on Num 12:12, which interprets Aaron's exclamation upon seeing that God had punished his sister Miriam by smiting her with leprosy: "Oh, do not let her be like one dead!" The midrash comment reads: "'Oh, do not let her be like one dead' (Num 12:12)! Aaron exclaimed, 'It is as if I have lost my sister! I cannot quarantine her. Neither can I declare her impure, nor can I declare her clean!' " (*Sifre al Bemidbar,* on Piska 105).[20] Thus we learn that Aaron believed he could not deal with the leprosy of those related to him. According to Lev 13–14, the priest is responsible for examining a person with leprosy, quarantining the person, and declaring the person clean after the leprosy has disappeared. According to the midrash, Aaron realizes that, as a sibling, the halakhah forbids him from examining, isolating, or declaring Miriam clean. He feels helpless about the situation and cries out in frustration that his sister is "as one dead."[21]

In both cases the halakhic ruling about a priest being barred from examining, isolating, and declaring clean a relative is affirmed. The Mishnah simply quotes the opinion of Rabbi Meir with no appeal to Scripture. The midrash, however, claims the same by appealing to Num 12:12 as scriptural proof. Here we see a fine example of how Mishnah and midrash can work together, while taking different approaches, to strengthen a point of halakhah.

The word *midrash* is related to the Hebrew verb *darash,* which in biblical Hebrew means "to seek, consult, inquire of."[22] Often in the Bible the verb is used in the context of seeking out a prophetic word from the God of Israel or pagan deities. For example, 1 Kgs 22 describes King Jehoshaphat of Judah and King Ahab of Israel making preparations for war against their common enemy the King of Aram. Before mobilizing against Aram, Jehoshaphat insists upon seeking a word from the Lord about their plans.

> Then the king of Israel gathered the prophets together, about four hundred men, and said to them, "Shall I go against Ramoth-gilead to battle or shall I refrain?" And they said, "Go up, for the LORD will give it into the hand of the king." But Jehoshaphat said, "Is there not yet a prophet of the LORD here that we may inquire [*darash*] of him?" The king of Israel said to Jehoshaphat, "There is yet one man by whom we may inquire [*darash*] of the LORD, but I hate him, because he does not prophesy good concerning me, but evil. He is Micaiah son of Imlah." (1 Kgs 22:6–8 NASB)

Midrash is always tied to the biblical text; one cannot engage in midrash without "darashing" the text or probing its full implication. Midrash represents the process, method, and rules of interpretation, which ancient Jewish teachers formulated not only for exposition, but also for seeking God through Scripture. (Hillel the Elder developed seven such principles for interpreting the Bible, which will be discussed later.) Midrash employs well-

---

[20] Horovitz, *Sifre,* 103. The translation is my own. Compare Paul Levertoff, trans., *Midrash Sifre on Numbers* (London: SPCK, 1926), 87. Reuven Hammer also translates the text: *The Classic Midrash: Tannaitic Commentaries on the Bible* (New York: Paulist, 1995), 261.

[21] See Hammer, *The Classic Midrash,* 261.

[22] See BDB, 205.

defined principles of hermeneutics to unravel the deeper meaning of the sacred text. As my mentor, Professor David Flusser, once remarked, "midrash may be compared to taking a lemon and squeezing every drop out of it." Midrash aims at squeezing every possible drop of meaning out of the biblical text. In a broad sense, Torah includes this whole process of interpretation and seeking the divine will through Scripture.

APPROXIMATE DATES OF RABBINIC TEXTS

These texts were compiled based on oral tradition toward the end of each period.

From the Tannaitic Period, from 20 B.C.E. to 220 C.E.

Mishnah (Oral Torah)	Tosefta (Supplements to Mishnah)
Mekhilta deRabbi Ishmael (on Exodus)	*Mekhilta deRabbi Simeon bar Yochai* (on Exodus)
Sifra, Torat Kohanim (on Leviticus)	*Sifre Bemidbar* (on Numbers and Deuteronomy)
Sifre Zuta (on Numbers)	*Sifre Devarim* (on Deuteronomy)

[*Seder Elijah, Tanna deBe Eliyahu,* date disputed, ethical midrash]

[Minor Tractates of the Talmud, date disputed]

From the Early Amoraic Period, from 220 C.E. to 400 C.E.

Genesis Rabbah	*Leviticus Rabbah*
Lamentations Rabbah	*Esther Rabbah*
	Jerusalem Talmud

From the Late Amoraic Period, from 400 C.E. to 500 C.E.

Pesikta of Rab Kahana	*Song of Songs Rabbah*
Ruth Rabbah	Babylonian Talmud

From the Post-Amoraic Period, from 500 C.E. to 900 C.E.

Midrash Proverbs	Midrash Samuel
Ecclesiastes Rabbah	*Tanchuma*
Numbers Rabbah	*Pesikta Rabbati*
Exodus Rabbah	Midrash on Psalms

[Minor Tractates of the Talmud, date disputed]

[*Seder Elijah, Tanna deBe Eliyahu,* date disputed, ethical midrash]

Origins of the Synagogue

As centuries passed, Judaism evolved and so did its primary language, Hebrew. During the intertestamental period, the verb *darash* assumed additional nuances of meaning that reflected a fundamental shift in Judaism. History impacted the people, their faith, and their language. In 586 B.C.E., the King of Babylonia destroyed Solomon's Temple and carried the Jewish people off into exile. While in Babylonia, the Jewish people had an opportunity to reflect on their covenantal relationship with God, the Torah entrusted to them at Mount Sinai, and the repeated warnings of the prophets. Acknowledging their wayward past, the people abandoned idolatry and turned again to the one true God. They began seeking God through immersing themselves in study of their sacred literature—the Bible. The reading and proper interpretation of the Bible began to assume a place of prominence in the Jewish religious experience.

The synagogue as an institution also emerged at about this time. One of its primary functions was to serve as a forum for the public reading of Scripture. Every weekend the Jewish people assembled in synagogues to hear a section of the Bible read aloud and then explained according to a lectionary cycle. In this context, *darash* came to mean seeking the divine will through an intense engagement with Scripture.[23]

As decades passed, this intense way of reading Scripture—otherwise known as *midrash*—became quite sophisticated. It also generated a mass of interpretations and traditions that became interwoven with the fabric of the biblical text. This mass of material had already swelled considerably by the time Jesus and his disciples arrived on the scene. One can gain glimpses of Jesus drawing from this reservoir of midrashic material in the Synoptic Gospels.[24] About 170 years after Jesus' death and resurrection (i.e., ca. 200 C.E.), the rabbis decided to start collecting, editing, and formatting this mass of material. They began collecting and writing down the ancient oral teachings and early midrashim, which explained the deeper meaning of the Bible.[25]

An important point to keep in mind is that, as a system, approach, or strategy for reading the Bible and ensuring its relevancy, midrash was birthed

---

[23] See Marcus Jastrow, *A Dictionary of the Targumim, the Talmud Babli and Yerushalmi, and the Midrashic Literature* (Peabody, Mass.: Hendrickson, 2005), 325.

[24] See, for instance, Jan W. Doeve, *Jewish Hermeneutics in the Gospels and Acts* (Assen, Netherlands: Van Gorcum, 1954); and E. P. Sanders, *Jewish Law from Jesus to the Mishnah* (Philadelphia: Trinity, 1990).

[25] See Schofer, *The Making of a Sage,* 68, "Rabbinic literature is filled with descriptions of the revelation at Sinai that dramatize and intensify the biblical narrative."

in the land of Israel, and it experienced its golden age between approximately 100 B.C.E. and 400 C.E., though certainly midrashic activities preceded and continued after this golden age. The sages and rabbis of Israel excelled in midrash. Although the torch of Jewish scholarship passed from the hands of rabbis in Israel to Babylonian academies like Sura and Pumbidetha about the fifth century C.E., the Babylonian scholars never eclipsed the midrashic creativity and activity undertaken at the earliest stages in Israel—the period of interpretation to which Jesus himself contributed. Midrash is the intensification of Torah. In this line of tradition, Jesus did not cancel the law and the prophets. Rather, he intensified Torah by his midrashic interpretation.

TANNAITIC AND AMORAIC MIDRASHIM

When speaking of the midrashim as rabbinic commentaries on Scripture, we can categorize them according to their formal characteristics and the historical period in which their contents were collected, edited, and formatted. Organizing them this way we can separate them into three groups: exegetical, homiletical, and ethical. Categorizing them according to historical periods, we can separate them into Tannaitic (20 B.C.E.–220 C.E.) and Amoraic (220–500 C.E.) midrashim.

For our purposes we will discuss the midrashim in terms of being Tannaitic or Amoraic. Our treatment will not be exhaustive, but introductory. Though their history is complex, some form of the Tannaitic midrashim probably were committed to writing by 220 C.E., similar to the Mishnah. The word Tannaitic refers to a period of time from about the time of Jesus' birth (ca. 4 B.C.E.), when Hillel and Shammai flourished, to 220 C.E. It comes from the Hebrew and Aramaic word *tanah,* which means "to repeat," and is related to the word *shanah,* which also means "to repeat," and from which the word *mishnah* is derived. There are five principle Tannaitic midrashim: *Mekhilta, Sifra, Sifre BeMidbar, Sifre Zuta,* and *Sifre Devarim.* These rabbinic commentaries are concerned with the five books of Moses and are categorized as exegetical midrashim.[26]

"Exegesis" and "exegetical" are words often heard in seminary classes. They come from the Greek *exago,* which means "to lead out," hence the idea of leading meaning out of a text. If something is exegetical, it has to do with the interpretation of a text. The structure of the exegetical midrashim reflects

---

[26] *Midrash Tannaim on Deuteronomy* is based on Cairo Geniza fragments. The *Midrash Hagadol* could also be included. The editions of the Tannaitic midrashim used today may have been written in their present form following the Mishnah. Originally they represented the perspectives of the schools of Akiva and Ishmael from debates of Torah study.

the structural arrangement of the Bible, because they move verse by verse through Scripture and offer a running commentary on it. For example, the Mekhilta is a commentary on Exodus, Sifra on Leviticus, Sifre BeMidbar on Numbers, and also Sifre Zuta on Numbers and Sifre Devarim on Deuteronomy. These texts are largely exegetical in content.

The personalities mentioned in this earliest group of midrashim are called *tannaim*, or "repeaters," because they were known for memorizing and repeating the Oral Torah. Aaron Hyman has estimated the Tannaim to have been about 420 in number.[27] These personalities were the driving force behind the growing mass of midrashic material during the Tannaitic period. Since the interpretation of the Bible impacts the interpretation of legal issues surrounding observance of Torah in daily living, the midrash is also naturally connected to Mishnah.

After the Tannaitic midrashim were committed to writing, a second group of rabbinic Bible commentaries emerged called the Amoraic midrashim. Like the Tannaitic midrashim, this later group takes its name from the historical period in which they were compiled and edited. The Aramaic word *amora* refers to a learned individual who stood beside a sage while he gave a public discourse, and served as his public announcement system; he would repeat loudly and perhaps clarify succinctly the content of the sage's lecture.

Picking up where the Tannaitic period ended, the Amoraic period spanned roughly the next two hundred years (220–500 C.E.). The Amoraic midrashim were in writing by 450 C.E. and may be thought of as Byzantine midrashim. They include both exegetical and homiletical commentaries. Some representative examples of Amoraic midrashim are *Bereshit (Genesis) Rabbah, Veyikra (Leviticus) Rabbah, Kohelet (Ecclesiastes) Rabbah, Eicha (Lamentations) Rabbah, Shir Hashirim (Song of Songs) Rabbah,* and *Pesikta of Rab Kahana.* The *Pesikta of Rab Kahana* is homiletical in content, revealing rabbinic preaching relating to religious life and the sacred calendar. Jewish festivals are the subject of sermons. The other Amoraic midrashim mentioned here follow an exegetical format with verse-by-verse discussion, but these texts generally contain more homily than their Tannaitic counterparts.

The rabbinic involvement with the biblical text in midrashic activity went beyond the Tannaitic and Amoraic periods. Even after the Muslim expansion from 640 C.E., rabbis continued to develop midrashim often based upon earlier texts; most of the materials in post-Amoraic midrashim are largely based upon the earlier teachings of the Tannaim and the Amoraim.

---

[27] Aaron Hyman, *Toldoth Tannaim Veamoraim* (3 vols.; Jerusalem: Boys Town, 1964), 1:8–16.

Of course the dating of midrashic works is debated among even the finest scholars. *Seder Eliyahu*, for instance, is dated by some scholars to the Tannaitic Period and by others to the ninth century C.E.! The ethical midrash does not ever mention a rabbi later than the Tannaim. Rich in stories, parables, and practical ethical teachings, *Seder Eliyahu* features a Hebrew style all its own. Since no Amora is mentioned, quite probably the core materials flow from the Tannaim even if the text underwent later revisions. So the Tannaitic midrashim are attributed largely to Tannaim, whereas the later Amoraic midrashim contain teachings and discussions attributed to both Tannaitic and Amoraic rabbis.[28] But even late midrashic anthologies dating to around 1200–1300 C.E., such as the *Yalkut Shimeoni* or the *Yalkut Machiri,* bring together various interpretations of the Bible from previous generations. Sometimes these midrashic collections even quote by name sources that have not survived to the modern period. One early Midrash quoted by the name *Yelamdenu,* "Teach us," our Master, is known only from secondary quotations in later sources. These ancient sources are known from quotations in later texts, in much the same way that Christian scholars know about the early Bishop Papias from quotations by the later church historian Eusebius.

THE CHAKHAMIM

After the Amoraic period, *midrashim* continued to be written. A distinction needs to be made, however, between the earlier Tannaitic and Amoraic midrashim and later *midrashim.* The scholars who are mentioned in the Tannaitic and Amoraic texts belonged to a specific social group of learned scholars who were called sages, or *chakhamim.* In Hebrew a *chakham* refers to a "wise or learned person." After 70 C.E. a *chakham* often carried the title of "Rabbi." After 70 C.E., this title may indicate that a sage had received rabbinic ordination. In Jesus' day this type of ordination is not widely attested; the title probably simply meant "my teacher," rather than an ordained member of the clergy. In Babylon, the sages were called "Rav."

As a social group, the *chakhamim* spanned the Tannaitic and Amoraic periods. At the end of the Amoraic period, however, the heads of the Babylonian academies eclipsed the *chakhamim* of Israel. After 450 C.E., scribes continued to collect and reshape material from earlier generations. In other words, later scribes and scholars recycled the earlier midrashic material that the *chakhamim* had produced, and wrote new midrashic commentaries based on older traditions. These newer rabbinic texts were also referred to as

---

[28] Amoraic teachers may appear in Tannaitic sources due to later interpolations or combining of later sources.

midrashim. Thus when speaking of midrashim, we could be talking about an early midrashic text from the Tannaitic and Amoraic periods or a later text from the time after the *chakhamim*. Some of these later midrashim were composed as recently as the ninth and tenth centuries.

Midrash Rabbah

Midrash Rabbah, or "The Great Bible Commentary," is a large and well-known collection of midrashim. These rabbinic interpretations of Scripture follow a verse-by-verse exegetical approach to commenting on the five books of Moses and the five *megillot*. In Hebrew, *megillot* means "scrolls," and as a proper noun refers to the books of Ruth, Esther, Lamentations, Song of Solomon (or Song of Songs), and Ecclesiastes. These scrolls are read and studied on Jewish holidays. Traditionally Lamentations is read for the ninth of the month *Av,* which commemorates the destruction of the Temple. Ruth is read for Pentecost; Ecclesiastes is read for Tabernacles; Esther for Purim; and the Song of Songs is read for Passover. Each of the midrashim in this collection is named after the book of the Bible on which it comments, hence the names *Exodus Rabbah, Deuteronomy Rabbah,* and so on. The earliest midrashim in *Midrash Rabbah* are Amoraic. Some of the later ones, such as *Exodus Rabbah* and *Numbers Rabbah,* were compiled between the sixth and twelfth centuries C.E.

English Name	Hebrew Name
Genesis Rabbah	*Bereshit Rabbah*
Exodus Rabbah	*Shemot Rabbah*
Leviticus Rabbah	*Veyikra Rabbah*
Numbers Rabbah	*Bemidbar Rabbah*
Deuteronomy Rabbah	*Devarim Rabbah*
Lamentations Rabbah	*Eichah Rabbah*
Ruth Rabbah	*Rut Rabbah*
Ecclesiastes Rabbah	*Kohelet Rabbah*
Esther Rabbah	*Ester Rabbah*
Song of Songs Rabbah	*Shir Hashirim Rabbah*

COMPARING RABBINIC LITERATURE WITH THE GOSPELS

One common criticism directed against using rabbinic literature for comparative study with the Gospels is the gap in time that exists between when Jesus lived and when a given rabbinic text was compiled and put into writing. The earliest rabbinic texts we have are the Mishnah, Tosefta,[29] and the Tannaitic midrashim.[30] Before the Talmud there was the Torah, and the midrashim interpret its significance in personal experience. All of these were written by around 220 C.E., and most scholars agree that they contain much earlier sources.[31]

While it is true that these texts reflect the concerns of the Jewish community in Israel during the late second and early third centuries C.E., the careful scholar must be sensitive to earlier materials. Consequently, to focus on reading rabbinic literature as the product of only one period, without recognizing the earlier history of many teachings, is a serious mistake. These texts should never be excluded from comparative study with the Gospels because, even if written in 220 C.E., the composite nature of rabbinic literature means that earlier sources were employed from a carefully preserved oral history that was passed down. Having moved like a glacier down a slope through time, rabbinic literature cycled through itself old traditions while also picking up new ones. In certain aspects a rabbinic text resembles an archeological tel, a hill or mound of a buried city of antiquity that archaeologists excavate and evaluate. Like a tel, which contains numerous levels or strata of civilization, a rabbinic text contains new and old material and everything in between. Scholars must rely on their expertise, tried methods of textual criticism, and comparative research with other texts in order to sort out which material is earlier and which is later.[32]

---

[29] The Tosefta, literally "addition or supplement," is parallel in its organization to the Mishnah and contains teachings not included in the Mishnah. As a supplement to the Mishnah, it often has parallel discussions on issues of religious observance, and at times explains and interprets the Mishnah.

[30] The Tannaitic Bible commentaries are really the foundation of all the oral tradition because they explore the deeper meaning of the Scripture and give practical application. The Tannaitic midrash on the five books of Moses are frequently called *Midrashe Halakhah.* Long before the Talmud was written, these midrashim taught how to apply the teachings of Torah to everyday life.

[31] Of course each document must be studied individually and the date and provenance for a text will produce fierce debate. Related to this issue is whether midrash preceded halakhah or whether halakhah emerged from the midrashic Scripture interpretation. Today probably the more popular view is that religious practice and halakhah were first, and that midrash was used to validate accepted observance. I tend to believe that observance flowed from Bible study. In any case, halakhah and midrash are closely interrelated in Jewish practice.

[32] In fact, much earlier material appears in the Amoraic literature in the form of *Baraitot,* "outside teaching," of early origin but excluded from Rabbi Judah's Mishnah. As noted in footnote 11 above, the eminent Talmudic scholar Michael Higger studied and collected the *Baraitot* in an important ten-volume work, *Otzar Habaraitot.*

Some New Testament scholars exclude the evidence of rabbinic literature in researching early Christianity. These same scholars, however, will study New Testament apocryphal documents or references in the writings of the church fathers that are contemporary with rabbinic sources. For example, Papias, the Bishop of Hierapolis, is often studied for information he reveals about the composition of the Gospels. Papias died around 130 C.E., about the time of Rabbi Akiva, and nothing Papias wrote has survived. Scholars study his writings as they were preserved by the church historian Eusebius, who died around 340 C.E. While some scholars accept quotations from Papias, cited by Eusebius, as valuable for New Testament study, they reject references to Hillel, who lived in 20 B.C.E., from the Mishnah, which was compiled in 220 C.E. This is not consistent scholarly method. I believe that it is poor scholarship to exclude the valuable evidence from rabbinic literature when studying the New Testament environment, because Jewish texts contain crucial historical and cultural information. Historical and critical methods must be used to evaluate all resources, including rabbinic literature.

DATING RABBINIC TEXTS

The sages made a concerted effort to pass down a saying or tradition in the name of its originator. It is not uncommon to see in the rabbinic literature a saying preceded by a string of two or three rabbis' names. The name of a rabbi quoted in a source is often used to date the saying.[33] If an encyclopedia which was printed yesterday quoted Franklin Delano Roosevelt as saying, ". . . the only thing we have to fear is fear itself," it would be historically inaccurate to date the statement to the time in which the encyclopedia was published. Roosevelt did not make that statement yesterday, with events of yesterday in mind. Rather, he made this powerful speech in his first inaugural address in 1933 when economic panic gripped the nation in the midst of the Great Depression; when most banks were closed, industrial production plummeted, unemployment soared, and farmers were facing dire circumstances. On the international scene, Adolf Hitler was starting his rise to power and there were growing uncertainties about Italy, Japan, and the Soviet Union. In the same way a rabbinic saying should be dated close to the time in which the rabbi making the statement lived, even though the state-

---

[33] See W. Bacher, *Tradition und Tradenten* (Leipzig: Gustav Fock, 1914), which is a classic that deals with attribution of a rabbinic teaching. Brief biographies of the rabbis appear in the *Encyclopedia Judaica*. See also, Birger Gerhardsson, *Memory and Manuscript: Oral Tradition and Written Transmission in Rabbinic Judaism and Early Christianity* (Grand Rapids, Mich.: Eerdmans, 1998), 91–121.

ment is published in a later source like the Mishnah. The rabbis were meticulous in the way they preserved their oral traditions and attributed a teaching to the one who taught it. The memorized oral tradition was preserved verbatim, as if it was written in text. You were considered wicked if you claimed another's teaching as your own wisdom.

The rabbis appealed to Scripture to support their habit of passing down a saying in the name of its originator. As part of their appeal they enlisted Esth 2:22 as a proof text. Rabbi Eleazar and Rabbi Chanina said, "Everyone who repeats a saying in the name of its originator brings redemption into the world, as it is said, 'And Esther said to the king in the name of Mordecai'" (*b. Megillah* 15a). As this comment demonstrates, the rabbis were neither dry nor straight-faced, often displaying a delightful sense of humor as they interpreted Scripture. After all, Esther was instrumental in bringing redemption to her people, which the rabbis connected to the honesty she modeled for them when she reported to the king in the name of Mordecai.

Dating rabbinic texts accurately is a challenging undertaking. Scholars are able to identify the rabbis of the talmudic literature and to learn about some of their life experiences, and dating a saying in the time period of the rabbi who teaches it is one method of approximating the date of a text.[34] The other factor that should be kept in mind is the time of the composition of the source in which the saying is quoted.[35] The final editing of the Mishnah is the latest date possible for sayings quoted from that text (ca. 220 C.E.). The scholar must also realize, however, that Rabbi Judah HaNasi did not write the Mishnah, but that he was the compiler. Other rabbis, especially Rabbi Meir, also worked tirelessly in this enormous task. Other rabbinic texts, such as the Tannaitic midrashim on the Pentateuch, were edited over this period of time. The Tosefta is a collection of legal discussions organized like the Mishnah. It provided supplements and further explanation on religious life and also originated during this era.

In the Talmud there is one explanation of how these texts were compiled and who is primarily responsible for editing the Tannaitic sources. If a saying is attributed to a particular rabbi, then the reader knows who taught the statement. But if the statement is anonymous, is it possible to theorize who may have taught it? In the Talmud, Rabbi Yochanan explains how the traditions were formulated into texts, "The author of an anonymous Mishnah is

---

[34] The student can look up a rabbi quoted in the *Encyclopaedia Judaica* or the *Jewish Encyclopedia* for general biographical information. E. P. Sanders noted, "Material attributed to a pre-70 Pharisee or to one of the earliest post-70 rabbis constitutes a body of evidence that most scholars accept as representing Pharisaism." See his *Judaism Practice and Belief,* 10.

[35] Scholars also recognize interpolations and conflation of sources.

Rabbi Meir, of an anonymous Tosefta is Rabbi Nehemiah, of an anonymous teaching in *Sifra* is Rabbi Judah [bar Illai], of an anonymous saying in *Sifre*, Rabbi Simeon [bar Yochai] and all are taught according to the perspective of Rabbi Akiva" (*b. Sanhedrin* 86a). Scholars debate the accuracy of Rabbi Yochanan's observation in this text. At face value, however, an anonymous saying in the Mishnah may be attributed to Rabbi Meir because he did most of the work in compiling it. An anonymous saying in the Tosefta may be attributed to Rabbi Nehemiah because of his efforts in collecting and editing the materials for the Tosefta, and so on.

HANDING DOWN TRADITIONS

Perhaps the best place in rabbinic literature to glimpse the dynamic of handing down traditions from one generation to the next is in the *Ethics of the Fathers* (*Avot,* the most famous tractate of the Mishnah; pious Jewish people read the *Ethics of the Fathers* during the afternoon on the Sabbath). The *Ethics of the Fathers* begins, "Moses received the Torah on Sinai, and delivered it over to Joshua; Joshua delivered it over to the elders; the elders to the prophets; and the prophets handed it down to the leaders of the great gathering together." These leaders from the great gathering together represent the spiritual giants of Israel who came after Ezra and Nehemiah (ca. 458–424 B.C.E.). Tradition credits them with establishing the foundation of the Jewish liturgy, editing several books of the Bible, and playing a lead role in fixing the Jewish canon.

Simon the Just was one of the last survivors of the great gathering together, and he passed on the oral tradition to Antigonos of Socho. Simon the Just should probably be identified with Simon the High Priest, the son of Onias who served from about 219 to 196 B.C.E. Interestingly, this historical figure is highly praised in Sir 50:1–21. In this apocryphal book, also known by the name Ecclesiasticus, we read, "The leader of his clan and the pride of his people was Simon the High Priest, son of Onias who in his life repaired the house and in his time fortified the Temple" (Sir 50:1).

Antigonos, about whom we know very little, passed the oral tradition to the *zugot,* or "pairs," who shared in the leadership of the Jewish community. The last pair, Hillel (active ca. 20 B.C.E. to 10 C.E.) and Shammai (ca. 50 B.C.E.–30 C.E.), marked the beginning of the Tannaitic period; they were the last of the *zugot* and the first of the Tannaim. Hillel and Shammai overlapped with the years when Jesus lived (ca. 4 B.C.E.–33 C.E.). Rabbi Judah the Prince, whom we have already mentioned (see discussion in Chapter Six, pp. 82–83), belonged to the final generation of the Tannaim, and marked the close of the Tannaitic period. The Tannaim handed down the oral tradition to the Amoraim.

Paul probably had a similar dynamic of handing down teaching in mind when he wrote 1 Cor 15:3: "For I have delivered to you as of first importance what I also received . . ." Being a Pharisee, the Apostle Paul would have been acquainted with the process in oral teachings of receiving tradition and passing it on with meticulous care to the community of faith.

Now being familiar with the opening section of the *Ethics of the Fathers,* we can see how new and old materials were cycled and recycled through rabbinic literature. We should also strive to view the literature, not as a collection of boring textbooks filled with data, but as living literature, built upon the Bible and centered around godly leaders with dynamic personalities and keen spiritual insight. Rabbinic literature resembles a richly woven, multicolored fabric. It comprises many diverse sayings, traditions, opinions, stories, parables, and comments upon Scripture that span approximately eight centuries of Jewish history, from 200 B.C.E. to 600 C.E. It is literature we can still enter into today, to debate and argue with these great personalities, issues, and interpretations of the biblical text. We will come away with precious insights mined from the depths of Scripture and the combined wisdom of great spiritual leaders.

Continuity of Faith from the Bible to the Mishnah

For the rabbis, the continuity of the Oral Torah and the living faith traditions of the Jewish people throughout the ages flow from the experience of ancient Israel in the Bible moving forward to the teachers of spiritual truth in the Mishnah. These years of transition are anything but silent in Jewish history. In fact, history itself must be centered on Torah and how it was received from a previous generation, and then passed on to faithful leaders, in succession, to the following generation. The master teacher and disciple-follower paradigm of education was carefully preserved. The burning question was: how to live a life pleasing to God? Only the continuity of faith taken from the tried and proven ways within a sacred tradition was able to answer this question. This book, the *Ethics of the Fathers,* portray this view of sacred history. Great Torah scholars are living links between the Bible and the Mishnah.

Living Links: The Zugot and their Successors

During the biblical period, the royal line and the priesthood ruled supreme, with the prophets calling for reform and spiritual awakening. In contrast, during the return to Zion, Ezra sought spiritual revitalization through

Torah learning and scholarly attainment (Ezra 7:10). Instead of relying upon the king, priest, or prophet, the people read and studied the law seeking to apply its teachings and form a community. The reforms of Ezra paved the way for the rise of pious sages who taught Torah to the people. The last of them were Yose son of Yoezer and Yose son of Yochanan, the first of the Zugot. These leaders were living links of a chain of tradition joining the past with the future.

The word *zugot* means "pairs," and refers to the presiding leader of the Sanhedrin and the Chief Magistrate of the Court, who served the Jewish people from approximately 160 B.C.E. to 20 C.E. Since rabbinic Judaism is the heir of the biblical faith of ancient Israel, the links of the chain of tradition that follows a line of transition from the Bible to the Mishnah was very important for the rabbis to establish. The rabbis were not interested in giving a carefully laid out historical timeline in a perfect chronological summary.[36] They were keenly interested in producing a cogent and credible overview of how the Oral Torah was accurately and precisely transmitted through the transitional periods of Jewish history. They did describe events, and some times modern scholars can suggest dates based upon the available facts, but the chief purpose in remembering the leaders in these formative periods was to stress the authority of the oral teachings for the practice of Judaism in their time. The legitimate successor to the biblical heritage must be the community of faith, which preserved the oral teachings that explained the true meaning of the written word. The writing of the Oral Torah into the Mishnah was the realization of faithful preservation of a tradition originating with Moses on Mount Sinai.

Immense attention and interest is focused on the teachings of these early pious leaders. Each leader taught profound truths about the pursuit of righteous living, pleasing God, and helping others in the description of the chain of transmission beginning with Moses on Mount Sinai. Moses passed the Torah to Joshua, and Joshua delivered it over to the elders and, so went the chain of tradition, in pure succession from the hands of one generation into the hands of the next. The message of each leader represents a pinnacle of achievement because they embody the combined wisdom of spiritual giants throughout the generations. Their sayings are representative samples of each succession of Torah education. When Simeon the Just teaches, "Upon three things the world is based: upon the Torah, upon the Temple service, and upon the practice of charity" (*Avot* 1:2), he is spanning the generations linking the Jewish community of faith with their biblical heritage. For more ex-

---

[36] See Jacob Lauterbach, *Rabbinic Essays* (Cincinnati: Hebrew Union College, 1951), 195–97.

amples of representative teachings, see the first chapter of the *Ethics of the Fathers* in the translation provided above (see Chapter Seven). Torah learning, praying to God, and helping others in charitable activities are the foundation of Jewish life throughout the ages—from the Bible, to the Talmud, and even to the present day. The following chart which provides the name of each leader of the pair "Zug" (sing. of *zugot*), shows the continuity of faith traditions and how one generation stands on the shoulders of an earlier generation's spiritual giants.

NASI, Leader	*AV BET DIN*, Judge
YOSE the son of YOEZER	YOSE the son of YOCHANAN
"Let your house be the meeting place for the wise."	"Let the poor be members of your household."
JOSHUA the son of PERACHYAH	NITTAI (MATTAI) the Arbelite
"Provide yourself with a teacher."	"Associate not with the wicked."
JUDAH the son of TABBAI	SIMON the son of SHETACH
"Do not play the part of the prosecuting attorneys."	"Be very searching in the examination of witnesses."
SHEMAYAH	AVTALYON
"Love work" but "hate lordship."	"Sages, be careful of the words you speak."
HILLEL	SHAMMAI
"Be of the disciples of Aaron, loving peace and pursuing peace."	"Say little and do much."

The Mishnah also reveals controversy that later would sharpen the distinction between the leader of the Sanhedrin and the Chief Magistrate, and foster diversity in a community that highly esteemed Torah scholarship. These positions may have entailed different responsibilities over the period under discussion, and quite probably the Mishnah projects a later organizational design of the Sanhedrin back upon earlier times (for more on this, see Chapter Four).

Be that as it may, the disputes concerning various matters are debated in successive time periods and each leader of the Zugot, the "pair," takes up a position that disagrees with his colleague. [37] One such dispute concerns the laying on of hands. The debate seems to have been about whether it is

---

[37] See also Young, *Jesus the Jewish Theologian*, 184–88.

permitted to lay hands upon the peace offering sacrifice to dedicate it in the Temple on a holiday, or whether such action would be considered work and thus forbidden on that sacred day. The only exception to the series of debates surrounding this issue is during the brief period when Menachem agrees with Hillel, before Shammai rises to prominence.

> Yose the son of Yoezer teaches, "One may not perform the laying on of hands." Yose the son of Yochanan teaches, "One may do so." Joshua the son of Perachyah teaches, "One may not." Nittai the Arbelite teaches, "One may." Judah the son of Tabbai teaches, "One may not." Simon the son of Shetach teaches, "One may." Shemayah teaches, "One may." Avatalyon teaches, "One may not." Hillel and Menachem did not differ. Menachem left and Shammai entered. Shammai taught, "One may not perform the laying on of hands." Hillel taught, "One may." The first one mentioned in each case is the presiding leader of the Sanhedrin while the second one mentioned is the Chief Magistrate of the Court (*m. Chagigah* 2:2).

So the two leaders represent opposing views. Judaism was far from being the monolithic legal authority that forced one view upon the people. Respect and honor were accorded to divergent opinions, and this seems to be one reason why two leaders are described in the literature; scholarship requires debate and opposing views.

The *Ethics of the Fathers* provides an overview of the collective wisdom of these pious leaders and demonstrates the continuity of Torah learning from the biblical period to the activities of the rabbis. Hillel and Shammai are considered to be the last of the Zugot but also the first of the Tannaim. The *Ethics of the Fathers* preserves Yose the son of Yoezer teaching: "Let your house be a meeting place for the wise; cover yourself with the dust of their feet, and drink in their words with thirst" (*Avot* 1:4). In the period of the Zugot, he emphasized piety and learning. In modern times, Abraham Joshua Heschel writes, "Piety, finally, is allegiance to the will of God . . . Piety is, thus, not an excess of enthusiasm, but implies a resolve to follow a definite course of life in pursuit of the will of God."[38] This modern expression of the essence of Jewish piety shows the way that Torah learning has gone from generation to generation, and how the early teachers embody the moral and ethical code from the biblical period.

Yose the son of Yoezer died a martyr's death. His nephew was the wicked priest Alcimus who served the Roman rule under the Seleucid government.[39]

---

[38] Susannah Heschel, ed., *Moral Grandeur and Spiritual Audacity* (New York: Farrar, Strauss & Giroux, 2001), 316.

[39] See Wilhelm Bacher, *Tradition und Tradenten,* 50. Bacher comments on the priestly line and family connection between Alcimus and Yose the son of Yoezer.

Alcimus is known in other historical sources because he was an enemy of
Judah Maccabee and other faithful Jews who fought against the pagan influence trying to undermine genuine Jewish faith and practice in the second-
century B.C.E. His Hebrew name was Yakim, or Eliakim, and he supported
the Seleucid domination of the people. Being a representative of the
Selucids, he opposed his uncle who was a dedicated leader of the pious ones
loyal to the Torah tradition (1 Macc 7:1–25; 9:1–73; 2 Macc 14:1–36).[40] In
1 Macc 7:5, Alcimus is described as the leader of some very bad company:
"Then there came to him [Demetrius] all the lawless and ungodly men of Israel; they were led by Alcimus who wanted to be High Priest." Demetrius I
Soter ruled from 162 to 150 B.C.E. and believed that the wicked Alcimus
would serve his purposes of putting down the ones who were faithful to
Torah observance. Contrary to accepted protocol, Alcimus was appointed to
be High Priest by Demetrius and served from about 162 to 159 B.C.E. According to the midrash, during the persecution carried out by the High
Priest Alcimus and the Seleucid overlords, Yose the son of Yoezer was crucified. His nephew, Alcimus, rode a horse and followed him to the place of
crucifixion. He ridiculed his saintly uncle. Even in death, according to the
midrash, Yose ben Yoezer reminded his nephew of the reward and punishment in the future life. He did not fear death for himself but warned his
nephew of the torment that would come down upon those who anger God.[41]
The episode in the midrash and the parallel historical sources provide a
clearer picture of the time and circumstance of the events surrounding the
life, teachings, and death of this outstanding leader in Jewish history.

THE CRUCIFIXION OF RABBI YOSE SON OF YOEZER

Yakum [Alcimus the High Priest] turned apostate. When Rabbi Yose son of
Yoezer was sentenced to be crucified, the enemy bound the crucifixion beam on
him as he was dragged off to execution on the Sabbath and Yakum was riding before him on his horse. Yakum taunted Yose, "See the horse my master gave me
and the horse your master gave you." Yose replied, "If such reward is given to
those like you who anger God, how much more then to those who do His will."
Yakum however was not to be outdone, "Is there anyone who has done God's will
more than you? And look what is happening to you!" he jeered. "If such suffering
comes to those who love God, how much worse will come to those who anger

---

[40] See also Josephus, *Ant.* 12:385–86, 391–97, 413; 20:235. The death of
Alcimus is not described as a suicide except in the rabbinic literature. On Alcimus
see Emil Schürer, *History of the Jewish People,* 1:168–73.
[41] *Genesis Rabbah* 65:22 (Albeck and Theodor, *Midrash Bereshit Rabbah,*
2:741–44) and the Midrash at the end on Ps 11. See also my article, "The Cross,
Jesus, and the Jewish People," *Immanuel* 24/25 (1990): 23–34.

Him," replied Yose. And those words pierced Yakum like the poison of a snake, and he went and committed suicide . . . (*Genesis Rabbah* 65:22).[42]

In the case of Rabbi Yose the son of Yoezer, scholars possess sources from the apocrypha, Josephus, and rabbinic literature that speak about the life and teachings of a sage who was the last of the "grape clusters" and the beginning of the Zugot. In death, he encouraged his wicked nephew to repent and return to the faith. According to the midrash, Alcimus was cut to the heart by his uncle's warning and demonstrated remorse by committing suicide. While the book of Maccabees agrees with the rabbinic story that Alcimus was evil and killed many pious Jews, it does not describe his death as a suicide but rather a divine punishment for wrong doing (1 Macc 9:55–56). With the aid of the historical references, scholars can see through the legend and find the man. Certainly the legend teaches students of rabbinic thought and literature much about righteous living, committed faith, and devoted piety during this crucial transitional period between the Bible and the Mishnah. Students of the New Testament, moreover, must learn history through the eyes of first-century Jewish leaders who emphasized more than mere dates and events, but could see the transmission of a Torah learning tradition through the combined activities of spiritual giants. Certainly a greater awareness and appreciation of the Torah tradition held sacred by a living people will enhance the scholarly understanding of the historical facts. A new sensitivity to Judaism in New Testament research will provide a clearer picture of the authentic context of first-century Christianity.

In sum, the Zugot, these great pairs of community leaders and Torah scholars are living links between Mount Sinai and later generations of faithful Jewish people who are loyal to their sacred history and tradition. The fascinating work, the *Ethics of the Fathers,* demonstrates the interconnectedness between the prophets and priests of the Bible and the spiritual giants who meticulously preserved the traditions of the Oral Torah. The Zugot and their teachings, as evidenced by the *Ethics of the Fathers,* have greatly impacted subsequent generations down through the intervening years. Later educators, scholars, rabbis and their disciples have trained others to preserve and pass on these precious oral teachings.

---

[42] Here I have only slightly revised the excellent translation of Chaim Pearl, Hayyim N. Bialik, and Yehoshua H. Rawnitzky, *Sefer Ha-aggadah: The Book of Jewish Folklore and Legend* (Tel Aviv: Dvir, 1988), 242. In the version of the story in the Midrash on Psalms it explains that Alcimus did indeed repent. In the earlier version of Genesis Rabbah the deep remorse for his actions is portrayed in how he committed suicide with the four accepted methods of the death penalty. Because of his repentance, Rabbi Yose sees Alcimus in the future life. The story illustrates the grace of God in Jewish thought: God receives the repentance of even the very wicked.

The Rabbi Introduces Talmudic Argument to a Country-Fellow

One day a country-fellow came to his Rabbi. "Rabbi," he said, in the tongue-tied fashion of the unlettered in the presence of the learned, "for a long time I have been hearing of Talmud. It puzzles me not to know what Talmud is. Please teach me Talmud."

"Talmud?" the Rabbi smiled tolerantly, as one does to a child. "You'll never understand Talmud; you're a peasant."

"Oh, Rabbi, you must teach me," the fellow insisted. "I've never asked you for a favor. This time I ask. Please teach me, what is Talmud."

"Very well," said the Rabbi, "listen carefully. If two burglars enter a house by way of the chimney, and find themselves in the living room, one with a dirty face and one with a clean face, which one will wash?"

The peasant thought for a while and said, "Naturally, the one with the dirty face."

"You see," said the Rabbi, "I told you a farmer couldn't master Talmud. The one with the clean face looked at the one with the dirty face and, assuming his own face was also dirty, of course he washed it, while the one with the dirty face, observing the clean face of his colleague, naturally assumed his own was clean, and did not wash it."

Again the peasant reflected. Then, his face brightening, said, "Thank you, Rabbi, thank you. Now I understand Talmud."

"See," said the Rabbi wearily. "It is just as I said. You are a peasant! And who but a peasant would think for a moment that when two burglars enter a house by way of the chimney, only one will have a dirty face?"

Nathan Ausubel, A Treasury of Jewish Folklore (New York: Crown Publisher, 1975), 3–4.

Those Who Are Near God, Fear God the Most!

Human beings may be close to God, but nevertheless, "Can there be comradeship with Heaven?" Rabbi Judah ben Tema would say: "Love Heaven, but fear Heaven." For the Bible says: "the Lord your God is a consuming fire, an impassioned God" (Deuteronomy 4:24).

Similarly, the school of Rabbi Akiva interpreted this verse: "Do not defile yourselves in any of those ways" (Leviticus 18:24)—"Whether you defile yourself in all of those ways, or only in some of them . . . for when I open the ledger, I shall demand payment for all of them."

Rabbi Johanan expounded in the same vein as Rabbi Akiva on this verse: "You are awesome, O God, in Your holy places" (Psalm 68:36)—"Do not read, 'Your holy places (mikdashekha)' but 'those who are sanctified by You (mekudeshekha).' When is God awesome? When God judges the saints strictly, God is feared, exalted, and praised." It is the nature of a human being to be more revered by those who are far from him than by those near to him. Not so with the Holy and Blessed One; God is revered by those who are near even more than by those who are far.

Abraham Joshua Heschel, *Heavenly Torah* (New York: Continuum, 2005), 170.

CHAPTER 7

Ethics of the Fathers

The *Ethics of the Fathers* is a moral code of conduct, filled with vivid, larger-than-life personalities. For Christians, it is a valuable source of Jewish teachings that links the spiritual world of the Old Testament with the New Testament era. What happened between the close of the canon for the Hebrew Bible and the first words of the New Testament? Some Christian scholars have referred to this time as the "silent years," but any casual overview of this crucial historical period will demonstrate that these years were anything but silent! In fact, the New Testament as a Jewish book, is closely connected to the theology, history, moral outlook, and cultural environment of the community and spiritual leaders mentioned in *Ethics of the Fathers.*

Sixty-five rabbis, spanning the time between the Hebrew Bible and the age of the Mishnah, are quoted in the *Ethics of the Fathers.* The book has been incorporated into the Mishnah and the Jewish Prayer Book even though it developed with a history all its own. These sixty-five rabbis form the foundation of the oral tradition.[1] They revere the one God of Israel in biblical revelation and recognize that each individual is created in the divine image and will be held accountable before the Almighty for his or her conduct of life, which will result in either reward or punishment in the world to come.

The history of the book covers the time of the great gathering together of the exiled people of Israel from Babylonian captivity during the time of Ezra, around 539 B.C.E., to the time of the Mishnah, around 220 C.E. The first five chapters were written before the Mishnah, and they reflect the way oral teachings were preserved by memorizing a Rabbi's message and passing the Torah learning achievements from one generation to the next. The sixth chapter was added later and emphasizes Torah learning, discipleship, and the fear of God in education. The moral outlook of these spiritual giants encompasses all of community and religious life. The ethics reveal what is of primary importance to each Torah Master. The insights into Jewish thought in this formative period are of monumental significance to all who wish to understand the beginnings of Christianity. The cultural environment of the

---

[1] See Saul Raskin, *Pirke Aboth* (New York: Academy of Photo Offset, 1940), 3.

Ethics of the Fathers opens a window through which learners can view the family life, spiritual walk, and communal organization of the Jewish people from the Bible to the Mishnah.

The *Ethics of the Fathers* has many names. Sometimes it is called *Avot,* "Fathers," according to the sound of the word in Hebrew. It is often referred to as *Aboth,* also translated "Fathers," but this way of spelling results from a different method of transliteration, which gives different English equivalents for each Hebrew letter.[2] The term *pirke,* "Chapters" or block quotations of sayings, is often added to the name, as in *Pirke Avot,* "Chapters of the Fathers." One may also call it the "Sayings of the Fathers." Many titles are used for the same book!

As the various names imply, the book contains wisdom sayings that are the spiritual heritage of a people. The "fathers" are their ancestors, who have provided a guide for a meaningful life within a community of faith. It is similar to a testament or a spiritual, moral, and ethical will designed to preserve the heritage of a people. Christians must recognize that Jesus belonged to his people and esteemed his spiritual heritage. The *Ethics of the Fathers* helps us to answer important questions about both. How did Jews think in this historical period? How did they read and interpret the Bible? How are Jesus' teachings similar? How are his teachings different? How can one describe the spiritual heritage of Jesus and his people? What spiritual insights can we learn from these outstanding leaders? What is their moral and ethical outlook? How have the issues changed over time and how does their wisdom speak throughout the ages? How do these teachings apply for today?

The *Ethics of the Fathers* is printed in every edition of the Jewish Prayer Book and pious Jews are encouraged to study its teachings during the Sabbath afternoon. It is printed in the Mishnah after the order *Nezikin.* No other one book outside of the Bible has had such a pervasive influence upon Jewish life. All students seeking to understand ancient Jewish thought and the beginnings of Christianity must study this document and ponder its message. For the convenience and edification of the reader, this crucial historical document is provided below.

These sayings and teachings of the rabbis provide significant parallels to the moral message of Jesus' Sermon on the Mount. For those familiar with the New Testament, a first-time read of the book will call to mind numerous passages from the writings of the apostles, who teach a similar ethical code of conduct based upon Scripture. This does not mean, however, that the major

---

[2] In Hebrew, the letter *bet* can be pronounced both like a "b" and a "v," depending on its placement in a word. The letter *tav* is sometimes written as "th" but is pronounced as "t." Sometimes it is transliterated as an "s" and the name becomes *Avos* or *Abos.*

significance of this ancient work is its connection to Christian thought and literature. The timeless message of these spiritual leaders speaks to all people in all times with great wisdom for current problems. Even if at times we disagree with their conclusion, their reverence for God and love for the Bible challenge us to examine the issues afresh and make us see the possible solutions to problems in a new light. Textual study is always relevant. In our study of the ancient text, we write a commentary in our hearts and minds.

Elie Wiesel reminds us,

> Commentary in Hebrew is *perush*. But the verb *lifrosh* also means to separate, to distinguish, to isolate—that is, to separate appearance from reality, clarity from complexity, truth from its disguise. Discover the substance, always. Discover the spark, eliminate the superfluous, push back obscurity. To comment is to reclaim from exile a word or notion that has been patiently waiting outside the realm of time and inside the gates of memory. When you pray, said the late Louis Finkelstein, you speak to God; when you study, God speaks to you. If study is discovery, commentary is adventure.[3]

Studying rabbinic literature for those who want to learn over and beyond the limits of the Jewish community is the discovery of a world that non-Jews do not know exists. Discovering a new world is pure adventure. Let the adventure begin.

ETHICS OF THE FATHERS

All Israel has a place in the world to come, as it is said, "Your people shall be all righteous; they shall inherit the land for ever, the branch of my planting, the work of my hands, that I may be glorified (Isaiah 60:21)."[4]

First Chapter

(1:1) Moses received the Torah on Sinai, and delivered it over to Joshua, Joshua delivered it over to the elders, the elders to the prophets, and the prophets delivered it to the men of the great gathering together. They said three things: "Be deliberate in judgment, raise up many disciples, and make a fence around the Torah."[5]

---

[3] Elie Wiesel, *Wise Men and their Tales* (New York: Schocken Books, 2003), xvii–xviii.

[4] This foreword to the Ethics of the Fathers does not appear in all the better manuscripts. One should compare it to the Apostle Paul's declaration, "All Israel will be saved" (Rom 11:26).

[5] The meaning of the word *Torah* is different here than the five books of Moses. The rabbis are describing both the Written and Oral Torahs (for more on Oral Torah see p. 23, n. 5).

(1:2) Simon the Just was one of the last survivors of the great gathering together. He used to say, "Upon three things the world is based: upon the Torah, upon the Temple service, and upon the practice of charity."

(1:3) Antigonos of Socho received the tradition from Simon the Just. He used to say, "Be not like servants who minister to their master upon the condition of receiving a reward, but be like servants who minister to their master not on the condition of receiving a reward, and let the fear of Heaven be upon you."[6]

(1:4) Yose the son of Yoezer from Tzeredah, and Yose the son of Yochanan from Jerusalem, received the tradition from them. Yose the son of Yoezer from Zeredah, said, "Let your house be a meeting place for the wise; cover yourself with the dust of their feet, and drink in their words with thirst."[7]

(1:5) Yose the son of Yochanan from Jerusalem, said, "Let your house be open wide, let the poor be the members of the household, and engage not in much gossip with women. The saying applies even to one's own wife; how much more then to the wife of one's neighbor." Hence the sages say, "Whoever engages in much gossip with women brings evil upon himself, neglects the study of the Torah, and will in the end inherit Gehinnom."[8]

(1:6) Joshua the son of Perachyah, and Nittai the Arbelite, received the tradition from them. Joshua the son of Perachyah said, "Provide yourself with a teacher, and find yourself a study companion, and judge all people upon the scale of merit."

The Apostle Paul uses similar language in 1 Cor 15:3: "For I delivered to you . . . what I also received." The words of the epistle would remind Jewish readers of the technical method used to pass the Oral Torah from one generation to the next.

[6] David Flusser comments, "In the days of Antigonos, the awe of God was synonymous with the love of God" (*Judaism and the Origins of Christianity* [Jerusalem: Magness Press, 1988], 472). Flusser connects this saying in ancient Jewish thought to the new sensitivity in the Christian message to divine grace (ibid.). One does not serve God to earn a reward. Grace is given as a result of divine favor. But the awe and love of God must guide the person of faith.

[7] Compare the discipling techniques used in the New Testament. Consider the phrase, ". . . shake off the dust from your feet" (Matt 10:14; Mark 6:11; Luke 9:5).

[8] On the whole, the rabbis highly esteemed women, in spite of some isolated harsh sayings. Here Yose the son of Yochanan mainly seeks to avoid temptation by keeping a distance from his neighbor's wife.

(1:7) Nittai the Arbelite[9] said, "Keep yourself far from a bad neighbor, associate not with the wicked, and abandon not the belief in divine retribution."

(1:8) Judah the son of Tabbai and Simeon the son of Shatach, received the tradition from them. Judah the son of Tabbai said, "Do not play the part of the prosecuting attorneys when the parties involved in the lawsuit are standing before you. Allow both of them to be regarded as guilty before you, but when they have left your presence, regard them both as innocent. The verdict has been received by them."

(1:9) Simeon the son of Shatach said, "Be very searching in the examination of witnesses, and be careful of your words, lest through them they learn to give false information."

(1:10) Shemayah and Avtalyon received the tradition from them. Shemayah said, "Love work, hate lordship, and do not make yourself known to the ruling power."

(1:11) Avtalyon said, "Sages, be careful of the words you speak, unless you cause the punishment of exile and be exiled to a place of evil waters. The disciples who come after you will drink from them and die, and then the Heavenly name will be profaned."

(1:12) Hillel and Shammai received the tradition from them. Hillel said, "Be of the disciples of Aaron, loving peace and pursuing peace, loving every single person, and drawing each one near to the Torah."[10]

(1:13) He used to say, "A name made great is a name destroyed: he who does not increase his knowledge decreases it. He who does not study, deserves to die; and he who makes a worldly use of the crown of the Torah shall waste away."

(1:14) He used to say, "If I am not for myself, who will be for me? If I am only for myself, what am I? If not now, when?"

(1:15) Shammai said, "Set a time for your study of the Torah. Say little and do much. Receive every person with a cheerful countenance."[11]

(1:16) Rabban Gamaliel said, "Find yourself a teacher, and quit doubting. Do not allow yourself to give tithes by a conjectural estimate."

---

[9] Nittai may well be a corruption of the Hebrew "Mattai," which is a shortened form of the name Matthew.

[10] Jesus taught, "Blessed are those who make peace" (Matt 5:9). Compare also 2 Cor 13:11 and Rom 12:18. Psalm 34:14 calls upon the faithful to "seek peace and pursue it" (NIV).

[11] Compare the exhortation, "Say little and do much," to Jas 1:19–27.

(1:17) Simeon his son said, "All my days I have grown up among the wise, and I have not found better service than silence. Not learning but doing is the main goal. Whoever is overly talkative leads to sin."[12]

(1:18) Rabban Simeon the son of Gamaliel said, "By three things the world is preserved: by truth, by judgment, and by peace, as it is said, ". . . *judge with truth and the judgment of peace [will be] in your gates* (Zechariah 8:16)."

Rabbi Chananya the son of Akashya taught, "The Holy one Blessed be He, was pleased to make Israel worthy. Hence He gave them abundance of Torah and many commandments, as it is said, '*The LORD was pleased for his righteousness sake to magnify the Torah and to make it glorious* (Isaiah 42:21).'"[13]

Second Chapter

(2:1) Rabbi asked, "Which is the straight path that an individual should choose? That which brings honor by following it and that which will cause others to esteem his or her manner of life. Be careful to observe a light precept as a weighty one, for you do not know the gain of reward you will receive for doing each precept. Count the loss incurred by the transgression of a precept against the reward secured by its observance, and the recompense you will receive for committing a transgression against the loss it involves. Contemplate three things, and you will not come under the power of sin: Know what is above you—a seeing eye, and a hearing ear, and recognize that all your actions are written in a book."[14]

(2:2) Rabban Gamaliel, the son of Rabbi Judah the Prince, said, "An excellent activity is the study of the Torah combined with some worldly occupation, for the labor demanded by them both makes the desire to commit sin to be forgotten. All study of the Torah without work must in the end be futile and become the cause of sin. Let all who are employed with the congregation act with them for Heaven's sake, for then the merit of their ancestors sustains them, and their righteousness endures for ever. Then as for you, [God will

---

[12] Jesus also emphasized "doing" above "hearing" or learning, for example, in Matt 7:24; Luke 6:47; and also James 1:22: "Be doers of the word and not hearers only."

[13] The saying of Rabbi Chananya at the conclusion of Chapter One is repeated in many versions of *Ethics of the Fathers* at the end of every chapter. Here we cite it only at the conclusion of the first chapter.

[14] Jesus also speaks in similar terms concerning a "least" commandment and also concerning the "weightier matters of Torah" (Matt 5:19; 23:23). In Greek and Hebrew the wording of these passages is essentially the same.

say], 'I account you worthy of receiving a great reward, as if you had done it all by yourselves.'"[15]

(2:3) "Be on your guard against the ruling power, for they who exercise it draw no person near to them except for their own interests. They appear as friends when it is to their own advantage, but in the hour of need they cannot be depended upon to help an individual."

(2:4) He used to say, "Do His will as if it were your will, that He may do your will, as if it were His will. Cancel your will before His will, that He may cancel the will of others before your will."[16]

(2:5) Hillel said, "Do not separate yourself from the gathering of the people.[17] Do not trust in yourself until the day of your death. Do not judge your neighbor until you put yourself in his or her place.[18] Do not say something which cannot be understood at once, in the hope that it will be understood in the end. Do not say to yourself, 'When I have leisure time, then I will study, because you may never find leisure.'"

(2:6) He used to say, "An empty-headed person cannot be a sin-fearing individual, nor can an ignorant person live a pious life. A bashful person is not able to learn and a hot-tempered person is not able to teach. A person consumed with business will never be able to grow wise. In a society where there are no noble people, strive to be a person of true substance."

(2:7) Moreover, he saw a skull floating on the surface of the water, he said to it, "Because you have drowned others, they have drowned you. In the end, the ones who drowned you shall themselves be drowned."

(2:8) He used to say, "With the increase of raw meat comes more worms; the increase of treasures causes more stress; the more women, the more witchcraft; the more maid-servants, the more lewdness; the more men-servants, the more theft, but with the increase of the study of Torah comes a more meaningful life; the more learning, the more wisdom; the more counsel, the more understanding; the more charity, the more peace. The one who has acquired a good name, does well and has earned a reputation by his or her hard work. But the one who has acquired the words of Torah, does even better because he or she has acquired life in the world to come."

---

[15] Jesus promised, "for great is your reward" (Matt 5:12).

[16] The New Testament speaks about the will of God (Matt 6:10; 26:39–42; Rom 12:2; 1 Thess 4:3; 5:18). See the common background in Ps 40:8, "I delight to do your will, O my God."

[17] See Heb 10:25, on not neglecting to gather together.

[18] See Matt 7:1–2; Luke 6:37; Rom 2:1; 14:13.

(2:9) Rabban Yochanan the son of Zakhai received the tradition from Hillel and Shammai. He used to say, "If you have learned much Torah, do not ascribe special merit to yourself because it was for this reason that you were created."[19]

(2:10) Rabban Yochanan the son of Zakhai had five disciples. They are: Rabbi Eliezer the son of Hyrcanus, Rabbi Joshua the son of Chananya, Rabbi Yose the Priest, Rabbi Simeon the son of Nathaniel, and Rabbi Eleazar the son of Arakh.

(2:11) In this way he [Rabban Yochanan the son of Zakhai] used to praise their good qualities, "Rabbi Eliezer the son of Hyrcanus is a plastered cistern, which loses not a drop; Joshua the son of Chananya—happy is she that gave birth to him; Yose the Priest is a pious man; Simeon the son of Nathaniel is a man who fears sin; and Eleazar the son of Arakh is like an ever-flowing stream of spring water."

(2:12) He used to say, "If all the sages of Israel were upon one scale of the balance, and Eliezer, the son of Hyrcanus, upon the other, he would outweigh them all. Abba Saul said in his name, 'If all the sages of Israel were upon one scale of the balance, and Eliezer, the son of Hyrcanus, also with them, and Eleazar the son of Arakh, upon the other scale, he would outweigh them all.'"

(2:13) He asked them, "Go out and see, what is the good way to which each individual should steadfastly walk?" Rabbi Eliezer replied, "A good eye." Rabbi Joshua answered, "A good friend." Rabbi Yose said, "A good neighbor." Rabbi Simeon said, "One who foresees the results of events and actions taking place." But Rabbi Eleazar responded, "A good heart." After listening to their answers, he explained to them, "I approve of the answer of Eleazar the son of Arakh more than yours because his words also include your other answers."[20]

(2:14) He asked them, "Go out and see which is the evil way that an individual should shun." Rabbi Eliezer said, "An evil eye." Rabbi Joshua said, "A bad friend." Rabbi Yose said, "A bad neighbor." Rabbi Simeon said, "One who borrows and does not repay and it is the same whether one borrows from a human being or from the omnipresent God, as it is said, 'The wicked borrows and does not pay back what is owed, but the righteous one is gracious and gives

---

[19] Compare Luke 17:10: "So you also, when you have done everything you were told to do, should say, 'We are unworthy servants; we have only done our duty'" (NIV).

[20] In the interpretation of the Parable of the Sower, Jesus extols the virtue of a good heart (Luke 8:15). See especially Young, *The Parable*, 251–76.

(Psalm 37:21).'" Rabbi Eleazar said, "A bad heart." After listening to their answers, he said to them, "I approve of the answer of Eleazar the son of Arakh more than yours because his words also include your other answers."

(2:15) They each said three things. Rabbi Eliezer said, "Let your friend's honor be as dear to you as your own. Do not be easily moved to anger. Repent one day before you die." Moreover he taught, "Warm yourself by the fire of the wise. Take care, however, of their glowing coals, because you could be burned. Their bite is the bite of a fox, their sting is the sting of a scorpion and their hiss is the hiss of a snake. All their words are like coals of fire."

(2:16) Rabbi Joshua said, "The evil eye, the inclination to do wrong, and the hatred one feels for other human beings drive a person out of the world."[21]

(2:17) Rabbi Yose said, "Let the possessions of your friend be as dear to you as your own. Prepare yourself for the study of the Torah, since the knowledge of it is not an inheritance of your own. Let all your actions be done for the sake of Heaven."

(2:18) Rabbi Simeon said, "Be careful to recite the Shema and to pray the Amidah. But when you pray, do not allow your prayer to become a fixed mechanical task, but rather it must be an appeal for mercy and grace before the Omnipresent, as it is said, '*For he is gracious and full of mercy, slow to anger, and abounding in loving kindness, and relenting of evil* (Joel 2:13).' Do not be wicked in your own heart."[22]

(2:19) Rabbi Eleazar said, "Study diligently the Torah. Know how to answer the unbeliever.[23] Recognize also before whom you work and who is the Master of your job and who will pay you the reward for your labor."

(2:20) Rabbi Tarfon said, "The day is short, the work is plentiful and the laborers are lazy; but the reward is great and the Householder is pushing hard."[24]

(2:21) He used to say, "It is not your duty to complete the work, but neither are you free to remove yourself from it. If you have studied much Torah, you will be given great reward. Your Employer is faithful to pay you the reward

---

[21] On the good and evil eye, see Matt 6:22–23; 20:15; Luke 11:34. Compare Deut 15:9; Prov 22:9; 23:6; 28:22.

[22] See Matt 6:7–8.

[23] See 2 Tim 4:2.

[24] Compare the saying of Jesus concerning the harvest and the laborers: Matt 9:37–38; Luke 10:2.

due for your work. Recognize that the grant of reward stored up for the righteous will be given in the future time."

Third Chapter

(3:1) Akavya the son of Mahalalel said, "Reflect upon three things, and you will not come under the power of sin: know where you came from, where you are going, and before whom you will have to give an account and a record of your actions in the future. From where did you come? You came from a putrefying drop. Where are you going? You are going to a place of dust, worms, and maggots. Before whom will you have to give an account and a record? You will give an account before the Supreme King of kings, the Holy One, blessed be He."

(3:2) Rabbi Chanina the Vice-High Priest said, "Pray for the welfare of the government, because if it was not for the fear of it, human beings would swallow each other alive."[25]

(3:3) Rabbi Chananya the son of Teradyon said, "If two sit together and fail to exchange with each other words of Torah, they are like a meeting of scorners, concerning whom it is said, '*The godly person sits not in the seat of the scorners* (Psalm 1:1).' If two sit together and exchange words of Torah with each other, the divine Presence abides in the midst of them; as it is said, '*Then they that feared the Lord spoke one with the other, and the Lord hearkened and heard, and a book of remembrance was written before him, for them that feared the Lord, and that thought upon his name* (Malachai 3:16).' Now, this Scripture enables me to draw this inference when two persons are involved. Where can it be inferred that even if one person diligently occupies himself or herself with the Torah, that the Holy one, blessed be He, assigns a suitable reward? Because it is said, '*Though one sits alone, and meditates in silence, even so he has given it to him or her* (Lamentations 3:28).'"[26]

(3:4) Rabbi Simeon said, "If three have eaten together at a table and have failed to share with one another words of Torah, it is as if they had eaten from sacrifices of dead bodies, concerning whom it is said, '*For all the tables are full of vomit and filthiness; the Omnipresent is not [among them]* (Isaiah 28:8).' But if three have eaten together at a table and have discussed among themselves the words of Torah, it is as if they had eaten at the table of the Omnipresent, to which it was said, 'He said to me, "*This is the table that is before the Lord*" (Ezekiel 41:22).'"

---

[25] 2 Tim 2:1–2; Rom 13:5–6.
[26] See Matt 18:20 and compare David Flusser, *Judaism and the Origins of Christianity,* 515–25.

(3:5) Rabbi Chanina the son of Chakhinai said, "The one who stays awake at night, and walks along the way alone while turning his or heart toward worthless matters, behold such a one will forfeit his or her own life."

(3:6) Rabbi Nechunya son of Hakanah taught, "Whoever receives upon himself or herself the yoke of the Torah, the yoke of the royal regime and the yoke of worldly care will be removed from him or her. But whoever breaks away from himself or herself the yoke of the Torah, will be burdened with the yoke of the royal regime and the yoke of worldly care."[27]

(3:7) Rabbi Chalafta the son of Dosa, of the village of Chananya, said, "When ten people sit together and busy themselves with the study of Torah, the Shechinah abides among them, as it is said, '*God takes his stand among the congregation of the godly* (Psalm 82:1).' How can it be proven that the same applies to five? Because it is said, '*He has founded his group* [understood as five in number here, but could also be translated literally as 'vaulted dome' or 'bundle'] *upon the earth* (Amos 9:6).' How can it be proven that the same applies to three? Because it is said, '*He judges among the judges* (Psalm 82:1).' How can it be proven that the same applies to two? Because it is said, '*Then they that feared the Lord spoke one with the other, and the Lord hearkened and heard, and a book of remembrance was written before him, for them that feared the Lord, and that thought upon his name* (Malachi 3:16).' How can it be proven that the same applies even to one? Because it is said, '*In every place where I cause my name to be remembered I will come to you and I will bless you* (Exodus 20:24).'"

(3:8) Rabbi Eleazar a man from Bertota taught, "Give to God of what is His, seeing that you and what you have belong to Him, and this is taught by David, who said, '*For all things come from You, and from Your own hand have we given back to You* (1 Chronicles 29:14).'"

(3:9) Rabbi Jacob said, "The one who is walking along the way and studying, but breaks off his or her study and says, 'How beautiful is that tree or how fine is that person,' of that one Scripture regards as if he or she was guilty enough to receive the death penalty."

(3:10) Rabbi Dostai the son of Yannai said in the name of Rabbi Meir, "Everyone who forgets one word of his or her learning, to that one the Scripture counts it as if the individual had lost his or her life, for it is said, '*Only take care for yourself, and keep your soul diligently, unless you forget the things which your eyes have seen* (Deuteronomy 4:9).' Now, one might suppose that the same result follows even if a person's review study has become overly difficult. But look at what is learned from the verse, '. . . unless they depart from your

---

[27] See Matt 11:28–30.

mouth all the days of your life' (Deuteronomy 4:9). Thus, a person is not guilty of death until he or she deliberately sets out to remove the learning of Torah from his or her heart."

(3:11) Rabbi Chanina the son of Dosa said, "The one in whom the fear of sin comes before wisdom, his or her wisdom shall endure; but the one in whom wisdom comes before the fear of sin, his or her wisdom will not endure."

(3:12) He used to say, "The individual whose works are greater than his or her wisdom, that one's wisdom shall endure; but the individual whose wisdom is greater than his or her works, that one's wisdom will not endure."

(3:13) He used to say, "With the one in whom the spirit of human beings is pleased, in that one, the Spirit of the Omnipresent is pleased, and with whomever the spirit of human beings is not pleased, in that one the Spirit of the Omnipresent is not pleased."

(3:14) Rabbi Dosa the son of Horkinas said, "Morning sleep, midday wine, children's chatter, and frequently going to the meeting places of the vulgar drive a person out of the world."

(3:15) Rabbi Eleazar Hammudai said, "The one who profanes sacred things, despises the festivals, embarrasses another to shame in public, annuls the covenant of Abraham our father, forces wrong interpretations upon the Torah, such a one, even though knowledge of the Torah and good deeds may be possessed by this individual, he or she will have no share in the world to come."

(3:16) Rabbi Ishmael said, "Accept the authority of a superior, be amicable to someone making a request, and receive all people with cheerful countenance."

(3:17) Rabbi Akiva said, "Hilarity and lightness of disposition accustom an individual to lewdness. The traditional interpretation is a fence for the Torah. Tithes are a fence for riches. Vows are a fence for asceticism and a fence for wisdom is silence."

(3:18) He used to say, "Beloved is each human being, for each person was created in the image of God. But it is by an even greater increase of love that it was revealed to humanity that each human being is created in the image of God, as it is said, 'For in the image of God made he humans (Genesis. 9:6).' Beloved are the people of Israel, for they were called children of the Omnipresent. But it was by an even greater increase of love that it was revealed to them that they were called children of the Omnipresent, as it is said, 'You are children for the LORD your God (Deuteronomy 14:1).' Beloved are Israel, for unto them was given the precious instrument [Torah]. But it was by an even greater increase of love that it was revealed to them that the precious instrument by which the world was created was turned over to them, as it is said, '*For I give you good teaching, my Torah do not abandon it* (Proverbs 4:2).'

(3:19) "Everything is foreseen, nonetheless freedom of choice is given. The world is judged by grace, and all is not according to the increase of the works performed."[28]

(3:20) He used to say, "Everything is given on loan and a net is spread out for all the living. The shop is open, the dealer gives credit, the ledger lies open, and the hand writes. Anyone who wishes to borrow may come and take out a loan but the collectors routinely make their daily round, and exact payment from each person whether that one is willing to pay or unable. They have something upon which they can depend but the judgment is a judgment of truth. Everything is prepared for the banquet."[29]

(3:21) Rabbi Eleazar the son of Azaryah taught, "Where there is no Torah, there is no way to conduct one's affairs. Where no one knows how to conduct the affairs of one's life, there is no Torah. Where there is no wisdom, there is no fear of God. Where there is no fear of God, there is no wisdom. Where there is no knowledge, there is no understanding. Where there is no understanding, there is no knowledge. Where there is no flour [for sustenance of bread], there is no Torah. Where there is no Torah, there is no flour."

(3:22) He used to say, "One whose learning is greater than his or her accompanying good works, to what is that one like? To a tree whose branches are many but whose roots are few. The wind comes, uproots it, and knocks it down to the ground, as it is said, '*So that one shall be like a shrub tree in the desert, and shall not see when good comes, but shall live in stony waste places in the wilderness, a salt land and not inhabited* (Jeremiah 17:6).' But the one whose good works are greater than his or her learning, to what is that one like? To a tree whose branches are few, but whose roots are many, so that even if all the winds in the world come and blow hard against it, it cannot be moved from its place, as it is said, '*And that one shall be like a tree planted by the waters; and that spreads out its roots by the river, and shall not fear when the heat comes, but its leaves shall be green and it shall*

---

[28] Other manuscripts read, "all is according to the increase of the works performed." See the Hebrew article by Shmuel Safrai, ". . . all is according to the increase of works performed," *Tarbiz* 53 (1984): 33–40.

[29] Compare the wording in the invitation in the Parable of the Great Supper, "Come; for all is now ready" (Luke 14:17).

not be troubled in the year of drought, neither shall it cease from yielding fruit (Jeremiah 17:8).'"[30]

(3:23) Rabbi Eleazar Chisma said, "The laws pertaining to the sacrifices of birds and the purification of women are essentials of Torah while astronomy and gematria[31] are the refinements of wisdom."

Fourth chapter

(4:1) Ben Zoma said, "Who is wise? The one who learns from all people, as it is said, *'From all my teachers I have gained understanding* (Psalm 119:99).' Who is mighty? The one who overcomes his or her inclination to do wrong, as it is said, *'The one that is slow to anger is better than the mighty, and the one that rules over his or her temper than the one that conquers a city* (Proverbs 16:32).' Who is rich? The one who rejoices over what he or she possesses, as it is said, *'When you eat the fruit of your hands, happy are you, and it shall be well with you* (Psalm 128:2).' Happy are you in this world, moreover, it shall be well with you in the world to come. Who is honored? The one who honors others, as it is said, *'For them that honor me I will honor, and they that despise me shall be lightly esteemed* (1 Samuel 2:30).'"

(4:2) Ben Azzai said, "Be quick to carry out even one of the least of the commandments, and run away from transgression. Doing one commandment will force you to do another. Doing a transgression will force you to do more wrong. The reward of doing a commandment is the commandment accomplished. The recompense of doing a transgression is the wrong of a transgression accomplished."

(4:3) He used to say, "Do not despise any person and do not quibble about circumstances. Every person has a time when he or she is needed and every circumstance plays some role in life."

(4:4) Rabbi Levitas of Yavneh said, "Be exceedingly humble of spirit, because the anticipated end of a human being is the worm."

(4:5) Rabbi Yochanan the son of Berokah said, "Whoever profanes the Name of Heaven in secret will suffer punishment openly in public. This happens whether the Heavenly Name is profaned in ignorance or on purpose."

---

[30] Compare the parable of Jesus concerning the wise and foolish builders: Matt 7:24–27; Luke 6:47–49.

[31] *Gematria* refers to the study of the letters of the Hebrew alphabet. Each letter has a numerical value and may have symbolic meaning by way of interpretation.

(4:6) Rabbi Ishmael, his son, said, "The person who learns in order to teach, that one will be enabled to both learn and teach. But to the one who learns in order to practice, that one will be empowered both to learn and to teach as well as to observe and to practice [God's will]."

(4:7) Rabbi Zadok said, "Separate not yourself from the assembling of the congregation.[32] Do not behave like those who argue the technicalities of legal codes. Do not make the Torah a crown by which you aggrandize yourself, nor a shovel by which you dig." So also Hillel used to say, "The one who makes a worldly use of the crown of the Torah shall waste away. Hence you may infer, that whoever derives a profit for himself or herself from the words of the Torah is contributing to his or her own destruction."

(4:8) Rabbi Yose said, "Whoever honors the Torah will be honored by others, but whoever dishonors the Torah will be dishonored by others."

(4:9) Rabbi Ishmael his son said, "The one who refrains from passing judgment on others will free himself or herself from hatred, stealing, and false oaths. But the one who presumptuously puffs himself or herself up in his or her heart when learning with and instructing others is foolish, wicked, and of an arrogant spirit."

(4:10) He used to say, "Judge not alone, for none may judge alone except One. Do not demand, 'Accept my view' because the authority to decide is theirs, and it is not up you to compel them to agree with your opinion."

(4:11) Rabbi Jonathan said, "Each individual who fulfils the Torah in the midst of poverty shall in the end fulfill it in the midst of wealth. But each individual who cancels the Torah in the midst of wealth shall in the end cancel it in the midst of poverty."

(4:12) Rabbi Meir said, "Lessen your work for worldly goods, and be busy in the Torah. Be humble of spirit before all people.[33] If you neglect the Torah, many causes for neglecting it will present themselves to you, but if you work in the Torah, He has abundant reward to give you."

(4:13) Rabbi Eliezer the son of Jacob said, "The one who does one precept has gained for himself or herself one advocate. The one who commits one transgression has gained for himself or herself one accuser. Repentance and good deeds are protection against punishment."

---

[32] Heb 10:25.
[33] Consider the words of Jesus, "poor in spirit" (Matt 5:3).

(4:14) Rabbi Yochanan the sandal maker said, "Every assembly which is for the Name of Heaven will in the end be established, but that which is not for the Name of Heaven will not in the end be established."

(4:15) Rabbi Eleazar the son of Shammua said, "Let the honor of your disciple be as dear to you as your own, and the honor of your associate be like the fear of your master, and the fear of your master be like the fear of Heaven."

(4:16) Rabbi Judah said, "Be cautious in study, for an error in study may lead to presumptuous sin."

(4:17) Rabbi Simeon said, "There are three crowns: the crown of Torah, the crown of priesthood, and the crown of kingdom; but the crown of a good name excels them all."

(4:18) Rabbi Nehorai said, "Go out to find a home of Torah learning.[34] Do not say that the Torah will come after you because your associates there will establish you in the possession of it, and *lean not upon your own understanding* (Proverbs 3:5)."

(4:19) Rabbi Yannai said, "It is not in our power to explain either the prosperity of the wicked or the sufferings of the righteous."

(4:20) Rabbi Matthew the son of Cheresh said, "Be the first to greet another with blessings of shalom. You should prefer to be a tail for lions than a head for foxes."

(4:21) Rabbi Jacob said, "This world is like a waiting room that precedes the world to come. Prepare yourself in the waiting room in order that you may enter into the hall."

(4:22) He used to say, "Better is one hour of repentance and good deeds in this world than the whole life of the world to come. Far better is one hour of blissful joy in the world to come than the whole life of this world."

(4:23) Rabbi Simeon the son of Eleazar said, "Do not make amends with anyone at the time of his or her anger. Do not comfort anyone at the time when his or her dead loved one lies before him or her. Do not question anyone at the time he or she is making a vow. Do not strive to see anyone at the time of his or her disgrace."

---

[34] Literally the Hebrew text reads, "Be exiled to a place of Torah." No one usually has a choice in a forcible exile. Hertz translated it, "Wander forth to a home of the Torah" (*Daily Prayer Book,* 677). The message of the teaching focuses on the urgent need for each person to actively seek a place of Torah training where interaction and assessment can be accomplished in a community.

(4:24) Samuel the younger used to quote, *"Rejoice not when your enemy falls, and let not your heart be glad when he stumbles, because when the LORD sees it and it displeases him, he will turn away his anger from him* (Proverbs 24:17–18)."

(4:25) Elisha the son of Avuyah said, "If one learns as a child, what is it like? Like ink written on clean paper. If one learns as an old person, what is it like? Like ink written on a blotted paper."

(4:26) Rabbi Yose the son of Judah of Kefar Babli said, "The one who learns from the young, to what is it like? To one who eats unripe grapes, and then drinks wine from his or her vat. But the one who learns from the old, to what is it like? To one who eats ripe grapes, and drinks old wine."[35]

(4:27) Rabbi Meir said, "Look not at the wine container, but at what is in it. There may be a new wine container full of old wine while an old container may not even have new wine in it."

(4:28) Rabbi Eleazar Hakapar said, "Jealousy, lust, and ambition drive a person out of the world."

(4:29) He used to say, "They that are born are destined to die. The dead are destined to be resurrected to life again. So all the living will be judged. They will come to know, to make known, and to be made conscious that He is God, He is the Maker, He is the Creator, He is the One who understands all, He is the Judge, He is the Witness, He is the Prosecutor, and He is the One who in the future will pronounce judgment. Blessed is the One with whom there is no unrighteousness, no forgetfulness, no preferential treatment given for anyone and no taking of bribes. Be aware also that everything will be decided according to the summation. Do not allow your imagination to give you hope that the grave will be a place of refuge for you. You were forced to be made, you were forced to be born, you are forced to live out your life, you are forced to die, and in the future you will be forced to give an account and a reckoning before the Supreme King of kings, the Holy One, blessed be He."

Fifth chapter

(5:1) By ten sayings the world was created. How do we learn this? Could it not have been created with one saying? It is to demonstrate the punishment that will be given to the wicked who seek to destroy the world that was

---

[35] Consider the saying of Jesus, "The old wine is better" (Luke 5:39). See also Young, *Jesus the Jewish Theologian,* 155–61.

created by ten sayings, as well—as the great reward that will be given to the righteous who preserve the world that was created by ten sayings.

(5:2) There were ten generations from Adam to Noah. This is to make known how long-suffering God is, because all those generations provoked Him to anger until he brought upon them the waters of the flood.

(5:3) There were ten generations from Noah to Abraham. This is to make known how long-suffering God is, because all those generations provoked Him to anger, until Abraham our father came, and received the reward that they all were destined to receive.

(5:4) By ten trials our father Abraham was tested, but he overcame them all. This is to make known how great was His love for our father Abraham.

(5:5) Ten miracles were performed for our ancestors in Egypt, ten were done at the Sea.

(5:6) Ten plagues did the Holy One, blessed be He, bring upon the Egyptians in Egypt, and ten were done at the Sea.

(5:7) With ten temptations did our ancestors test the Holy One, blessed be He, in the wilderness, as it is said, ". . . *they have put me to the test these ten times, and have not hearkened to my voice* (Numbers 14:22)."

(5:8) Ten miracles were performed for our ancestors in the Temple: no woman miscarried from the smell of the holy meat; the holy meat never became rotten; no fly was ever seen in the slaughter house; no unclean accident ever happened to the high priest on the Day of Atonement; the rain never put out the fire of the wood piled upon the altar; the wind never prevailed against the column of smoke that arose from the altar; and there was never found a disqualifying defect in the *omer* [of freshly harvested barley, offered on the second day of Passover], or in the two loaves [from the first fruits of the wheat harvest, offered on Pentecost], or in the showbread [twelve loaves of unleavened bread put on display before the LORD in the Temple] even though the people stood closely pressed together, they found ample space to prostrate themselves; no one was ever injured by a snake or a scorpion in Jerusalem; no one ever said to a pilgrim, 'The available space is insufficient for me to stay over night in Jerusalem.'"

(5:9) Ten things were created on the eve of Sabbath between the setting and rising of the sun: "*the mouth of the earth* (Numbers 16: 32)"; "*the mouth of the well* (Numbers 21:16)"; "*the mouth of the donkey* (Numbers 22:28)"; "*the rainbow* (Genesis 9:13)"; "*the manna* (Exodus 16:4)"; "*the rod* (Exodus 4:17)"; the *shamir* worm; the letters of the written word; the writing; and the tables of stone. Some claim that the destroying spirits, the tomb of Moses, and the ram of Abraham our father were then created, and still others argue that tongs also were made with tongs.

(5:10) There are seven characteristics of an uncultured individual and seven of a wise person. The wise person does not speak in front of someone who is greater in wisdom and does not interrupt someone else who is talking. This individual is not hasty to answer. The wise one asks pertinent questions according to the subject matter, and answers them honestly. The wise speaks concerning the first point first, and addresses the last concern last. When he or she does not understand, the wise person says, "I do not understand it." The wise recognizes the truth. The reverse of all these characteristics is to be found in an uncultured individual.

(5:11) Seven kinds of punishment enter into the world on account of seven major transgressions. When some people give their tithes and others do not, then famine ensues from drought. Some people suffer hunger while others are full. When they all decide not to give tithes at all, a famine ensues from civil disorder and drought. If they resolve not to give the dough-cake (Numbers 15:20), a deadly famine comes. So a pestilence may come into the world to fulfill those death penalties threatened in the Torah which is not given over to human court systems, and for the breaking of the laws regarding the produce of the seventh year (Leviticus 25:1–7). The sword enters into the world on account of the suppression of justice, the perversion of justice, and those who interpret the Torah not according to its true meaning. Deadly prey animals come into the world on account of vain swearing and the profaning the divine name. Exile comes into the world on account of idolatry, immorality, murder, and the neglect of rest for the land during the release year.

(5:12) During four seasons of time pestilence increases: in the fourth year, in the seventh, at the conclusion of the seventh year, and at the conclusion of the Feast of Tabernacles in each year. In the fourth year, it increases on account of failure to give the tithe to the poor in the third year (Deuteronomy 14:28–29). In the seventh year, it increases on account of failure to give the tithe to the poor in the sixth year; at the conclusion of the seventh year, on account of the failure of observing the law regarding the fruits of the seventh year, and at the conclusion of the Feast of Tabernacles in each year, for robbing the poor of the grants that are legally assigned to them.

(5:13) There are four types of characters among people: the one who says, "What is mine is mine and what is yours is yours," this is an average type of character—some say, this is a type like that of Sodom; the one who says, "What is mine is yours and what is yours is mine," is ignorant; the one who says, "What is mine is yours and what is yours is yours," is a saint; the one who says, "What is yours is mine and what is mine is mine" is a wicked person.

(5:14) There are four types of people who lose their tempers: The one whom it is easy to provoke and easy to pacify, this one's loss disappears in his or her gain; the one whom it is hard to provoke and hard to pacify, this one's gain disappears in his or her loss; the one whom it is hard to provoke and easy to pacify, this one is a saint; the one whom it is easy to provoke and hard to pacify—this one is a wicked person.

(5:15) There are four qualities in disciples: the one who learns quickly but forgets quickly, his gain is canceled by his loss; the one who learns slowly but forgets slowly, his loss is canceled by his gain; the one who learns quickly and forgets slowly, this one possesses a good portion; the one who learns slowly and forgets quickly, this one possesses an evil portion.

(5:16) There are four types of attitudes among those who give charity: one who desires to give, but that others should not give, this one's eye is evil towards what belongs to others [since giving of charity brings blessing to the giver]; the one who desires that others should give, but will not give himself or herself, that one's eye is evil against what belongs to him or her; the one who gives and wishes that others will give is a saint; the one who will not give and does not wish others will give is a wicked person.

(5:17) There are four types of characters who attend the house of study: the one who goes and does not practice, who will receive the reward for going; the one who practices but does not go, who will receive the reward for practicing; the one who goes and practices, this individual is a saint; the one who neither goes nor practices, this is a wicked person.

(5:18) There are four qualities among those who learn from the wise: they may be compared to a sponge, a funnel, a strainer, or a sieve: a sponge, which soaks up everything; a funnel, which lets it in from one end but then pours it out at the other; a strainer, which purifies the wine as it passes through and keeps back the dregs; a sieve which lets out the bran but retains the fine flour.

(5:19) When love is dependent upon some transitory motive, with the passing away of that motive, the love too will pass away. When love is not dependent upon a transitory motive, however, it will never pass away. What example of love was dependent upon a transitory motive? Such was the love of Amnon and Tamar. But what love was not dependent upon a transitory motive? Such was the love of David and Jonathan.

(5:20) Every debate which is for the sake of the name of heaven shall be established in truth, but every debate which is not for the sake of the name of heaven shall not be established. Which debate was for the sake of the name of heaven? Such was the debate between Hillel and Shammai. Which debate, moreover, was not for the sake of the name of heaven? Such was the debate caused by Korah and all his company.

(5:21) Whoever leads many people in a society to be righteous, upon that individual no sin shall come; but he who leads many people in a society to commit sin, will not even be given the opportunity to repent. Moses was righteous and caused many people to become righteous. The righteousness of the many was laid upon him, as it is said, "*He executed the righteousness of the Lord and his judgments with Israel* (Deuteronomy 33:21)." Jeroboam, the son of Nebat, sinned and caused many people to sin. The sin of many people was laid upon him, as it is said, " . . . because of the sins of Jeroboam which he sinned and which he caused Israel to sin (1 Kings 15:30)."

(5:22) Whoever has these three attributes is of the disciples of Abraham our father, but whoever has three other characteristics comes from the disciples of Balaam the wicked. A good eye, an attitude of humility, and meekness of spirit are attributes possessed by the disciples of Abraham our father. An evil eye, an arrogant attitude, and egotistical conceit are the characteristics possessed by the disciples of Balaam the wicked. What is the difference between the disciples of Abraham our father and those of Balaam the wicked? The disciples of Abraham our father are provided for in this world and inherit the world to come, as it is said, "*That I may cause those that love me to inherit wealth and that I may fill all their treasuries* (Proverbs 8:21)." The disciples of Balaam the wicked inherit Gehinnom and descend into the pit of destruction, as it is said, "*But you, O God, will bring them down to the pit of destruction, people who shed blood and who are full of deceit shall not live out half their days. But I will trust in you* (Psalm 55:24)."

(5:23) Judah the son of Tema said, "Be strong as a leopard, light to fly like an eagle, agile to run like a deer, and brave as a lion, to do the will of your Father who is in heaven." He used to say, "The bold-faced individuals are for Gehinnom, but the shame-faced are for the Garden of Eden. May it be your will, O LORD our God and God of our ancestors, that the Temple may be rebuilt speedily in our days, and give us our part in your Torah."

(5:24) He used to say, "At five years of age one has reached the time for the study of the Bible, at ten for the study of Mishnah, at thirteen for the fulfillment of the commandments, at fifteen for the study of the Talmud, at eighteen for marriage, at twenty for seeking a livelihood, at thirty for entering into one's full vigor, at forty for understanding, at fifty for giving counsel, at sixty, one reaches old age, at seventy the gray haired head, at eighty the gift of renewed strength (Psalm 90:10), at ninety one bends over under the weight of years, at a hundred, it is as if one were already dead and had passed away from the world."

(5:25) Ben Bag Bag said, "[Immerse yourself in the study of Torah], turn it and turn it over again, for every thing is in it. Contemplate it, grow gray and old over studying it. Do not move away from learning it, for you cannot have a better manner of life than this."

(5:26) Ben He He said, "According to the work done, is the reward received."

Sixth chapter

The sages taught the following in the style of the Mishnah, Blessed be He that made choice of them and their Mishnah.[36]

(6:1) Rabbi Meir said, "Whoever works in learning the Torah for its own sake merits many benefits, but, in fact, the whole world is indebted to such a one, who is called friend, beloved, a lover of the Omnipresent, a lover of humanity. Such an individual is clothed with meekness and reverence. This one is prepared to become righteous, saintly, upright, and faithful. Such an individual will keep far from sin, and will be brought near to virtue. Through such a one the world receives the benefits of counsel, applied wisdom, understanding, and strength, as it is said, "*Counsel is mine, and applied wisdom, I am understanding and power is mine* (Proverbs 8:14)," and also to such an individual will be given sovereignty and dominion, discerning judgment, and the secrets of the Torah are revealed to this one, who will be made like an ever-flowing fountain, and like a river that goes on and on with ever-sustained vigor. This person practices modesty and long-suffering, and will forgive insults. This person will be considered distinguished, and will be ennobled over and beyond all his or her activities.

(6:2) Rabbi Joshua the son of Levi said, "Every day a voice from heaven echoes from Mount Sinai, proclaiming these words, 'Cursed are human beings because of their contempt for the Torah, for whoever does not work in obeying the Torah is said to be under the curse,' as it is said, '*As a ring of gold in a swine's snout, so is a beautiful woman who lacks discretion* (Proverbs 11: 22).' Moreover, it says, '*The tables were God's work, and the writing was God's writing, engraved upon the tablets* (Exodus 32:16).' Do not read here *charut* [engraved], but *cherut* [freedom], for no person is free but the individual who works in obeying the Torah. But whoever works to obey the Torah, behold

---

[36] "Made choice of them" refers to the divine election of Israel.

that one shall be highly esteemed, as it is said, '*And from Mattanah to Nachaliel, and from Nachaliel to Bamoth (Numbers 21:19).*'"[37]

(6:3) "The one who learns from another person a single chapter, a single rule, a single verse, a single expression, or even a single letter, should give honor to the one who taught it, for so you find with David, King of Israel, who learned only two things from Ahitophel, and yet regarded him as his master, his guide, and his familiar friend, as it is said, '*But it was you, a man, mine equal, my guide, and my familiar friend (Psalm 55:13).*' Now, is this not an argument from a minor premise to a major? If David, the King of Israel, who learned only two things from Ahitophel, regarded him as his master, guide, and familiar friend, how much more should a person who learns from another human being one chapter, one rule, a verse, an expression, or even a single letter bestow honor upon the person who taught it? Moreover honor is nothing but Torah, as it is said, '*The wise will inherit honor (Proverbs 3:35),*' and also '*the blameless shall inherit good (Proverbs 28:10).*' So then there is nothing good except for Torah, as it is said, '*For I give you good doctrine, you must not abandon my Torah (Proverbs 4:2).*'"

(6:4) "This is the way of life through which one may gain learning from the study of the Torah: a morsel of bread with salt you must eat, a little water by measure you must drink, you must sleep upon the ground, and you will live a life of trouble while you work to learn the Torah. If you do this, '*Happy you shall be and it shall be well with you (Psalm 128:2).*' You will be happy in this world, and it shall be well with you in the world to come."

(6:5) "Do not seek greatness for yourself, and do not court honor. Let your works exceed beyond your learning. Do not desire the delicacies of the king's table. Your table is greater than theirs. Your crown is greater than theirs. After all your Employer is faithful to pay you the reward for your work."

6:6) The Torah exceeds in value over the priesthood and even over royalty. Royalty requires thirty qualifications, the priesthood twenty-four, but the learning of Torah is acquired by fortyeight actions. These are they: by study; by attentive listening; by distinct pronunciation; by understanding with the

---

[37] The words *mattanah, nachaliel,* and *bamoth* from Num 21:19 refer to "gift," "heritage or inheritance from God," and "highlands," respectively. The verse seems to reference the "gift of Torah," which is the precious inheritance from the Lord. When put into practice, obeying Torah will lead a person out of the low wastelands up to the highlands, or a place of security. Hence one could loosely translate the verse as meaning, "From the gift of Torah learning a person gains a God-given inheritance which leads upward to spiritual heights."

mind; by discernment of the heart; by awe; by reverence; by meekness; with joy; with purity; by serving wise spiritual leaders; by connecting oneself to colleagues; by sharp debate with disciples; by a calm attitude; with Scripture study; by Mishnah memorization; by limiting business dealings; by using discretion in one's intercourse with the world; by limiting pleasure; by a minimum of sleep; by limited conversation; by refraining from too much laughter; by long suffering; by a good heart; by attaining a greater faith along with wise spiritual leaders; by acceptance of suffering; recognizing one's place and being satisfied with joy in accepting one's lot in life; building a fence around one's personal concerns and claiming no credit for one's accomplishments; being loved; loving the Omnipresent; loving other people; loving just causes; loving the straight paths; loving constructive criticisms bringing reproof; removing oneself away from seeking honor for one's actions; not becoming arrogant with one's achievements in learning; not relishing in the power to make decisions about religious life; taking upon one's shoulder the yoke carried by a friend; judging another with favor; leading another to the truth; establishing another in the way of peace; being focused in one's study; asking and answering; diligently listening and adding to one's learning; learning with the purpose of teaching; learning in order to practice; making one's teacher wiser; concentrating attention upon what one has learned; reporting a teaching in the name of the one who said it. In this way of life you have learned, "Whoever teaches a truth in the name of the one who said it brings redemption into the world, as it is said: 'Esther told the king in Mordecai's name' (Esther 2:22)."

(6:7) "Great is the Torah, which gives life to those that practice it both in this world and also in the world to come, as it is said, 'For they are life for those who find them, and health to all their flesh (Proverbs 4:22),' and it is said, 'It shall be healing for your body, and refreshment to your bones (Proverbs 3:8),' and it is said, 'It is a tree of life to them that take hold of it, and all of those who uphold it will be blessed (Proverbs 3:18),' and it is said, 'For they shall be a garland of grace upon your head, and necklaces about your neck (Proverbs 1:9),' and it is said, 'For by me your days will be multiplied, and the years of your life will be increased (Proverbs 9:11),' and it is said, 'Long life is in its right hand and in its left hand are riches and honor (Proverbs 3:16),' and it is said, 'For length of days, years of life, and peace they will add to you (Proverbs 3:2).'"

(6:8) Rabbi Simeon the son of Judah, in the name of Rabbi Simeon bar Yochai, said, "Beauty, strength, riches, honor, wisdom, old age, a gray-haired head, and children are fittingly appropriate for the righteous and fittingly appropriate in the world, as it is said, 'A gray-haired head is a crown of glory, if it be found in the way of righteousness (Proverbs 16:31),' and it is said, 'The glory of young people is their strength, but the adornment of old folk is their gray haired head (Proverbs 20:29),' and it is said, "The crown of the wise is their riches (Proverbs 14:24),' and it is said, '*Children's children are the crown of old people, and the adornment of children are their parents (Proverbs 17:6),*' and it is said, '*Then the moon shall be confounded and the sun ashamed, for the Lord of hosts will reign in Mount Zion and in Jerusalem, and his glory shall appear before his elders (Isaiah 24:23).*'" Rabbi Simeon the son of Menasya, said, "The sages enumerated these seven qualities as being characteristics of the righteous and all of them were realized in Rabbi Judah the Prince, and in his sons. The Holy One, blessed be He, made five possessions for Himself in this world, and these are they, the Torah, heaven and earth, Abraham, Israel, and the house of the sanctuary. How do we learn this of the Torah? Because it is written, '*The Lord possessed me at the beginning of his way, before his works of old (Proverbs 8:22).*' How do we learn of heaven and earth? Because it is written, 'Thus saith the Lord, '*The heaven is my throne, and the earth is my footstool, where therefore is a house you could build for me? Where is a place for me to rest? (Isaiah 66:1).*' Moreover it is said, '*How many are your works, O LORD! In wisdom you have made them all, the earth is full of your possessions (Psalm 104:24).*' How do we learn of Abraham? Because it is written, '*He blessed him, and said, 'Blessed be Abram of the Most High God, possessor of heaven and earth' (Genesis 14:19).*' How do we learn of Israel? Because it is written, '*Till thy people pass over, O LORD, till the people pass over whom you have acquired (Exodus 15:16).*' Moreover it is said, '*As for the saints who are upon the earth, they are the noble ones in whom is my total delight (Psalm 16:3).*' How do we learn of the house of the sanctuary? Because it is written, '*The place, O LORD, where you have made for you to dwell in, the sanctuary, O LORD, which your hands have prepared (Exodus 15:17),*' and it says, '*He brought them to the border of his sanctuary, to this mountain which his right hand had acquired (Psalm 78:54).*'"

(6:9) Rabbi Yose the son of Kisma said, "I was once walking by the way, when a man met me and greeted me. I returned his greeting. He said to me, 'Rabbi, from what place do you live?' I said to him, 'I come from a great city of sages and scribes.' He said to me, 'If you are willing to live with us in our town, I will give you thousands upon thousands of gold coins, precious stones, and pearls.' I said to him, 'Even if you were to give me all the silver, gold, precious stones, and pearls in the world, I would not live in any other place than where a home is made for the Torah.' Hence it is written in the book of Psalms by the hands of David, King of Israel, '*The law of your mouth is better for me than thousands of gold and silver pieces (Psalm 69:72),*' and not only so, but at the time of one's departure neither silver nor gold nor precious stones nor pearls accompany an individual, but only Torah learning and good works, as it is said, '*When you walk about, it will guide you, when you lie down to sleep it shall watch over you and when you wake up it will talk with* you (Proverbs 6:22).' The words, '*When you walk about, it shall watch over you,*' refer to the grave. The words, '*when you wake up it shall talk with you,*' refer to life in the world to come. Moreover it is said, '*The silver is mine, and the gold is mine (Haggai 2:8).*'"

(6:10) Whatever the Holy One, blessed be He, created in His world He created for the purpose of His glory, as it is said, "*Everything that is called by my name, it is for the purpose of my glory. Truly I have created it, I have formed it, and I have made it (Isaiah 43:7).*" Moreover it declares, "*The LORD reigns for ever and ever (Exodus 15:19).*"

Historical Transitions within Jewish Thought

In the course of its history, Rabbinic Judaism underwent numerous changes. Taken as a whole, its early phases have a greater affinity in certain respects to biblical Judaism than to the later phases of Rabbinic Judaism. For example, in the beginning of the rabbinic epoch, the laws of the sacrificial cult and of ritual purity, so important in the Torah, also played an important role in Rabbinic Judaism. The termination of the sacrificial cult, the centralized Sanctuary, the high-priesthood and many other laws and institutions due to the destruction of the Temple in Jerusalem, resulted in significant changes in the forms and ways of religious life of Palestinian and Diaspora Jewry. However, these changes did not cause an essential modification of the character of "mainstream" Judaism.

Alexander Guttmann, *Rabbinic Judaism in the Making* (Detroit: Wayne State University Press, 1970), xi.

Face-to-Face with God

The mystic is conscious of God as an indwelling Father in his soul, as an indwelling spirit of goodness in the world. His aim and purpose is to know this indwelling Father, to realise this spirit of goodness, and by these means to unite himself to God in as close a bond as it is possible for any human being to effect . . . For what is the acme of all religious teaching, but the fact that man is face to face with God, that he hears His voice and feels His presence, that he can only find his truest sanctification, his being's highest and holiest joy from the Presence of God. There is no religion in which the word "love," and the idea it stands for, does not occupy a commanding place. And it is mysticism that pushes love to the forefront. The mystic's idea is communion with God. His soul reaches out in living yearning to embrace God. And he knows that he has found God, because he has felt the thrill of His answering love.

J. Abelson, *The Immanence of God in Rabbinical Literature* (London: Macmillan, 1912), 4–5.

CHAPTER 8

The Amidah Prayer

Prayer is central to the spiritual life of the Jewish people. The breath of life for worship in the Temple during the time of Jesus were the prayers to God. More than mere words, they were expressions of the "service of the heart," deep heart yearnings for vital communion with God. Some form of "The Prayer" was recited daily in the morning, noon, and evening, in the Temple liturgy.

Three names—"The Prayer," "Shemoneh Esreh or 18 Benedictions or Prayer Petitions," and "Amidah"—all refer to this daily prayer, which continues to be prayed in the synagogue today, with some modifications, along with the study of the Torah portion.[1] The prayer is prayed with pious devotion as the Torah portion is studied, day by day and week by week, according to the cycle of the Jewish liturgical calendar. The Mishnah notes that the pious ones of old would spend an hour preparing the heart *before* they prayed to God, in order to make certain that they would indeed direct their hearts toward heaven. Even if they were disturbed by a life-threatening emergency like a snake wrapping itself around an ankle, they would not stir from their concentration. The call to prayer is Psalm 51, which emphasizes remorse for sins committed, true repentance, and purity of mind. A person prays that God will open one's lips so that one's praise will be acceptable and spiritually meaningful.

The Amidah also contains petitions for personal needs, including spiritual awakening, healing of the body, financial blessing, and community concerns. The Gospels make it clear that Jesus devoted much time to prayer (e.g., "But he withdrew to the wilderness and prayed," Luke 5:16). The Gospels also show Jesus praying before making decisions like choosing the disciples or even during times of intense ministry activity, but they do not give the reader much information about the words he prayed.

---

[1] Originally the Temple was the place for prayer and the synagogue was the place for Torah study. After the destruction of the Temple in 70 C.E., prayers from the Temple began to be prayed in the synagogue. See Shmuel Safrai, "The Synagogue and its Worship," in *Society and Religion in the Second Temple Period* (ed. Michael Avi–Yonah and Zvi Baras; Jerusalem: Massada, 1977), 78–89.

What follows is an introduction to the most foundational prayer in Jewish tradition, the Amidah, which may answer some of these and other related questions. What was the content of Jewish prayer during the time of Jesus? Did Jewish prayer impact the way that Jesus prayed or the way that he taught his disciples to pray? Did the early church pray like first-century Jews? How did the people prepare to worship? What is prayer in Hebrew thought? What can be learned about prayer by comparative study of liturgy?

Most Christians do not consider the Jewish Prayer Book as a source for understanding the prayer life of Jesus or the early church. The prayers of ancient Israel, however, both in the Hebrew Bible and the Jewish Prayer Book, lay a firm foundation for the earnest heart seeking intimate communion with God through prayer. The Amidah is one such prayer. There should be little doubt that Jesus and the disciples prayed some form of this prayer many times.[2] In Acts, the early church gathered in the Temple and participated in the worship, which means that they prayed this prayer. They broke bread together and prayed the prayer in home fellowships. The Amidah is also considered to be a private prayer for the individual. The Prayer is much more than making requests, because it concludes with a pure song of thanksgiving that invites a real spiritual awakening in the inmost feelings of the worshipper.

The Hebrew name *Amidah* means "standing," and refers to the posture of the prayer. One stands while praying this prayer because it helps one concentrate. Standing erect with feet together during the prayer shows respect. The worshipper faces the direction of the Holy of Holies in Jerusalem. During the opening blessing which signifies God's working of miracles in history, it is customary to bend the knees when saying, "Blessed," bow forward when saying, "are You," and then to stand erect again when saying, "My LORD." This signifies entering into the presence of royalty.[3] Sometimes worshippers take three small steps forward when commencing the Amidah, in the same way people show respect when entering the presence of an earthly monarch. After concluding the prayer, they take three small steps backwards, like an individual who is leaving the presence of a king.

The Hebrew name *Shemoneh Esreh* means "eighteen," and refers to the original number of blessings contained in the prayer. Today the prayer actually contains nineteen benedictions, or prayer petitions, but retains its name. (Most scholars believe that Benedictions 14 and 15 were originally one prayer, but later were divided into two separate petitions making nineteen

---

[2] Compare Louis Finkelstein, "The Development of the Amidah," *JQR* 16 (1925–1926): 1–43, 127–70; see also Safrai's critique, "The Synagogue and its Worship," 78–89.

[3] See Donin, *To Pray As a Jew*, 40, 71–72.

prayers instead of eighteen.[4]) David Flusser has demonstrated that originally the words of this prayer petition spoke against those schismatics who caused divisions and broke away from the community seeking an ascetic holiness (in Hebrew *perushim*, "Pharisees").[5] This usage of the term *Pharisee* pre-dates the rise of the Pharisee movement mentioned in the Gospels and other first-century literature (see discussion of Pharisees in Chapter Two) and refers to the basic meaning of the term, which is to be separate, set apart.[6] Recognized authority on Jewish prayer, H. Donin, argues that the benediction was originally formulated to mention the Samaritans, in Hebrew, *shomrim*.[7] This approach has much to commend it, since the Samaritans caused much suffering to the Jewish people during the return to Zion under Ezra (see Ezra 4:1–24; 9:1–15; Neh 4:1–23). It would be natural to pray for protection from enemies like the Samaritans in that day. Today the benediction mentions "slanderers," which refers to those who betray the righteous into the hands of oppressive governments and cause great suffering to the Jewish people. The benediction asks God for protection from those who would harm and injure the faithful. The Amidah is an old prayer that has undergone many revisions in its long history. The vitality of Jewish faith is seen in how prayer has adapted to face current challenges.

The prayers of Israel follow the cycle of daily life experiences. Hence, studying the Daily Prayer Book can be the most illuminating start for exploring the Jewish roots of Jesus' life and teachings. In Hebrew, the Prayer Book is called *Siddur*, which means "set order." There is an order for prayer that follows the order of one's life. As A. Steinsaltz explains, "The Siddur is not merely a book containing the liturgy of the synagogue, but a

---

[4] See Ismar Elbogen, *Jewish Liturgy: A Comprehensive History* (trans. R. Scheindlin; Philadelphia: Jewish Publication Society, 1993), 47–49. One should compare the Hebrew version of Sir 51:21–35 with the Amidah. For instance, the prayers to God to gather the exiles, build Jerusalem, and cause the horn (symbolizing strength) of the house of David to sprout are all paralleled in an ancient version of these blessings. The similarity between Sirach, Benediction 15, and Luke 1:68–69 is striking. See David Flusser, "Prayer at the Time of the Second Temple," *Society and Religion in the Second Temple* (Jerusalem: Massada Publishing, 1977), 19–22.

[5] David Flusser, "Prayer at the Time of the Second Temple," 23–24. While Flusser observes that different versions of the prayer mention diverse enemies, such as heretics, slanderers, perpetrators of wickedness, and the arrogant, "At all events, it is evident that the essence of the heretics' prayer preceded Christianity and that it was originally a kind of defense of the people against those endangering their existence."

[6] See *t. Berakhot* 3:25. Compare the important discussion by Saul Lieberman, *Tosefta Kefushutah* (15 vols.; New York: Jewish Theological Seminary, 1955–1977), part 1, *Zera'im*, 53–54 (Hebrew).

[7] See Donin, *To Pray As a Jew*, 92.

comprehensive collection of prayers and benedictions relating to every aspect of Jewish life."[8]

> The order of prayers relates not only to the weekdays and festivals, but to the entire life cycle: from birth until death, upon reaching maturity and entering marriage, the Jew is accompanied by prayers and benedictions. Nearly every sorrowful or joyous event, of everyday life or of special occasions, is reflected in the prayer book, since the Siddur is the book of Jewish life, in which everyone is involved and to which everyone relates.[9]

On holidays and Sabbaths a shortened form of the Amidah is prayed, consisting of the first three blessings and last three benedictions. A prayer about the festival or occasion is inserted in between the two sets of three blessings. Even though this would make up only seven benedictions, the shortened form is still called the Sabbath, or Festival Shemoneh Esreh, or Eighteen Benedictions. The middle thirteen petitions deal more with requests than with blessings. On holidays and Sabbaths, each individual is encouraged to focus on praise to God rather than making demands. Although praying for specific needs is certainly crucial, as can be seen in the thirteen intervening petitions prayed three times a day every day of the week.

Some scholars have even suggested that the prayer Jesus teaches his disciples to pray is a shortened form of the eighteen benedictions; there are clear parallels to the Lord's Prayer in the Siddur and especially in the Amidah. The rabbis also emphasized the kingdom of heaven in prayer, which is similar to Jesus seeking the divine rule in every aspect of life by teaching his followers to pray "Thy kingdom come."[10] One rabbi taught that any prayer that does not mention the kingdom is no prayer (*t. Berakhot* 1:8; *b. Berakhot* 40b).

Studying the diverse prayers in the nineteen petitions of the Amidah enables one to begin to grasp the Jewish view of God. Prayer begins with an understanding of the divine character. Indeed the first petition of the nineteen portrays God acting through history by working miracles and establishing a relationship with a family. The order of the prayer reminds worshippers that they are entering into the presence of the King of kings, to offer praise before making requests, and to offer some form of thanksgiving before leaving the King's presence.

---

[8] Rabbi Adin Steinsaltz, *A Guide to Jewish Prayer* (New York: Schocken, 2000), 4. Steinsaltz insightfully observes, "No other Jewish book contains, as does the Siddur, the entirety of Judaism." Prayer reveals the life of the people.

[9] Steinsaltz, *A Guide to Jewish Prayer*, 4.

[10] In my book, *Jewish Background,* I argue that a better translation of this petition would be "Continue establishing your kingdom." This is illustrated by rabbinic parables and the Kaddish, the Jewish prayer. See also the fine books by Frédéric Manns, *Jewish Prayer in the Time of Jesus* (Jerusalem: Franciscan Printing, 1994), and Di Sante, *Jewish Prayer.*

THE AMIDAH PRAYER

The prayer is as follows:[11]

Call to Prayer	"O Lord, open my lips, and my mouth shall tell your praise." Psalm 51:15

Acknowledging God's Character

1. The God of Creation and Giver of Love	Blessed are You, O LORD our God and God of our ancestors, God of Abraham, God of Isaac, and God of Jacob, the great, mighty and revered God, the most high God, who graciously gives loving-kindness. You create all things; You remember the pious actions of the patriarchs, and in love will bring a redeemer for their children's children for Your Name's sake. O King, Helper, Savior, and Shield. Blessed are You, O LORD, the Protector of Abraham.
2. The God Who Works Miracles	You are LORD, are all-powerful for ever, You resurrect the dead, You are mighty to save. You sustain the living with loving-kindness, resurrect the dead with great mercy, support the falling, heal the sick, release the prisoners, and uphold Your faithfulness to them that sleep in the dust. Who is like You, Lord of mighty acts, and who resembles You, O King, who orders death and restores life, and causes salvation to come forth? And You are faithful to resurrect the dead. Blessed are You, O LORD, who resurrects the dead.
3. "Holiness" and the Name of God	We will sanctify Your Name in the world even as they sanctify it in the heavens, as it is written by the hand of Your prophet: And they called one unto the other and said, *Holy, Holy, Holy is the LORD of Hosts: the whole earth is full of His glory.* Those over against them say, Blessed— *Blessed be the glory of the LORD from His Place.* And in Your Holy Words it is written, saying, *The LORD reigns for ever, your God, O Zion, unto all generations. Praise you the LORD.* Unto all generations we will proclaim Your greatness, and to all eternity we will tell of Your holiness. Your praise, O our God, shall not cease from our mouth for ever, for You are a great and holy God and

---

[11] The translation of the prayer is done by the author. For comparison, the reader is encouraged to examine Hertz, *Daily Prayer Book,* 130–59.

King. Blessed are You O LORD, the holy God. You are holy, and Your Name is holy and the holy ones praise You every day. Blessed are You, O LORD, the holy God.

Seeking Spiritual Insight and Awakening

4. Request for Understanding	You favor people with knowledge, and teach human beings understanding. O favor us with knowledge, understanding, and applied wisdom from You. Blessed are You, O LORD, gracious Giver of knowledge.
5. Returning to God for Repentance	Make us return, O our Father, unto Your Torah. Draw us near, O our King, back into Your service, and bring us again in perfect repentance into Your presence. Blessed are You, O LORD, who delights in repentance.
6. Request for Forgiveness	Forgive us, O our Father, for we have sinned. Pardon us, O our King, for we have transgressed, because You do pardon and forgive. Blessed are You, O LORD, who is gracious and forgives a multitude of wrongs.

Requesting Divine Help for Personal Needs

7. Request for Freedom from Affliction	Look upon our affliction and fight for our cause. Redeem us speedily for Your Name's sake because You are a mighty Redeemer. Blessed are You, O LORD, the Redeemer of Israel.
8. Request for Healing	Heal us, O LORD, and we shall be healed. Save us and we shall be saved. You are our praise. Provide a perfect healing for all our wounds; because You, almighty King, are a faithful and merciful Physician. Blessed are You, O LORD, who heals the sick of Your people Israel.
9. Request for Financial Prosperity	Bless this year for us, O LORD our God, together with every kind of the produce there is from it, for our well being. Provide a blessing upon the face of the earth. Satisfy us with Your goodness, and bless our year like other good years. Blessed are You, O LORD, who blesses the years.

Seeking Divine Help for the Jewish People, Society, and Community Needs

10. Request to Gather the Exiles of Israel to Their Homeland	Blow the great shofar horn for our freedom. Raise the standard to gather our exiles, and bring us together from the four corners of the earth. Blessed are You, O LORD, who gathers the dispersed of Your people Israel.

11. Prayer Seeking the Establishment of the Kingdom of Heaven	Restore our judges as at the beginning, and our counselors as in former times. Remove from us sorrow and sighing. Reign over us, O LORD, You alone, in loving-kindness and tender mercy, and justify us in judgment. Blessed are You, O LORD, the King who loves righteousness and justice.
12. Request for Protection from Enemies	Let there be no hope for slanders and let all wickedness perish as in a moment. Let all Your enemies be speedily cut off. May You root out, break off, bring down, and cause the ruin of the reign of evil speedily in our days. Blessed are You, O LORD, who breaks the enemies and humbles the arrogant.
13. Request for Mercy upon God's People	Let Your kind mercies rush toward the righteous and the pious, toward the elders of Your people the house of Israel, toward the remnant of their scribes, toward true proselytes, and toward us, O LORD our God. Give a good reward to all who faithfully trust in Your Name. Set our portion with them forever, so that we may not be put to shame because we have trusted in You. Blessed are You, O LORD, the support and security of the righteous.

Seeking Deliverance and Restoration for the Divine Plan and Future Hope

14. Request for the Rebuilding of Jerusalem	With tender mercies return to Jerusalem, Your city, so that Your Presence will abide in her midst as You have promised. Rebuild her soon in our days as an everlasting building, and speedily establish in her the throne of David. Blessed are You, O LORD, who builds Jerusalem.
15. Prayer for the Branch of David	Speedily cause the Branch of David, Your servant, to spring forth. With your saving power, raise up the horn of his strength because we wait for Your salvation all the day. Blessed are You, O LORD, who causes the horn of salvation to spring forth.
16. Request for Prayers to Be Answered	Answer our voice, O LORD our God. Free us and have mercy upon us, and accept our prayer in compassion and favor because You are God who answers prayers and supplications: from Your presence, O our King, turn us not empty away; because You hear with mercy the prayer of Your people Israel. Blessed are You, O LORD, who answers prayer.

Praise and Thanksgiving for Divine Help

17. Request to Restore Temple Service	Accept with divine favor, O LORD our God, Your people Israel and their prayer. Restore the worship to the inner sanctuary of Your house. With compassion receive in favor both the offerings of Israel and their prayer; and may the worship of Your people Israel be ever acceptable to You. Let our eyes witness Your return with compassion to Zion. Blessed are You, O LORD, who restores His divine presence to Zion.
18. Giving of Thanks to God for His Mercy	We give thanks to You, for You are the LORD our God and the God of our ancestors forever and ever. You are the Rock of our lives, the Shield of our salvation throughout every generation, we will give thanks to You and proclaim Your praise for our lives, which are committed into Your care, and for our souls, which are under Your charge, and for Your miracles, which are daily with us, and for Your wondrous acts and Your benefits, which are worked at all times, evening, morning, and noon. O You who are all-good, whose mercies do not fail; You who are all merciful, whose loving-kindnesses never cease, we have hope in You. Because of all this, let Your name, O our King, be blessed and be highly exalted continually, forever and ever. All living beings will give thanks to You, selah, and they will praise Your name in truth, the God of our Salvation and of our help, selah! Blessed are You, O LORD, the Good One is Your name, and so to You it is fitting to give praise.
19. Request for Peace	Give peace, well being, blessing, grace, loving-kindness and mercy to us and to all of Israel, Your people. Bless us, O our Father, even all of us together, with the light of Your countenance because by the light of Your countenance You have given us, O LORD our God, the Torah of life, the love of mercy and righteousness, blessing, loving-kindness, life, and peace. May it be good in Your sight to bless Your people Israel at all times and in every hour with Your peace. Blessed are You, O LORD, who blesses Your people Israel with peace.

Studying Jewish prayer is essential for understanding rabbinic literature. In addition, for Christians exploring events in the life of Jesus, one should consider that the birth, circumcision, naming of a child, purification of the mother, redemption of the firstborn, presentation in the Temple, blessings recited over food, blessing recited when witnessing a miracle, prayers for divine protection, prayers against being lead into temptation, prayers for God's reign, prayers during a Passover meal, and even the prayer of a dying person (Ps 31:6, "Into thy hands I commit my spirit") are all in some way discussed and reflected in the Jewish Daily Prayer Book.

Curiously on the one hand, Christian scholars rush to examine carefully late texts in apocryphal writings, from the newly published Gospel of Judas, to the Gospel of Philip, or even the well-known and widely-quoted Gospel of Thomas, in their quest for more information about Jesus, while on the other hand, the study of Jewish prayer is neglected or ignored altogether. Seldom have New Testament scholars thought to study seriously the spiritual faith experience of the Jewish people for insight into the life and teachings of Jesus and the early apostles. Quite probably the Jewish Prayer Book would do more to illustrate the life of Jesus and the religious community in which he thrived, than the Gospel of Peter. Here I must emphasize that all the evidence needs to be studied—including the non-canonical writings of second-and third-century Christian communities. Good methodology for some New Testament scholars, however, passes as the rejection of all the evidence derived from rabbinic literature because it is considered too late to be relevant. But at the same time, this sound academic method embraces other source materials from the church fathers to the apocryphal texts. This approach puts the Jewish rabbis of old into a ghetto, along with all their prayers, writings, and teachings in hand, and then builds a tall fence around all the evidence from their faith tradition with a sign at the gate warning all, "Entrance Strictly Forbidden!" This fence must come down.

Directing Your Heart in Prayer

One must not stand up to pray "the Prayer" except with heartfelt respectful awe. The early Pious ones used to direct their hearts toward heaven for an hour before they would commence praying. Even if the king would give one a greeting, one should not stop praying to return the greeting. Even if a snake would curl itself around one's ankle, one must not stop praying.

   m. Berakhot 5:1

The Shema—"Hear" and "Obey"

"Hear O Israel, the LORD our God the LORD is one."

Deut 6:4

The Shema consists of three sections of the Torah (Deuteronomy 6.4–8; 11.13–22; and Numbers 15. 37–42). It is a proclamation of the existence and Unity of God; of Israel's complete loyalty to God and His commandments; the belief in Divine Justice; the remembrance of the liberation from Egypt, and its corollary, the Election of Israel. These are the foundation pillars of the Jewish Faith.

J. Hertz, *The Authorized Daily Prayer Book* (Bloch Publishing: New York, 1985), 118.

CHAPTER 9

Maimonides' Thirteen Principles of Jewish Faith

The thirteen principles of faith are printed in every Jewish prayer book and are recited as a liturgical hymn at the conclusion of a Friday or Festival service.[1] The recitation of these fundamentals of faith during the synagogue service is known as the *Yigdal,* meaning "let [God] be exalted." In many ways, these principles can be compared to the Apostles' or the Nicene Creeds for Christians, because they embody Judaism's fundamental pillars of traditional belief.

MAIMONIDES

Maimonides (1135–1204 C.E.) compiled and composed the thirteen principles of Jewish faith. He is also known in Hebrew as Rabbi Moshe ben Maimon, or simply Rambam, based on the acronym of his Hebrew name. He is considered to be one of the most erudite and foremost spiritual sages of all time. Commonly one hears the Jewish folk saying from a monument erected in honor of Maimonides, "From Moses to Moses, there was no one like Moses,"[2] because he is often compared in greatness to the Moses of the Bible.[3] Certainly among medieval Jewish thinkers and leaders he towers above his peers in history.

---

[1] Abraham Z. Idelson, *Jewish Liturgy* (New York: Schocken, 1975), 74. The hymn is ascribed to Daniel ben Judah of Rome. Some rites use the *Yigdal* in the daily service. Here we have translated the summary of the entire thirteen principles from the synagogue liturgy. For a full discussion of the entire text, see the important study by J. David Bleich, *With Perfect Faith: The Foundation of Jewish Belief* (New York: KTAV, 1983), 619–87.

[2] Abraham Joshua Heschel, *Maimonides* (New York: Farrar, Straus and Giroux, 1982), 247.

[3] David Novak, "The Mind of Maimonides," *First Things* (Feburary, 1999): 27–33. See also Fred Rosner, *Moses Maimonides* (New York: Feldheim, 1975).

Raising of Lazarus, Luke 7:12–15
(Wood Engraving by Bernard A. Solomon)

Maimondes was born in Cordova, Spain, the son of a renowned judge and scholar of Jewish law. He lived in Fez, Morocco for a time and visited Israel where he prayed on the Temple Mount and in the Cave of Machpelah, the burial site of the patriarchs and matriarchs in Hebron. He moved to Egypt and flourished in Cairo, eventually being appointed as personal physician to the Sultan of Egypt. As a physician to the ruling class of Egypt, Maimonides won favor and respect for the Jewish community. His people recognized his wisdom and abilities, and he became the leader of the Jewish community in Egypt. His letters, written opinions, and religious philosophy became widely discussed throughout the world.

Maimonides made decisive rulings for the practice of the Jewish law in the area of halakhah. He was an expert Bible commentator, religious philosopher, scientist, and physician. Living under Muslim rule, he considered many issues that impacted the Jewish community as a minority group in a diverse society. He wrote extensively on Jewish practice and how to properly observe the commandments. In Judaism today, his influence is greatly felt in his well-written and researched work, *Mishnah Torah,* or *Yad Chazakah,* "Strong Hand," a monumental examination and codification of the Oral Torah. His insightful analysis deals with the correct application and meaning of the Torah for the daily practice of the Jewish faith. He also wrote a major philosophical and religious work called *The Guide for the Perplexed,* as well as many other works. Maimonides was a man of tremendous energy, who worked diligently as a physician but also contributed greatly to Jewish scholarship, and provided decisive leadership for the entire Jewish community.

PROGRESSIVE INTERPRETATIONS

While Orthodox Judaism holds Maimonides' Thirteen Principles as sacred and unchangeable, some scholars in the modern progressive movements of Judaism have made changes and adaptations to them in order to make them more relevant for their own teachings. In Reform Judaism, for instance, the divine inspiration of the Torah is questioned, the "Messiah" is anticipated as a future age where people will seek a more just and equitable society, and the doctrine of the resurrection is viewed with uncertainty because it cannot be scientifically proven and because there are other possible views of the afterlife—if indeed there is life in a future existence.[4] Reform Judaism, therefore, emphasizes social justice in the tradition of the Hebrew prophets, rather than the traditional beliefs and practices held sacred by the Orthodox; that is, Jewish faith and practice is made relevant for today through action.[5]

When non-Jews encounter Judaism it is sometimes difficult to summarize the basic beliefs because Judaism stresses such diversity. However, the thirteen principles of belief are a good place to begin studying Jewish theology. Almost all the Jewish faithful affirm these principles, or at least explain how they deviate from them or interpret them in light of modern applications of their faith tradition. While there was some harsh opposition to Maimonides even in his lifetime, his ability to synthesize theological belief based upon the Bible and tradition gained unparalleled acceptance. The unity within the diverse Jewish communities that resulted from his teachings provided a universally recognizable identity to expressions of Jewish faith based upon a succinctly articulated belief system. This was no small achievement.

COMMONALITIES WITH CHRISTIANITY

Most Christian theologians would share the fundamental beliefs espoused by Maimonides. The thirteen principles of faith illustrate significant

---

[4] See Simcha P. Raphael, *Jewish Views of the Afterlife* (Northvale, N.J.: Jason Aronson, 1994), 244–58.

[5] On the beliefs and practices of the Reform movement, see W. Gunther Plaut, *Growth of Reform Judaism* (New York: World Union for Progressive Judaism, 1965). Plaut has also written an informative and insightful commentary, *The Torah a Modern Commentary* (New York: Union of American Hebrew Congregations, 1981).

similarities between Christianity and Judaism: the divine creation of the world, the incorporeal nature of the Creator, the dignity of every human being, the sanctity of life, the authority and inspiration of Scripture, prayer to God alone, reward for the righteous, punishment for the wicked, and the bodily resurrection of the dead. Principle 2, for example, affirms the unity of God (which would rule out discussions of the Christian doctrine of the Trinity for Maimonides), while Christian theology affirms belief in the triune God who is one and must be accepted as an essential unity. Principle 3 affirms that God does not have a body, he is not physical; similarly, Jesus tells the woman of Samaria, "God is Spirit, and those who worship him must worship in Spirit and truth" (John 4:24). Principle 4 describes God as the first and the last, recalling similar terminology in the New Testament, " 'I am the Alpha and the Omega' says the Lord God, who is and who was and who is to come, the Almighty" (Rev 1:8). Like Maimonides' Principle 13, the Apostle Paul strongly argues for a bodily resurrection (1 Cor 15), and he applies this belief about physical matter to spiritual concerns: the wicked who are living actually are walking dead, and the righteous who have died in the Lord are living because of the resurrection.[6]

MAIMONIDES' PRINCIPLES AND THE MESSIAH

The major difference between Maimonides' Principles and Christian theology is Principle 12, which affirms the belief in the future coming of the Messiah. Christians share with Orthodox Jews the belief that, in the future, the Messiah will come; the question is whether this will be the first or second coming. For Christians also believe that the Messiah has already appeared in the person of Jesus of Nazareth. Orthodox Jewish scholar David Flusser, who served on the faculty of the Hebrew University, has said, "I do not think that many Jews would object if the Messiah—when he came— was the Jew Jesus."[7]

---

[6] See *b. Berakhot* 18 a–b and Bleich's discussion on Principle 13, *With Perfect Faith,* 619–88; cf. Jesus' defense of the resurrection from the Torah in Matt 22:23–33; Mark 12:18–27; Luke 20:27–40.

[7] In private communication, I have heard Prof. Flusser make this and similar statements. While I am sure that some members of the Jewish community would object strongly to the idea that Jesus could turn out to be the Messiah after all, it is significant to Christians that a leading Jewish scholar would advance such a view. He was once asked what the Messiah would say to reporters when asked, after he finally did come, if it was his first or his second coming. Prof. Flusser responded with characteristic humor: "First he would look at the Jewish community and then at the Christians all waiting with anticipation. Then he would answer, 'No comment,' and show love to all."

The future messianic hope expressed by the early Christians was not so far removed from the vision described by Maimonides. In the conclusion of his monumental work the, *Mishnah Torah,* Maimonides tries to outline hope for the future by speaking about his strong faith in the coming days of the Messiah. He envisions the messianic days as a time when

> No hunger will be experienced there, no war, no envy and no competition. Basic decent goodness will abundantly increase influencing all. Delightful things will be available everywhere like the dust. The single occupation of everyone in the entire world will be to know the LORD. In accord with the age, great sages of wisdom will arise who will comprehend the hidden matters. Moreover, they will attain a knowledge of their Creator, as it is within the potential power of every human being, even as it was written, "For the earth will be full of the intimate knowledge of the LORD, even as the waters cover the sea" (Isa. 11:9). (Maimonides, *Mishnah Torah, Melakhim* and *Milchamot* 12:5)[8]

Maimonides warns against setting the date for the coming of the Messiah, in the same way that Jesus teaches his disciples that no one knows the day or the hour (Matt 24:36). Each person should wait expectantly for the unknown time of Messiah's coming. A similar point is made by Rabbi Abraham Isaac Kook (1868–1935), who provided spiritual leadership as the Ashenazi Chief Rabbi for the Jewish people during the days before the founding of the State of Israel. He teaches, "Just as a lookout doesn't leave his post even when everything is quiet and nothing seems to be happening, but stands ready to detect enemy movement and to react to it at a moment's notice, so do we maintain a state of constant spiritual alertness and readiness, so we may respond when the time comes. These are the two components of awaiting salvation" (*Olat Re'iya* I 279–80).[9]

Donin emphasizes the concept of waiting in the daily prayers, for the worshipper affirms the belief in the messianic hope when praying, " 'for Thy deliverance do we constantly hope' teaches us the concept of *anticipating deliverance* even when there are no signs of it in daily events."[10] Holocaust survivors have remembered those who died in the concentration camps, recalling the last words that many faithful Jews said before they died. Sometimes they were silent. Other times they uttered the words of the *Shema,* "Hear O Israel, the LORD our God, the LORD is one" (Deut 6:4). Some would recite the twelfth principle of Jewish faith, expressing an

---

[8] I have used for my translation, *Mishnah Torah,* with introduction by Yehudah Hacohen Maimon, based upon the Rome printed edition (Jerusalem: Mosad Derav Kook, 1986), 693.

[9] Quoted by Donin, *To Pray As a Jew,* 95.

[10] Donin, *To Pray as a Jew,* 95.

unconquerable hope when facing an excruciating death: "I believe by complete faith, in the coming of the Messiah, and even though he tarry, with all that, I will still wait expectantly for him each day that he will come."[11]

THIRTEEN PRINCIPLES OF JEWISH FAITH

Principle 1   I believe by complete faith that the Creator, blessed be His name, is the Creator and Guide for all created beings. He alone made, makes, and will make all that is created.

Principle 2   I believe by complete faith that the Creator, blessed be His name, is a Unity, and there is no union in any way like Him. He alone is our God, who was, who is, and who is to be.

Principle 3   I believe by complete faith that the Creator, blessed be His name, is not a body, is not affected by physical matter, and nothing whatsoever can compare to Him [or be compared with Him].

Principle 4   I believe by complete faith that the Creator, blessed be His name, is the first and is the last.

Principle 5   I believe by complete faith that the Creator, blessed be His name, to Him alone is it fitting to make prayer and to another prayer shall not be made.

Principle 6   I believe by complete faith that all the words of the prophets are true.

Principle 7   I believe by complete faith that the prophecy of Moses our teacher, may peace rest upon him, was true and that he was the father of all prophets that preceded him as well as all that came after him.

Principle 8   I believe by complete faith that the whole Torah now found in our hands was the exact same one given to Moses, may peace rest upon him.

Principle 9   I believe by complete faith that this is the Torah, and it shall not be changed and it shall not be replaced with another from the Creator, blessed be His name.

---

[11] See Telushkin, *Jewish Literacy*, 180.

Principle 10 I believe by complete faith that the Creator, blessed be His name, knows every action done by each human being as well as all their thoughts, as it was said, "It is He that fashions their hearts together and He ponders all their deeds" [Ps 33:15].

Principle 11 I believe by complete faith that the Creator, blessed be His name, rewards all who keep His commandments and punishes all those who transgress His commands.

Principle 12 I believe by complete faith in the coming of the Messiah, and even though he tarry in waiting in spite of that, I will still wait expectantly for him each day that he will come.

Principle 13 I believe by complete faith that there will be a resurrection of the dead at the time that will be pleasing before the Creator, blessed be His name, and the remembrance of Him will be exalted forever and for all eternity.

These thirteen principles of faith, though composed after the Talmudic period, form the foundation for ancient Jewish belief. Jewish theology is ever evolving and always encouraged live debate and interaction. But when non-Jews seek a foundation stone for the basic belief system, these sacred tenets of faith serve to explain Israel's faith experience rooted in the Bible and expressed in the rich diversity of Talmudic thought. Many aspects of these principles underpin Jewish biblical interpretation and the methodology developed in hermeneutics.

The Tenacious Prayer

Rabbi Leazar observed a fast but no rain fell. Rabbi Akiva observed a fast, and rain descended. He went in and said to them, "I will tell you a parable. To what may the matter be compared? To a king who had two daughters. One was tenacious and the other was gracious. When the tenacious one wanted something and came before him, he said: Give her what she wants so she will get out of here. But when the gracious one wanted something and came in before him, he lengthened his dealings with her because he enjoyed listening to her conversation."

y. Ta'anit 66d

On Forgiveness before the Day of Atonement

This is almost the last chance to ask forgiveness of people one has hurt; it is a time for giving restitution to those we have wronged and forgiving those who have hurt us. One should forgive freely, with a full heart. The way of the Israelites is to be slow to anger and quick to be pacified.

Rabbi Irving Greenberg, *The Jewish Way* (New York: Touchstone Book, 1993), 204, 206.

CHAPTER 10

Hillel's Seven Principles of Bible Interpretation

The biblical word possesses the power both to unite and to divide. Whether the study of the Bible will unite people together with common views or divide them in total disharmony depends upon their method of interpretation. In fact, although Jewish and Christian communities share common views concerning the inspiration and authority of the Hebrew Bible, they approach the interpretation of the sacred text from very different perspectives. Even within the same religious community people disagree as to how to interpret the Bible and apply its message.

The foundation of Scripture study and exposition, however, both in rabbinic literature and New Testament, is rooted in the Second Temple period and the multi-faceted methods of interpretation developed by the Jewish people. One of the most important places to begin to understand the principles of interpretation is the system developed by Hillel the Elder (flourished ca. 20 B.C.E. to 10 C.E.). He enumerated seven distinct techniques for exposition that could be used to understand and apply the Torah in everyday life. These are rules of exegesis.

Hillel's method of interpretation has greatly impacted rabbinic thought. His approach can be seen in the interpretation of the Hebrew Bible contained in the New Testament. The writers of the New Testament used Jewish hermeneutics when they studied the Bible, in large part because many of them *were* Jewish.[1] Here we will define these seven principles as they appear in rabbinic literature to gain insight into the Jewish method of interpreting the Bible. First and foremost, these rules of interpretation, or exegesis, focus on the Bible itself: the biblical text must be used to interpret the biblical text. Words in one text must be studied and compared to other texts where the same words appear. These insightful formulations attributed to Hillel the Elder are drawn from the Bible in order to interpret and to apply the Bible to everyday life situations within the community of faith. The community,

---

[1] See Doeve, *Jewish Hermeneutics*.

moreover, is involved in the work of exposition and application. The preacher has one eye on the text, and the other eye on the congregation. Midrash breathes fresh meaning into the old text and makes it live for a new generation facing problems in a contemporary life setting. The great biblical scholar Martin Noth called the work of interpretation a "re-presentation" of the text.[2] The interpreter is presenting again the old message for a new time.

In Judaism the process of "re-presentation" must be made legitimate by accepted methods and rules. Whether one accepts the view of Rabbi Ishmael that the words of the text must be interpreted as mere human speech, or Rabbi Akiva's prevailing view that every letter and nuance has a spiritual meaning in the deeper mystery of divine inspiration, the proper technique of Bible interpretation must be used if the results are to be accepted as legitimate by the community. Interpreting Scripture with Scripture according to the method of Hillel gained wide acceptance by those involved in the laborious task of Bible commentary. Jewish midrash, or biblical exposition, explores the deeper meanings of the text. The method behind midrash is a sophisticated conceptual way of thinking about God and the sacred text inspired by Him.

HILLEL'S METHOD IN PRACTICE

According to one account in the Talmud, Hillel the Elder became the leader of the Jewish people during the Second Temple period because of his penetrating interpretation of Torah and the authoritative learning he received from his teachers, Shemayah and Avtalyon. A burning question relating to ritual observance had arisen because the festival of Passover and the Sabbath were to fall on the same day: if one observed the Sabbath, the Passover would be violated; if one observed the Passover, the Sabbath would be profaned. What was to take precedence, the observance of Passover or the keeping of the Sabbath rest? The family that was then establishing the rule of conduct for the Jewish community was that of Bathyra, a member of the ruling aristocracy, but its members did not know the answer to the urgent question. If they came to the wrong interpretation, the whole community would either profane the Sabbath or violate the Passover.

---

[2] Martin Noth, "The 'Re-presentation' of the Old Testament in Proclamation," in Claus Westermann, ed., *Essays on Old Testament Hermeneutics* (Richmond, Va.: Westminster John Knox, 1963), 80. Noth contrasts "re-presentation" with historical and critical exegesis. See also the discussion by Daniel Patte in *Early Jewish Hermeneutic in Palestine* (Missoula: Scholars, 1975), 4–5.

When they heard about Hillel and his innovative teachings of Torah, they sought him out hoping that he might give a definitive answer to this question, and determine whether the entire Jewish community would observe the Passover according to Scripture. The account in b. Pesachim 66a tells how Hillel solved the problem by using his methods of biblical interpretation.[3] First Hillel observes that there is a similar wording in two different passages of Scripture, one that deals with the daily sacrifice and the other with the Passover. Both texts use the phrase, "In its appointed time." In Hebrew, *bemoado,* "In its appointed time," is used both in Num 28:2—a passage about the daily offering—and also in Num 9:2—a passage concerning the Passover. This means that an analogy must be drawn from the two uses of the same words. This rule of interpretation shows the connection between these two texts, even though they appear chapters apart from each other. This analogy is called, *gezerah shavah* in Hebrew, and literally means that the two phrases are "cut from the same block."[4] They are equal in how they are to be interpreted. So if the daily sacrifices are considered more important than the Sabbath rest, then also the Passover must override the Sabbath. After all, the Bible uses the same wording, "In its appointed time," for daily offering and for the observance of Passover.

THE SEVEN PRINCIPLES AND THE NEW TESTAMENT

In the Gospels, reference is made to the same method when the passage, "You shall love the LORD your God" (Deut 6:5), is linked to, "You shall love your neighbor as yourself" (Lev 19:18). Both verses begin with the phrase, "You shall love," indicating that they form an analogy because they are both cut from the same block. The passage from Deut 6:5 deals with one's relationship to God and the passage from Lev 19:18 treats one's relationship with other people. Even though the passages appear in different books and in divergent contexts, they are connected together because of the analogous wording. They summarize the demands of Torah in terms of the proper

---

[3] Many of these hermeneutical principles are paralleled in the New Testament. See the fine work of Doeve, *Jewish Hermeneutics,* and also Patte, *Early Jewish Hermeneutic.*

[4] See Doeve, *Jewish Hermeneutics,* 65–66. The objective analogy, or *hekesh,* compares the daily offering that is also slaughtered on the Sabbath with the Passover offering. Since both are whole offerings, the objective analogy shows that they are both permissible on the Sabbath.

relationship with God and with other people. So also the daily sacrifices override the observance of Sabbath. If the daily sacrifices override the observance of Sabbath, how much more will the observance of Passover take precedence over the keeping of the Sabbath rest. The analogy based upon similar wording of two different passages of Scripture makes this interpretation clear. After all, the words, "In its appointed time," appear in Scripture for both the daily offering and for the Passover.

The method of reasoning that claims this type of interconnectedness between verses in the biblical text is not acceptable within Western, systematic treatments of theological issues. Nevertheless, it is widely used in rabbinic literature and was certainly accepted by the early Jewish Christians in their approach to the sacred text. Hillel's first hermeneutical principle, *kal vechomer,* that is, "the light and the heavy," is an argument based upon the minor premise as also applicable in the case of a major premise. It is a principle based on the question, "how much more?" [5] As Hillel explains, if the punishment for not observing the Passover is more severe than the punishment for not carrying out the daily sacrifice, then the command to observe Passover takes precedence. In other words, if the punishment for not observing Passover is being cut off, whereas the punishment for neglecting the daily sacrifice does not carry a punishment of being cut off, then, according to the minor premise, one must assume that the daily sacrifice overrides the Sabbath. This then leads to the formulation of a major premise, namely that observing the Passover takes precedence over keeping the Sabbath.[6]

Another example relates to the people of Israel. If they disobey God, how much more will they disobey Moses (Exod 32:7–11).[7] If they will not obey God who is supreme, they will not obey Moses who is human. In the Sermon on the Mount, Jesus teaches that, since God takes care of the birds of the air, how much more will he take care of each individual who is created in His image (Matt 6:25–30). In parabolic form, Jesus teaches that if an unjust judge can be moved to help a defenseless widow because of her persistent pleas for justice, how much more will the righteous God be moved to help the faithful when they pray (Luke 18:1–8). The argument from a minor premise to a major one is used in Greek logic as well, and certainly there is Hellenistic influence which can be detected in

---

[5] Probably the older way to refer to this principle was *ad achad kamah vekamah,* "until one how many, many more?"

[6] See Patte, *Early Jewish Hermeneutic,* 109–12.

[7] See the Jewish interpretations in Menahem Kasher, *Torah Shelemah* (45 vols.; New York: Talmud Institute, 1951–1983), 21:100–102. See Lauterbach, *Mekhilta Derabbi Ishmael,* 1:252.

the rabbinic thought and literature.[8] The Hellenistic influence, however, becomes absorbed in the Hebrew culture and often takes on an entirely new identity.

THE SEVEN PRINCIPLES OF BIBLICAL INTERPRETATION

Principle 1   *Kal vechomer* (literally, "light and heavy"): The argument from a minor premise to a major one.

Principle 2   *Gezerah shavah* (literally, "cut equally"): The teaching based upon an analogy or inference from one verse to another.

Principle 3   *Binyan av mikatuv echad* (literally, "building a teaching principle based upon one verse"): The main proposition is derived from one verse.

Principle 4   *Binyan av mishnai katuvim* (literally, "building a teaching principle based upon two verses"): The main proposition is derived from two verses.

Principle 5   *Kelal uferat–perat vekelal* (literally, "general and specific–specific and general"): Teaching from a general principle to a specific one, or from a specific principle to a general one.

Principle 6   *Keyotza bo bamakom acher* (literally, "As comes from it in another place"): A teaching based upon what is similar in another passage.

Principle 7   *Devar halamed meinyano* (literally, "A word that is learned from its own issue"): A matter that is learned from its own subject. (*Sifra,* Introduction 1.7, *t. Sanhedrin* at the end)

THE SEVEN PRINCIPLES EXPLAINED

So the first principle of interpretation involves proof from a minor premise to a major premise. The second principle uses an analogy based upon the same wording in two different texts where the interpreter applies

---

[8] See David Daube, "Rabbinic Methods of Interpretation and Hellenistic Rhetoric," *HUCA* 22 (1949): 239–64. Compare also Peder Borgen and Søren Giversen, eds., *The New Testament and Hellenistic Judaism* (Peabody, Mass.: Hendrickson, 1997).

the same meaning to both passages. The third principle develops an approach to interpretation based upon the teaching in one verse, and that generalization becomes a proposition based upon the one verse's message; the Bible is used to interpret the Bible. The fourth principle uses the same approach but develops a generalization based upon two verses.

The fifth principle develops a teaching from a general rule to a specific application; the particular rule will have a more universal meaning when applied to various cases. One example can even be seen in Paul's writings to the Galatians. First he quotes the general rule to "love your neighbor as yourself" from Lev 19:18. Then he gives specific guidelines about how to apply this rule in daily living (Gal 5:14–23).[9] Yose the son of Yoezer (160 B.C.E.) is considered the first to use this principle in rabbinic literature. He challenged the prevailing teachings of the "early elders," (Hebrew: *zekanim reshonim*), who taught that not only did touching a dead body render a person unclean, but also touching anything that had been in contact with the dead body.[10] Yose taught that only coming in contact with the dead caused ritual uncleanness. (His liberal position earned him the nickname, "the Permitter.") Citing the general principle of Scripture, namely that the dead body renders the person who comes in contact with it unclean (Lev 5:3a; Num 19:11), he then noted the specific cases from Scripture, which enumerated three details and referred to the carcasses of wild animals, cattle, or a reptile (Lev 5:2b). Therefore items that came in contact with the dead do not cause ritual uncleanness.[11] The general principle that contact with the corpse of a dead person causes uncleanness, then, is limited by the specific details in referring to contact with carcasses of wild animals, cattle, and reptiles. Hence an object which came into contact with the dead cannot transfer its impurity. This is the argument from a general principle to the specific details of a teaching in its practical application.

The sixth principle explores the meaning of one verse by comparing it to another passage and making an analogy, hence a similar teaching may be learned from a parallel text. The seventh principle deals with how an interpreter learns information about a matter from its own content and subject. The text is thoroughly examined in its context, and the conclusion is drawn from that context.

---

[9] See Young, *Paul the Jewish Theologian,* 75–76, 88–93.

[10] It may well be that Jesus' reference to "men of old" in the Sermon on the Mount (Matt 5:21) is actually a reference to a collection of halakhic teachings like that referred to here as the "early elders." Like Yose the son of Yoezer, Jesus refers to their literal interpretation and then offers an innovative approach to the text based upon the true fulfillment of the transcendent meaning of Torah.

[11] See Lauterbach, *Rabbinic Essays,* 219–21. See *Sifra* on Lev 5:2.

These seven principles may be seen in different passages of midrash. They reflect Jewish methods of interpreting the Bible. Midrash seeks the deeper meaning and practical application of the Bible by using highly developed exegetical techniques. Jesus himself also utilizes a method of interpretation which intensifies the deeper meaning of the Torah. He quotes from the Ten Commandments and then makes application through practical interpretation. Later, Rabbi Ishmael expanded these seven principles of Hillel to thirteen, and then Rabbi Eleazar enlarged the scope of hermeneutical principles to include thirty-two different applications. Here in this brief introduction to rabbinic thought and literature, the foundation of seven principles are enumerated as a foundation for further study.

The Existence of Evil and the Goodness of God

There are those who sense the ultimate question in moments of wonder, in moments of joy; there are those who sense the ultimate question in moments of horror, in moments of despair . . .

How did Abraham arrive at his certainty that there is a God who is concerned with the world? Said Rabbi Isaac: Abraham may be "compared to a man who was traveling from place to place when he saw a *palace in flames.* Is it possible that there is no one who cares for the palace? He wondered. Until the owner of the palace looked at him and said, 'I am the owner of the palace.' Similarly, Abraham our father wondered, 'Is it conceivable that the world is without a guide?' The Holy One, blessed be He, looked out and said, 'I am the Guide, the Sovereign of the world.'"

The world is in flames, consumed by evil. Is it possible that there is no one who cares?

The world is in need of redemption, but the redemption must not be expected to happen as an act of sheer grace. Man's task is to make the world worthy of redemption. His faith and his works are preparation for *ultimate redemption.*

Abraham Joshua Heschel, *God in Search of Man* (New York: Farrar, Strauss and Giroux, 1993), 367 and 380.

PART III

Introduction to the Rabbis

After exploring rabbinic thought and literature, it is time to meet the rabbis. Jewish thinking is biblically based and the literature is a commentary, not only on the Bible, but also on life. So the spiritual giants who live large on the pages of the Talmudic literature give all people inspiring examples regardless of their faith traditions. Outstanding personalities created the rabbinic literature. They were living links in a vital chain of teaching from Moses on Mount Sinai to their present community service. As Lawrence Shiffman observes, "The student of Torah becomes a link in the unbroken chain which connects the Jewish people to revelation at Sinai."[1] Torah learning and practical application made these community leaders great. Not only did they study Torah and teach, but they also lived their lives as a model for others. They fasted and repented on the Day of Atonement, observed the Sabbath and festivals at the appointed times, and gave charity to others in need at all times. They practiced what they preached and left a spiritual legacy. Everyone should become familiar with some of the rabbis and come to appreciate their contribution to human civilization. They loved Torah, and taught their disciples to love God and esteem others.

---

[1] Lawrence Schiffman, *From Text to Tradition: A History of Second Temple and Rabbinic Judaism* (Hoboken, N.J.: KTAV, 1991), 243.

The Greatest Duty of the Jew

It must already have become evident to the reader that the Talmud has its roots in the Hebrew Scriptures. For almost every thought and every utterance warrant is sought in the sacred text. Duty of the 'As it is said' or 'as it is written' follows practically every statement. The Rabbis, whose teachings comprise the Talmud, would have denied that they were originators of Jewish thought. All they would have admitted was they were excavators in the inexhaustible mine of the divine Revelation contained in the Scriptures and brought to light treasures that lay hidden beneath the surface.

To study the inspired Writings, to meditate upon them, to extract from them all they could be made to produce was, accordingly, the chief privilege as it was the greatest duty of the Jew.

Abraham Cohen, *Everyman's Talmud: The Major Teachings of the Sages* (New York: E. P. Dutton, 1949), 125.

CHAPTER 11

Meet the Rabbis

We have described rabbinic thought and literature, but long before anything was written down, the oral tradition was preserved by "walking books." Rabbinic literature is really comprised of scholars who immersed themselves in holy Scripture and passed the teachings of Torah down from generation to generation. Here we will meet some of the outstanding, animated personalities mentioned in it.

The chain of Torah learning from one generation to the next can be followed in the charts and illustrations provided here. Beginning with Moses on Mount Sinai, the revelation of oral teachings was preserved from one family to the next. A Torah master mentored disciples, and those disciples eventually wrote down the oral teachings. The charts of the literature seek to acquaint the reader with the names of various books and the places they occupy in rabbinic literature. The charts of the rabbis attempt to organize the teachings of Talmudic literature around some outstanding personalities.

As noted earlier, the sages mentioned in talmudic literature may be divided into primarily two groups, the Tannaim and the Amoraim. We will begin with an Amoraic sage and work back in time to the period of the Tannaim, concluding with Hillel the Elder.

THE AMORAIM

The Amoraim were influential scholars and teachers who were active in community life, from the completion of the Mishnah around 220 C.E. to the close of the talmudic period with the compilation of the Jerusalem and Babylonian Talmuds in the fourth and fifth centuries. The term *amora* refers to the function of amplifying the lecture of the sage by repeating his teaching to the disciples in a louder voice, explaining and interpreting the oral tradition as Torah is being expounded. The Amoraim became proficient preachers and creative scholars. The Amoraic scholar clarified and interpreted the teachings of the Tannaim but was not permitted to dispute or contradict their authority. Here are but a few names of the leading Amoraim who far outnumbered the Tannaim. They commented upon the earlier Tannaitic teachings that were written in Hebrew, and employed Aramaic for many of their discussions. Thus the talmudic literature reveals that Hebrew continued to be used long after the destruction of Jerusalem and into the third and fourth centuries C.E., when Aramaic gained greater use.

Among the many distinguished Amoraim (see summary list below), five deserve special mention.

RABBI JOSHUA BEN LEVI

Rabbi Joshua ben Levi (beginning of the third century C.E.) was a leading scholar, preacher, and interpreter of Torah who lived in the land of Israel. He became the head of the academy at Lydda, and flourished during the transition from the Tannaim to the Amoraim. Humility was a virtue he praised for drawing a person nearer to the divine presence. Rabbi Joshua was renown as one who told stories with a message. Many parables have been attributed to his sermons and Torah interpretations. He taught that studying Torah helped alleviate sufferings: "If a person is traveling and has no companion, let that one become immersed in Torah learning . . . if a person has a head ache, let that one become immersed in Torah learning . . . if a person feels throat pain, let that one become immersed in Torah learning" (b. Eruvin 54a).

RABBI YOCHANAN BEN NAPCHA

Rabbi Yochanan ben Napcha, who also lived in the land of Israel, flourished in the second half of the third-century C.E. He was born in Tzipori (Sepphoris), and though he inherited fields and vineyards from his parents, he sold them in order to study Torah. He achieved major recognition for his Torah learning and became the head of the academy of learning in Tiberias. He was a major influence in the compilation of the Jerusalem Talmud. He emphasized giving charity, Torah study, and praying. He said that one should pray continually and that prayers should be recited in Hebrew because the ministering angels who deliver the prayers do not understand Aramaic (b. Berakhot 21a and b. Shabbat 12b).

RABBI SIMEON BEN LAKISH (RESH LAKISH)

Rabbi Simeon ben Lakish (often abbreviated in the midrashim and Talmuds as Resh Lakish) was a contemporary of Rabbi Yochanan. He seems to have been a convert to Judaism who became a great Torah scholar and community leader. He viewed Torah study itself as obeying a great commandment in the Bible, and possessed a concern for the less fortunate in society. As a young man he apparently found himself in desperate financial straits. In order to survive, he sold himself as a gladiator, a profession that sometimes proved highly lucrative. Having participated in some deadly contests, he showed exceptional courage and strength. As a former gladiator he brought some colorful background experiences into the academies of Torah learning. According to Jewish tradition, prior to disciplining himself to study Torah, Resh Lakish was an unruly rogue. Once in a fit of rage, his colleague, Rabbi Yochanan, recalled publicly Resh Lakish's former life of banditry. According to the tradition, Rabbi Yochanan felt so badly about humiliating Resh Lakish that he became ill and died (*b. Baba Metzi'a* 84a).

In another story from the Babylonian Talmud (*b. Baba Metzi'a* 84a), while walking along the banks of the Jordan River, Resh Lakish spied what he thought to be a vulnerable, naked maiden bathing. Charged with uncontrollable lust, he pole vaulted with his spear into the water, only to find himself embracing a wet Rabbi Yochanan. In the end, Rabbi Yochanan prevailed upon Resh Lakish to devote his life to Torah, and as an incentive he even gave his daughter to him in marriage. Rabbi Yochanan obviously realized the great potential this young man possessed for Torah scholarship. His marriage to a godly woman was a powerful influence for good.

Although he had been reckless in his youth, Resh Lakish changed his ways and emerged as a model of piety and scholarship. He had a strong sense of equity and shunned partiality. He also was a man of strong convictions. For example, once when he encountered a Jewish tourist from Babylon visiting the land of Israel, he severely criticized him for not having followed Ezra and Nehemiah's lead in returning to Jerusalem (*b. Yoma* 9b).

Resh Lakish stressed a holy lifestyle and observed the force of the evil impulse: "Every day a person's evil impulse threatens to control him or her, and tries to destroy him or her" (*b. Sukkah* 52b). In personal piety he taught, "The one who commits adultery with the eye, has already committed adultery with the body." His teaching resembles in spirit what Jesus says, "I say unto you that everyone who looks at a woman lustfully has already committed adultery with her in his heart" (Matt 5:28).

RAV (ABBA BEN AIVU)

Rav (Abba ben Aivu) was a Babylonian Amora who flourished at the beginning of the third century. Rav came from an illustrious family and was able to study in the land of Israel. He sat at the feet of Rabbi Judah the Prince (see discussion in Chapter Six, pp. 82–83) and was involved in Torah learning with Rabbi Yochanan in Tiberias. He went back to Babylon to serve the large Jewish community in the Diaspora. He established and became the head of the prestigious academy at Sura, in modern Iraq. Rav praised

Torah learning as the essence of living a life of faith. He opposed a false sense of religiosity that denied pleasure in life, teaching that "Each person is destined to give an account for all that his or her eye saw but has not eaten" (*y. Kiddushin* ch. 4, hal. 12, 66d). One will be judged not only for sins committed against Torah but also for pleasures in life that were neglected because of a false religious abstinence. The sense of joy in living comes from the creation. God created the world and pronounced His work good. Each person is responsible for enjoying the goodness of God and will be judged for seeing but not eating.

RAV ASHI

Rav Ashi (335–428 C.E.), also called Rabbana, was the outstanding scholar and leader of the Jewish community in Babylon, who was appointed the head of the academy at Sura. Many disciples and scholars centered their activities around Rav Ashi's teachings. He is credited with editing the Babylonian Talmud, which was a monumental achievement even if the completion of the entire project took place after his death. The work was conducted with the support of Rabina, who is sometimes viewed as the last representative of the Amoraic sages. The Talmud laments that, with the deaths of Rav Ashi and Rabina, "authentic teaching is concluded" (*b. Baba Metzi'a* 85b). Rav Ashi's contribution to Jewish life cannot be underestimated. He was able to assemble together the vast materials of earlier Amoraic teachers and systematize them into the tractates of the Mishnah. He was well liked by his contemporaries and honored for his rich contributions to Torah learning. He stressed a humble attitude in personal conduct because, "Every person who is full of arrogance will in the end be humbled" (*b. Sotah* 5a).

LIST OF AMORAIM

I have adapted this summary list from Shmuel Safrai's work "Amoraim" in the *Encyclopaedia Judaica* (ed. Cecil Roth; 17 vols.; Jerusalem: Keter, 1972), 2:866.

LAND OF ISRAEL   **BABYLON**

First Generation: 220 C.E.–250 C.E.

Rabbi Chanina bar Chama—   Rav (Abba bar Aivu)—
    Flourished in Tiberias and   Founder/Head of the Academy of
    Sepphoris   Sura
Oshaya Rabbah—   Samuel—
    Head of the Academy of Caesarea   Head of the Academy of Nehardea

Rabbi Yanni—
Disciple of Judah HaNasi

Rabbi Joshua ben Levi—
Head of the Academy at Lydda

Karna: "Judge of the Diaspora"

Mar Ukba: Judge and Community
Leader—
Famous for giving charity
anonymously

Second Generation: 250 C.E.–290 C.E.

Rabbi Yochanan ben Napcha: Head of
the Academy at Tiberias—
Credited with editing much of the
Jerusalem Talmud

Rabbi Simeon ben Lakish (Resh
Lakish)

Rabbi Eleazar ben Pedat—
Head of the Academy at Tiberias

Rav Huna—
Head of the Academy of Sura
Stressed Torah Study and Prayer

Rav Judah bar Ezekiel—
Founder / Head of the Academy of
Pumbedita

Rav Hammuna

Third Generation: 290 C.E.–320 C.E.

Rabbi Ammi—
Head of the Academy at Tiberias

Rabbi Assi—
Head of the Academy at Tiberias

Rabbi Abbahu—
Head of the Academy of Caesarea

Rabbi Zeira

Rav Chisda—
Head of the Academy of Sura

Rabbah bar Rav Huna—
Head of the Academy of Sura

Rabbah bar Nachmani—
Head of the Academy of Pumbedita

Rav Joseph bar Chiya—
Head of the Academy of Pumbedita

Fourth Generation: 320 C.E.–350 C.E.

Rabbi Jonah—
Head of the Academy at Tiberias

Rabbi Yose—
Head of the Academy at Tiberias

Rabbi Jeremiah

Rabbi Haggai

Abbaye—
Head of the Academy of Pumbedita

Rava ben Joseph—
Founder / Head of the Academy of
Machoza

Rami bar Chama

Rav Zeira

Fifth Generation: 350 C.E.–375 C.E.

Rabbi Mani—
Head of the Academy at Tiberias

Rav Papa—
Head of the Academy of Naresh
near Sura

Rabbi Yose bar Bun   Rav Huna bar Rav Joshua

Rabbi Tanchuma bar Abba   Rav Zevid—
                                          Head of the Academy of Pumbedita

Sixth Generation: 375 C.E.–425 C.E.

Rav Ashi—
    Head of the Academy of Sura in
    Matah Mehasya
    Credited with compiling the Baby-
    lonian Talmud
Ravina
Mar Zutra
Ameimar

Seventh Generation: 425 C.E.–460 C.E.

Mar bar Rav Ashi (Tabyomi)—
    Head of the Academy of Sura
Rav Yeimar—
    Head of the Academy of Sura
Rav Geviha of Bei-Katil—
    Head of the Academy of Pumbedita

Eighth Generation: 480 C.E.–500 C.E.

Ravina II bar Huna—
    Head of the Academy of Sura
    His death marked the end of the
    Amoraic Period
Rav Yose—
    Head of the Academy of Pumbedita
Achai bar Rav Huna

THE TANNAIM

The Tannaim were scholars, teachers, and community leaders who flourished from the time of Hillel and Shammai, around 20 B.C.E., until the written compilation of the Mishnah, around the time of Judah the Prince in 220 C.E. The word *Tanna* means "someone who learns by repetition;" that is, reciting the oral tradition by heart. The destruction of Jerusalem in 70 C.E. and the Bar Kokhba revolt, which ended in 135 C.E., are major landmark dates in assessing the life and times of the Tannaim. They spoke and taught primarily in Mishnaic Hebrew.

RABBAN YOCHANAN BEN ZAKHAI

Rabban Yochanan ben Zakhai (Yochanan son of Zaccahaeus) was a younger contemporary of Jesus. He survived the devastation of Jerusalem's destruction in 70 C.E., and assumed an important leadership role after the Temple was destroyed, establishing a study center in Yavneh. Yavneh became a major center of Jewish culture, learning, and Torah scholarship. Rabban Yochanan ben Zakhai sat at the feet of Hillel the Elder. He was a faithful disciple, learning Hillel's heart for people and the teachings of Torah. As Rabban Yochanan ben Zakhai learned Torah and practiced his faith in action, he emphasized loving God and showing a sincere love for others, even the Romans who were increasingly hostile toward the Jewish people and their traditions.

The crucial problem of the day was the Jewish Zealots who wanted greater autonomy. Their militant opposition to Roman incursions into the personal life and religious freedom of the people created a clash between civilizations which resulted in war and in the destruction of the Temple. Rabban Yochanan ben Zakhai rejected the violence of the Zealots and pursued the path of peaceful co-existence. When Jerusalem was besieged by the Romans and no one was permitted to leave the city, he faked his own death in order to meet with the Roman general Vespasian who was soon to be named Caesar. Trapped inside the walls of Jerusalem, Rabban Yochanan pretended to be sick. Then he laid down in a funeral casket acting as if he had died. He had two of his disciples, Rabbi Joshua and Rabbi Eleazar carry the coffin to the gates of Jerusalem. The guards did not wish to let them pass. But because it was forbidden to bury a dead person inside the holy city and out of honor for the esteemed Jewish leader, they allowed the coffin to pass through the gate. Outside Jerusalem, Rabban Yochanan ben Zakhai went to General Vespasian. He prophesied that he would become emperor. As a result, he obtained favor from Vespasian who did indeed become Caesar during the siege. His son Titus took over the war effort and succeeded in destroying the holy city of Jerusalem and the Temple in 70 C.E. while his father returned to Rome. In their meeting, Rabban Yochanan ben Zakhai asked Vespasian for the town of Yavneh where he could disciple his followers and raise up a remnant community of Jewish leaders and Torah scholars. He asked Vespasian, "Give me Yavneh and its sages!" He wanted to preserve the dynastic line of Hillel through Gamaliel and reestablish the Sanhedrin in a new location (*b. Gittin* 56a–b). He explained, "I ask from you only Yavneh. Let me go there and teach my disciples, and there set up a place for prayer, and there fulfill all the commandments prescribed by the Torah" (*Fathers according to Rabbi Nathan,* Version A, ch. 4). The general, soon to be Caesar, granted the Jewish leader's request. G. Alon suggested that Vespasian sent Rabbi Yochanan ben Zakhai to a detention camp for Jerusalem refugees. The camp

was located in Yavneh and would have given a place for Jewish people who
were willing to live under Roman sovereignty (G. Alon, *The Jews in their
Land in the Talmudic Age* [Jerusalem: Magnes Press, 1984], 1:97). While his
theory is somewhat different from the midrash, it would explain the possible
historical circumstances around the beginnings of Rabban Yochanan ben
Zakhai's activities at Yavneh. A message was sent calling upon all who had
learned to come and teach and upon all who had not studied Torah to come
and learn.[1]

Hillel the Elder emphasized in his teachings, that each individual must
pursue peace, and so, must seek to build bridges of understanding between
people with disagreements, "Be of the disciples of Aaron, loving peace and
pursuing peace, loving every single person, and drawing each one near to the
Torah" (*Avot* 1:12). Rabban Yochanan ben Zakhai followed the instruction
of his Master teacher. He was known for his warm-hearted greetings. No one
ever greeted him first. He would be the first to reach out to each person with
a cordial greeting of shalom, "It has been reported concerning Rabban
Yochanan ben Zakhai that no individual ever greeted him with the blessing
of 'Peace' first, even a heathen in the market place" (*b. Berakhot* 17a).

The reference to the "heathen" standing in the market place in this passage is quite revealing. Rabban Yochanan ben Zakhai did not differentiate
between a pagan and a Jew, he treated all with equal congeniality and collegi-
ality. Even if he encountered a Roman soldier or someone who might be defined as an enemy of the Jewish people, he maintained a humanitarian
attitude of kindheartedness in interpersonal relationships with all. In truth,
this is the essence of Hillel's humane approach. Rabban Yochanan ben
Zakhai would have been quite young in his encounters with Hillel and it
would seem that the elder teacher had a great impact upon the young scholar
who no doubt grew up within the school of thought attributed to the house
of Hillel. Rabban Yochanan ben Zakhai declared, "If you have learned much

---

[1] See *b. Berachot* 63b and *Song of Songs Rabbah* 2:5,3. The two sources do not
agree in all details. The Talmud relates the event to Yavneh after Jerusalem's destruction and the Midrash connects the saying to Usha after the Bar Kochba rebellion.
See Gedalia Alon, *The Jews in their Land in the Talmudic Age* (2 vols.; Jerusalem:
Magnes, 1980–1984), 2:664. Though the evidence is stronger for the tradition to
be associated with the midrash, a similar type of call could have been associated with
Yavneh. Those who had learned must teach Torah to those who had failed to take
advantage of study previous to the persecution. Torah learning is viewed as the key
to survival as a people. In all events, Gamaliel and others came to Yavneh, which is
often referred to as a "vineyard" in the rabbinic literature. The "Vineyard of Yavneh"
became a place of spiritual growth and renewal following the disaster that had devastated the Jewish people. Later Yochanan ben Zakhai moved to Beror Chayil and established an academy of Torah scholarship there

Torah, do not ascribe special merit to yourself because it was for this reason that you were created" (*Avot* 2:9). In this respect, he is not far from the teachings of Jesus who taught in a similar vein that even if one obeys God and the teachings of the Bible, "We are unworthy servants; we have only done our duty" (Luke 17: 10 NIV). According to legend, Hillel the Elder saw greatness in the young Yochanan ben Zakhai and gave a prophecy about his future role as a source of wisdom and Torah learning for all generations to come. When Hillel was sick some eighty pairs of his disciples came to visit him. The young Yochanan waited outside in the courtyard in characteristic humility. Of all his disciples, Hillel wanted to see Yochanan. He asked, "Where is the youngest of you? After all, he is the father of wisdom and the fount of [Torah learning] for all future generations. Needless to say, he is the greatest one among you" (*y. Nedarim* 39b, ch. 5, hal. 6). By dealing with crisis and providing magnanimous leadership which exemplified the best in Jewish tradition, Rabban Yochanan ben Zakhai succeeded in fulfilling the prophecy of his Master teacher. Playing a pivotal role in Jewish history, truly he has become the "father of wisdom and fount of [Torah learning] for all future generations."

RABBI JOSHUA BEN CHANANYAH

Rabbi Joshua ben Chananyah (first and second centuries C.E.) was one of the five disciples of Yochanan ben Zakhai, who proclaimed about his disciple, "happy is she who gave him birth." His mother carried him to the synagogue in his cradel when he was a small baby. She wanted him to hear the Bible read and studied. She hoped that he would be a great rabbi and Rabban Yochanan ben Zakhai referred to her happiness (*Avot* 2:11). Rabbi Joshua ben Chananyah was probably about thirty-years-old when the Temple was destroyed. He describes some of the ceremonies and celebrations of the Temple. He often disputed with Rabbi Eliezer ben Hyrcanus on issues of community life based on different views of Bible interpretation. One time they argued about a female proselyte who had an immoral past. Rabbi Joshua argued that she should be received into the Jewish faith as a convert, against Rabbi Eliezer's objection (*Ecclesiastes Rabbah* 1:8, 4). Rabbi Joshua taught that "righteous Gentiles share a place in the world to come" (*t. Sanhedrin* 13:2). He emphasized humility and an attitude of kindness toward others, which is seen in his teaching, "an evil eye [stinginess], an evil impulse, and hatred of other people drive a person out of the world" (*Avot* 2:16).[2]

---

[2] Rabbi Joshua was so well-liked by his colleagues that when the presiding leader Rabban Gamaliel insulted his dignity, they forced Gamaliel to be removed from office and replaced by Rabbi Eleazar ben Azaryah (*b. Berakot* 28a). See Wiesel, *Sages and Dreamers*, 202–10.

Rabbi Eliezer ben Hyrcanus

Rabbi Eliezer ben Hyrcanus (first and second centuries C.E.) was one of the five disciples of Yochanan ben Zakhai who called him "a plastered cistern, which loses not a drop" (*Avot* 2:11). Rabbi Eliezer and the preceding Rabbi Joshua ben Chananyah, carried their beloved Master teacher Rabban Yochanan ben Zakhai out of besieged Jerusalem in a coffin to the camp of Vespasian. Rabbi Eliezer possessed an extensive knowledge of early Jewish traditions and ancient legal lore. He is known for his teaching, "Let your friend's honor be as dear to you as your own. Do not be easily moved to anger. Repent one day before you die" (*Avot* 2:15). He also taught, "The one who has bread in his basket today and says, 'What will I eat tomorrow?' behold that one is of little faith" (*b. Sotah* 48b). This saying is parallel to Jesus' teaching in the Sermon on the Mount that the one who is anxious about what to wear or what to eat demonstrates little faith (Matt 6:25–30).

A Sampler from Rabban Yochanan ben Zakhai and His Disciples

He asked his disciples,
"Go out and see, what is the good way to
which each individual should steadfastly walk?"

RABBI ELIEZER BEN HYRCANUS	His known characteristic—
He answered, "A Good Eye."	"A plastered cistern which loses not a drop."
RABBI JOSHUA BEN CHANANYA	His known characteristic—
He answered, "A Good Companion."	"Happy is she who gave birth to him."
RABBI YOSE THE PRIEST	His known characteristic—
He answered, "A Good Neighbor."	"He is a saintly man."
RABBI SIMEON BEN NATHANIEL	His known characteristic—
He answered, "One Who Sees What Will Be."	"He is fearful of sin."

RABBI ELEAZAR BEN ARAKH   His known characteristic—

He answered, "A Good Heart."   "He is an ever flowing spring."

RABBI AKIVA

Rabbi Akiva (first and second centuries C.E.) is considered by many scholars to be the outstanding scholar and community leader of his time. He greatly influenced the development of Jewish legal discussions and also captivated the hearts of his listeners with colorful stories and creative Bible interpretations. As a poor, unlearned shepherd, he fell in love with Rachel, the daughter of a wealthy landowner. The celebrated love story recounted in the Talmud tells about how they overcame family opposition to their marriage and extreme poverty.

Akiva began his studies at age forty. He took a special interest in the poor and raised money to alleviate human suffering. He stressed in his life experience and teaching that, "Whatever God does is for the best" (*b. Berakhot* 60b–61a). He also taught that, "Everything is foreseen, nonetheless freedom of choice is given. The world is judged by grace, and all is not according to the increase of the works performed" (*Avot* 3:19). He emphasized that each individual is created in the divine image and that people must love one another as they love themselves. In explaining the creation story in Genesis, Akiva noted, "Beloved is each human being, for each person was created in the image of God. But it is by an even greater increase of love that it was revealed to humanity that each human being is created in the image of God" (*Avot* 3:18; cf. Gen 1:27).

In teaching Torah, Rabbi Akiva stressed humility. Like Jesus, he stressed humble service to others as the mark of true noble character. In fact, the teaching of Rabbi Akiva on the subject of humility for an occasion like a wedding feast or a special celebration is remarkably similar to Jesus' saying in the Gospels. Rabbi Akiva encourages his followers, "Take your place two or three seats below your place of honor so that you will be invited to move up to a higher position. After all, it is better for them to say to you, 'Come up higher' than for them to say to you, 'Move down lower'" (*Leviticus Rabbah* 1: 5).[3] In a similar way, Jesus teaches, "When someone invites you to a wedding feast, do not take the place of honor, for a person more distinguished than you may have been invited" (Luke 14:8 NIV). Rabbi Akiva also stressed joy in expressing one's faith even in the midst of adversity and hardship. On one occasion he and his disciples traveled to Jerusalem. When they came to

---

[3] Margulies, ed., *Midrash Vayikra Rabbah,* 1:16–17. See also Freedman and Simon, eds., *Midrash Rabbah,* 1:5, English translation, 4:9).

Mount Scopus where they could see the holy city in ruins after the Romans had destroyed Jerusalem, they all cried with anguish and tore their garments in grief. As they came nearer the city, they saw a fox run out of the destroyed sanctuary where the Holy of Holies formerly stood. The other rabbis wept, but Rabbi Akiva laughed. They were astonished and offended. They asked how Rabbi Akiva could laugh when the Temple was in ruins and wild animals inhabit the most holy of all places. But Rabbi Akiva viewed the ruins from his deep faith. He explained that the same teachings of Scripture that foretold the destruction also speak about the restoration. Hardship and severe suffering sometimes comes before revitalization. If the Bible was true in what it predicted about the destruction of Jerusalem, how much more must the teachings of Scripture be true in predicting the holy city's future redemption (*b. Makkot* 24b; *Sifre Deuteronomy*, Piska 43). In his life, Rabbi Akiva seemed to draw strength from times of his adversity and weakness. Even during the intense persecution of Hadrian, Rabbi Akiva could reach deep into the recesses of his inner life, discover unknown personal fortitude, and then bring out a noble response to suffering that was characterized by faith and joy. He would give thanks to God for both the good and the bad in his personal experience (*b. Berakhot* 60b–61a).

Akiva raised up many disciples. He seems to have supported Bar Kokhba as a messianic figure, and refused to stop teaching Torah when the government issued decrees against Torah learning (for more on these events, see Chapter Six). According to tradition, he was martyred during the Bar Kokhba revolt (132–135 C.E.) while reciting the Shema prayer (Deut 6:4–9).[4]

RABBI SIMEON BAR YOCHAI

Rabbi Simeon bar Yochai (second century C.E.) is one of the five principal disciples of Rabbi Akiva. He studied under Akiva for thirteen years at Akiva's school in Bene Berak. He survived the terrible war during the Bar Kokhba revolt and helped to revive the teachings of Judaism after the defeat. He believed that suffering played an important role in the life of an individual who lives by faith, and that suffering does indeed have a purpose, at times, and can even possess a redemptive quality. He taught that God had given the people of Israel three precious gifts. These are the Torah, the Land of Israel, and the world to come. All three of them, however, can only be obtained through a measure of suffering (*b. Berakhot* 5a). He is known for saying, "If all Israel would properly observe two Sabbaths according to Torah teachings, they would at once be redeemed" (*b. Shabbat* 118b).

---

[4] On Akiva's life and teachings, see the fine book, L. Finkelstein, *Akiba: Scholar, Saint and Martyr* (New York: Atheneum, 1975).

Rabbi Meir

Rabbi Meir (second century C.E.) became one of the leaders of the Jewish community of faith following the Bar Kokhba revolt. He is cited by name more than any other scholar in the Mishnah. Though Rabbi Judah the Prince is credited with compiling the Mishnah, much of the teaching materials are derived from Rabbi Meir's work.

Rabbi Meir is thought to be the child of converts to Judaism. He possessed a brilliant mind and was able to interact with major issues relating to Torah interpretation and religious observance. In his personal piety and teaching he stressed study, work, and prayer. He taught, "Lessen your toil for worldly goods, and be busy in the Torah. Be humble of spirit before all people. If you neglect the Torah, many causes for neglecting it will present themselves to you, but if you labor in the Torah, He has abundant reward to give you" (*Avot* 4:12).

A Sampler from Rabbi Akiva and His Disciples

RABBI AKIVA

He supported the Bar Kokhba Revolt.
Rabbi Akiva started his education at age forty.
Rabbi Akiva was the outstanding scholar of his day.
Rabbi Akiva said:
"If soft water cuts hard stone, the words of Torah can penetrate my heart."

RABBI MEIR

After disagreeing with the Nasi, all subsequent statements made by him were noted anonymously.

He is the most quoted sage in the Mishnah.

He emphasized work, study, prayer

RABBI YOSE BEN CHALAFTAH

He was a co-leader with Judah Ha Nasi.

He was known for his considerable influence and was respected by all.

RABBI SIMEON BAR YOCHAI

Judah Ha Nasi studied under him.

"If Israel were to keep two Sabbaths according to the Law they would immediately be redeemed."

Some legends attributed the compilation of the *Zohar* ("Splendor"—an important work of Kabbalah or mysticism) to him.

RABBI JUDAH BAR ILAI

He was known as a pious man.

He was the first to establish as a rule, a single witness as a condition for a widow to remarry.

RABBI ELEAZAR BEN SHAMMUA

He was known to be the happiest of the sages.

He esteemed others, "Let the honor given to your disciple be as precious to you as your own."

BERURYAH

Beruryah (second century C.E.) was the wife of Rabbi Meir and the daughter of famous Rabbi Chananyah ben Teradeyon. While she is not considered a rabbi or Tanna, she is an outstanding example of a community activist and spiritual leader. She engaged in halakhic discussion with the leading rabbis of the time; in fact, she is credited with the proper approach to halakhah in two arguments. In the first instance, Rabbi Tarfon and the sages disagreed over the issue of ritual purity, so Beruryah expressed her opinion. When the discussion was reported to Rabbi Judah, he praised her answer over and above the ruling of Rabbi Tarfon and the sages, noting "Fittingly correct did Beruryah rule" (*t. Kelim Baba Metzi'a* 1:6). In the second instance her interpretation of religious law was accepted above the ruling of her brother, who was an outstanding Torah scholar (*t. Kelim Baba Kamma* 4:17).

Beruryah was a true scholar. According to one account, every day she would study 300 halakhic rulings made by 300 different great Torah sages in Israel. She devoted herself to this type of intensive research for three years (*b. Pesachim* 62b). By actively participating in Torah learning, she developed her understanding of religious law. The rabbis listened to her teachings, and honored her for her pious lifestyle and innate kindness. Beruryah also was a Bible interpreter. On one occasion, her husband, Rabbi Meir, was very disturbed by a band of cutthroat brigands who had invaded their neighborhood. He became so exasperated with them that he prayed his interpretation of Ps 104:35, "May the sinners be annihilated." He based his reading on the root word for "sinners" in Hebrew, which is *chata;* the plural form is *chotaim.* His saintly wife pointed out a mistake in his reading of the text which, at that time, was printed without vowels and therefore open to more than one translation. Whereas he read *chotaim,* "sinners," she argued that the proper reading should be *chataim,* "sins." Rabbi Meir agreed with her exegetical interpretation: he should pray Ps 104:35 with the correct translation, "Let the sins be annihilated." His prayers were answered and the troublesome neighbors repented.

Rabbi Meir and Beruryah experienced the most severe tragedy any parent can live through, the death of both their sons. They died on the Sabbath, while Rabbi Meir was away teaching in the House of Study. Beruryah placed their dead bodies in the bed. She wanted to prepare her husband for the tragic news. When he returned home, she waited till after the Sabbath and prepared food. She asked him, "Earlier in the day a certain man came and entrusted me with a valuable treasure as a trust. The owner of the precious treasure came back later and asked for his deposited trust to be returned. Should I give it back to the owner or keep it?" Rabbi Meir answered that she must return the valuable treasure to its owner. Then she led him to the bed. Upon seeing his dead sons he cried out in anguish, "My son, my son!" Beruryah comforted him by saying, "Did you not teach me that we must return a precious treasure to its Master? 'The LORD gives and the LORD takes away.'" In this way Beruryah comforted her bereaved husband (midrash on Prov 31).

RABBI TARFON

Rabbi Tarfon (first and second century C.E.) was from priestly descent (he tells about standing in the Temple as a youth). He was a respected colleague of Rabbi Akiva, and was known for his ability to answer difficult questions relating to Jewish faith and practice using his extensive knowledge of the Scriptures, Mishnah, midrash, Aggadah, and legal lore. Once, an argument arose as to whether study of Torah or the action of doing good works was more important. Rabbi Tarfon argued against Rabbi Akiva that action takes precedence over study (*b. Kiddushin* 40b). His emphasis on action is similar to the words of Jesus that one must hear *and* obey (see Matt 10:1–4; Mark 3:13–19); study and action go together (*Sifre Deuteronomy,* Piska 41).[5] Obedience is stressed in the life of a disciple. Moreover, Jesus teaches that the fields are white and ready to be harvested (Matt 9:37–38; Luke 10:2). In a similar saying, Rabbi Tarfon teaches, "The day is short, the work is plentiful and the laborers are lazy; but the reward is great and the Householder is pushing hard" (*Avot* 2:20).

---

[5] See Hammer, *Sifre,* 82–84. The consensus of the rabbis was with the opinion of Rabbi Akiva, however, namely that study is more important because study leads to action.

SUMMARY LIST OF TANNAIM

First Generation of Tannaim

From Jerusalem to Yavneh (20 B.C.E. to 80 C.E.)

From the Schools of Hillel and Shammai to Rabban Yochanan ben Zakhai and His Colleagues

Second Generation of Tannaim

Yavneh and Torah Learning in Galilee (80 to 110 C.E.)

Ramban Gamaliel of Yavneh with Rabbi Eliezer ben Hyrcanus and Rabbi Joshua ben Chananyah

Third Generation of Tannaim

Usha, Persecution, and the Bar Kokhba Revolt (110 to 135 C.E.)

Rabbi Akiva, Rabbi Ishmael, and Their Colleagues

Fourth Generation of Tannaim

Shefaram (135 to 170 C.E.)

Rabbi Meir, Rabbi Judah bar Illai and Their Colleagues

Fifth Generation of Tannaim

Bet Shearim, Sepphoris, and the Compilation of the Mishnah (170 to 220 C.E.)

Rabbi Judah HaNasi and His Colleagues

HILLEL THE ELDER

Hillel the Elder, from the house and lineage of David, flourished around 20 B.C.E. He became the leading scholar of his day and his teachings have greatly influenced Judaism throughout the generations and have even influenced Christianity; Hillel's grandson, Rabban Gamaliel, taught the Apostle Paul (Acts 22:3).

Hillel's approach to faith was one that valued humane compassion for all peoples, and placed less importance on stringent interpretations of Torah observance. The School of Hillel was concerned with how the interpretation of Scripture would make life more enjoyable through greater freedom in obeying Torah. His approach was anthropocentric. Hillel the Elder carried on terse debates with his influential counterpart, Shammai, and his disciples. Shammai, in general, was more intensely involved with rigid observance of Torah, without much consideration for how his interpretation impacted people. He was more theocentric.

In fact, over 300 sharp disagreements are recorded in the Talmudic literature, and demonstrate the intense clash over issues of Torah interpretation between the School of Hillel and his disciples and the School of Shammai. For example, one of their debates surrounded the lighting of the Hanukhah lamp to commemorate the rededication of the Temple that took place in 164 B.C.E. According to Shammai, one should light all eight lamps on the first day of the festival, and one less each following day until the final day of the celebration, when only one lamp should be lighted. The festival of Hanukhah, then, should end with only one light. By way of contrast, Hillel taught that one should observe the festival by lighting one lamp on the first night of Hanukhah and one more each night, until one finishes the celebration with all eight lamps lighted. The festival of Haunkhah, then, should end illuminated by the most light, with the growing light representing an increase of holiness. Both approaches are considered to be the very words of the living God. Because God revealed Torah and gave His revelation to His people for interpretation, He blesses their deliberations concerning Torah observance, and sanctions their discussions pertaining to the deeper meaning of sacred Scripture.

Hillel's views are considered more worthy of practice, primarily because he and his disciples honored the divergent views of Shammai and his disciples. Hillel's attitude was more acceptable to God. His patience and kind temperament are legendary in the Talmudic literature. Shammai is remembered for his short fuse and quick displeasure to impertinent questions. Would Jesus have lighted one lamp on the first night or eight? At times Jesus seems to be closer to Hillel and his interpretation of Torah, but on some issues he seems closer to Shammai.[6]

Hillel the Elder reached out to others in his sphere of influence to encourage Torah learning. He is known for his kindness and his winsome personality, by which he would draw secular-minded Jews under the wings of the divine presence.

He [Hillel] would stand at the gate of Jerusalem and meet people going to work. He questioned them, "How much will you make at work today?" One

---

[6] See James Charlesworth, ed., *Hillel and Jesus: Comparisons of Two Major Religions* (Minneapolis: Fortress, 1997). The chapter contributed by David Flusser (71–107) shows the new sensitivity for love of God and others in both the teachings of Hillel and Jesus.

person would answer, "A denarius." Another replied, "Two denarii." Then he would ask them, "What will you do with your earnings?" They would reply, "We will buy what we need to live." Then he challenged them, "Why don't you come follow me and acquire knowledge of the Torah. Then you will receive life in this world as well as life in the future world?" In this way Hillel lived all his days and was able to bring many people under the wings of Heaven. (*Avot R. Nat.*, vers. B, ch. 26)[7]

Hillel was not willing to sit in an academy of learning and allow the people of Jerusalem to live out their lives without God. He would go out to the streets and encourage people to study Torah and live a life pleasing to the Almighty.

Hillel's humane approach stressed the creation of humanity in the divine order of the universe. Every individual is created in the divine image and is of inestimable value in the sight of God. On one occasion, Hillel declared, "If I am here, all is here!" (*b. Sukkot* 53a). This proclamation might seem egotistical and out of character for a religious leader whose reputation for kindness and humility was widely acknowledged. Hillel's declaration, however, was meant to teach that each person created in the image of God could make the same statement with equal validity.

On another occasion when Hillel was leaving his disciples, he explained that he was going to perform an important religious duty. His disciples probably thought that he was going to visit the sick, comfort a grieving person, or distribute charity to a needy family. After questioning Hillel further they discovered that he was going to the bath house, for his own pleasure. The disciples were shocked. Is bathing a religious duty? Hillel explained his teaching with a parabolic illustration. The matter may be compared to a king who owns a statuary, which contains different statues of the king. The king pays his servants to clean and care for the statues. How much more will God reward every individual, created in His image, for taking care of himself or herself? So taking a bath, in Hillel's theology, is actually fulfilling an important religious duty.

The Talmud describes a number of differences between Hillel and Shammai. For example, Shammai studied the commandment, "Remember the Sabbath day and keep it holy;" for him, the holiness of the day was observed by doing everything to keep it sacred. He would go to the market and buy the best foods and store them away for the Sabbath. The celebration of the day of rest, then, would be made sacred by the finest meal of the week. Hillel also observed the Sabbath rest, but he wanted to stress the sacredness of all of life—by the way he lived every day. Hillel interpreted Ps 68:20—

---

[7] See Nahum Glatzer, *Hillel the Elder: The Emergence of Classical Judaism* (New York: B'nai B'rith Hillel Foundations, 1956), 50–51.

"Blessed be the Lord, day by day"—to teach that each person must uphold the reverence of living for God each day. Today is the day that one should sanctify the presence of God.[8] He praised God day by day and so he refused to make the Sabbath more holy by reserving the finest foods for the day of rest. David Flusser suggests that Jesus may have had this in mind when he taught his disciples to pray, "Give us this day our daily bread" (Matt 6:11; Luke 11:3).

The patience of Hillel and his humane approach is contrasted with Shammai's short fuse by the Talmudic legend of a non-Jew who decided to abandon idolatry, believe in the one God of Israel, and convert to Judaism. The non-Jew, however, wanted to make a stipulation. He wanted to be taught the entire Torah while standing on one foot. Since, according to Jewish tradition, the laws in the written legal code add up to 613 commandments and the oral tradition would constitute even more memorization and recitation of halakhah, the stipulation of learning all upon one leg was impossible. The man went to Shammai and made his request, "I will believe in the God of Israel and abandon idolatry on the condition that you teach me the whole Torah while standing on one foot." Shammai, who was holding a builder's cubit measuring rod in his hand at the time, became angry and whacked the would-be convert with his rod, driving him away for asking such a foolish question. Hillel's response to the man, as well as Jewish law, was quite different. When the would-be convert approached Hillel and asked him the same question Hillel answered him with respect and dignity, "What you do not want someone to do to you, do not do to him or her. The rest of the Torah is commentary upon this principle. Now go and learn it!" For Hillel, one did not have to memorize all the legal codes to understand the guiding principle that summarized the essence of the Torah.

Hillel's answer reminds students of the Gospels of the words of Jesus, "Do unto others as you would have them do unto you, for this is the Torah and the prophets" (Matt 7:12; Luke 6:31). His reference to the Torah and the prophets is powerful: fulfillment of the Torah's legal codes is accomplished by observing a single simple principle. Hillel taught the negative version of the Golden Rule, "Do not do to someone else," while Jesus taught positively to "Do unto others." In some ways they teach the same principle, but in different words. Perhaps the negative version is connected to the Ten Commandments, which contain the words, "You shall not . . ." (Exod 20:1–21; Deut 5:1–21).

As one of my students at the Hebrew University pointed out to me, however, these two versions of the Golden Rule are not synonymous. She

---

[8] See Young, *Jewish Background,* 23–27.

was an Orthodox Jew and a native Israeli. In Hillel's version, she observed, the individual must refrain from injuring another. In Jesus' version, each person is responsible for those who are in need. Doing to others really means that to observe the essence of the Torah and the prophets is to feed the hungry, visit the sick, be there for those who are in prison, and care for the needs of those less fortunate. After all, if you were hungry, you would want someone to give you food. Doing unto others embraces the Jewish concept of *tikun olam;* that is, "repairing a world" that is broken and in need of healing. I believe this is the fulfillment of Jesus' teachings concerning the kingdom of heaven. The kingdom message means that God's dynamic power is released as people obey the commandments. They participate in divine sovereignty by obeying God and reaching out to people created in the divine image who are suffering.

Created for Torah Study

Rabbi Eleazar taught, "Every person is created for labor, as it is written, 'Yet a person is born for labor (Job 5:7)' . . . But I still do not know whether 'for labor' means Torah study or worldly occupation. But since it is taught, 'This book of the Torah shall not depart from your mouth (Josh. 1:8)'—I must decide that every individual was created for labor in Torah learning."

b. Sanhedrin 99b

The Oral Torah and a Pagan Convert

Our Rabbis tell a story: One time a pagan came before Shammai. He asked him, "How many Torahs do you possess?"

"Two, the written Torah and the oral Torah," answered Shammai.

"I can believe you in regard to the written Torah," replied the pagan, "but not in regard to the oral Torah. I will come to faith in the God of Israel and convert to Judaism, with the only condition that you teach me the written Torah alone without the oral." Shammai reprimanded him harshly and sent him away in anger.

But when the same pagan went before Hillel with the same request, he was accepted as a convert. On the first day after his coming to faith in the God of Israel, Hillel taught him the first four letters of the Hebrew alphabet, *alef, bet, gimel* and *dalet.*

But on the next day, Hillel taught him the same letters but reversed the order. The pagan objected, "But yesterday you did not teach them to me in this order!" Hillel explained, "Since you are willing to rely upon my oral teaching to know the order of the letters for the alphabet, then you must also rely upon me with my teaching you the Oral Torah."

b. Shabbat 31a

Both Torahs Were Revealed on Mount Sinai

In the opening words of Maimonides' introduction to the Mishnah, God gives the Written Torah to Moses, and also reveals an extensive commentary that treats every word, issue, and nuance in the sacred text and explains how it could be applied in daily living. Thus, the traditional Jewish view traces the Oral Torah back to Mount Sinai. The monumental importance of this view for a correct understanding of Judaism and the beginnings of Christianity cannot be overemphasized. Both the Christian and Jewish communities share faith in the Bible, and the experience of reading the sacred text draws them together. But for the Jewish faithful, the written word can never be properly understood without its oral explanation. The Bible is a book filled with embedded meanings that transcend time and speak to every generation. So well has Abraham Joshua Heschel described the inexhaustible treasures buried in the sacred word. The illustration below portrays the divine revelation of two Torahs, both what was written and also what was said to Moses upon Mount Sinai

> Moses received the Torah on Sinai, and delivered it over to Joshua, Joshua delivered it over to the elders, the elders to the prophets, and the prophets delivered it to the men of the great in-gathering. They said three things: "Be deliberate in judgment, raise up many disciples, and make a fence around the Torah." (*Avot* 1:1)

WHAT WAS WRITTEN

Irrefutably, indestructibly, never wearied by time, the Bible wanders through the ages, giving itself with ease to all men, as if it belonged to every soul on earth. It speaks in every language and in every age. It benefits all the arts and does not compete with them. We all draw upon it, and it remains pure, inexhaustible and complete. In three thousand years it has not aged a day. It is a book that cannot die. Oblivion shuns its pages. Its power is not subsiding. In fact, it is still at the very beginning of its career. The full meaning of its content having hardly touched the threshold of our minds; like an ocean at the bottom

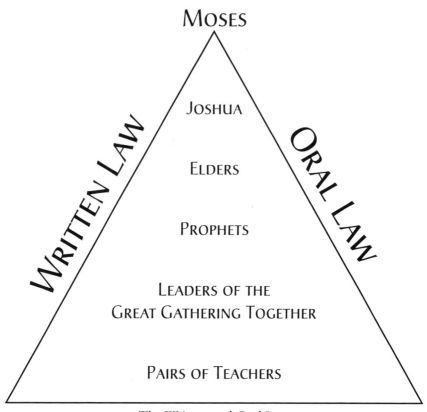

The Written and Oral Law

of which countless pearls lie, waiting to be discovered, its spirit is still to be unfolded. Though its words seem plain and its idiom translucent, unnoticed meanings, undreamed-of intimations break forth constantly. More than two thousand years of reading and research have not succeeded in exploring its full meaning. Today it is as if it had never been touched, never been seen, as if we had not even begun to read it.[1]

The revelation of Torah to Moses on Mount Sinai is the foundation of Jewish faith and practice. The pious Jew chooses a course of life and pursues the fulfillment of God's will by obedience to the commandments. But the

---

[1] Heschel, *God in Search of Man*, 242. This quotation shows how a Jewish philosopher and theologian is caught up in childlike wonder at the divine mystery embedded in the biblical revelation. Although a great Hebrew scholar, each time he reads a text it is as if he is reading it for the first time. See also Samuel H. Dresner, *I Asked for Wonder: A Spiritual Anthology* (New York: Crossroads, 2000), and Susannah Heschel, *Moral Grandeur*, 396.

words of the Torah can be interpreted in different ways, and the oral commentary that accompanied the revelation to Moses on Mount Sinai is the unwritten guidebook that must be preserved in memorized form by committed disciples who pass it on from one generation to another.

The Oral Torah is of almost equal importance in Jewish thought to what is written, largely because it reveals the meaning of the recorded text and is upheld by its authority. Still it is not considered to possess the same authority as the Written Torah. In ancient Judaism, the Oral Torah was highly valued and carefully preserved. This tradition reveals God's will from the written word. The oral teachings are sacred and must be preserved with care. The exact wording of the Torah teacher must be learned by heart, recited with precision, and passed on to worthy scholars who will keep the living waters of Torah flowing from one generation to the next. The Christian scholar Birger Gerhardsson has written the definitive work on the oral transmission of Torah learning within the Jewish community. He suggests this way of transmitting teaching most probably impacted the way the words of Jesus were committed to memory by his disciples. Rabbinic Judaism focused on the oral teachings and preserved them for future learners of Torah.

WHAT WAS SAID

The difference between the Written and Oral Torahs is in how they were transmitted. The written word was read, the oral word was recited. The disciple would repeat the exact words to the Torah master. Sometimes the teaching would be repeated at least four times, or as many times as was necessary (*m. Eduyot* 1:3; *b. Eruvin* 54b).[2] It was essential that a Torah teaching preserve the name of the authority that taught it; one was obligated to remember a saying of Hillel in the name of Hillel. As E. P. Sanders observes, "Scholars of all schools accept attributions to a named Pharisee or rabbi as being fairly reliable: a rule attributed to Shammai probably reflects his view."[3] Modern scholars

---

[2] See the *Mekhilta* on Exod 21:1 in Lauterbach, *Mekhilta Derabbi Ishmael*, 3:1. See also Gerhardsson, *Memory and Manuscript*, 130–36.

[3] Sanders, *Judaism Practice and Belief,* 10. See the entire context, where Sanders discusses the issues of dating the rabbinic literature based upon attribution. The issue is hotly debated among scholars. Some wish to reject all rabbinic literature from consideration as possible comparative material for early Christianity, largely because it was written after the first century. I believe good scholarship analyzes all the evidence. Sanders argues for a scientific analysis and assessment of the rabbinic texts. Not all attributions are to be believed, but the transmission process in ancient Judaism worked diligently to accurately preserve a teaching with the proper authority, so an attribution should not be dismissed without solid scientific evaluation.

may date a rabbinic text by the name of the sage giving a teaching, so the attributions within the oral Torah are of immense value.

> Our concentration upon Rabbinic Judaism is due to the fact of its being the leading, and the most influential, current within Judaism at the beginning of the Christian era, and to the fact of its position of dominance becoming definitive during the centuries immediately following; but it is also due to the fact that within this group the oral Torah was held to be sacred and authoritative, and was therefore transmitted with reverence, with care, and by means of a method which was so conscious that it is described in the source material.[4]

Sometimes the attributions may be accepted as accurate, at other times there may be reasons why they should be questioned. A rabbinic saying may be questioned because of a clear inconsistency in the chain of transmission (e.g., Hillel could not quote Rabbi Akiva, given that the former was active nearly one hundred years before the latter). Also some late rabbinic sources reveal a lack of accuracy. But even a so-called late rabbinic source could preserve accurately an earlier teaching of Hillel that might not be referenced in other sources that survived into our hands. The author of a rabbinic collection like the *Yalkut Shimoeni,* for instance, possessed books in his library from ancient Jewish records that have not been preserved for modern scholars. The modern reader only has access to the quotations from these sources made in the *Yalkut.* Christian historians use the church history written by Eusebius in a similar way.

To what extent can the collective memory of the community of rabbinic authorities and Jewish sages be considered reliable? Truly much of the Tannaitic literature is near in time to the compilation of the New Testament, and one can see parallels between the memory of disciples and the manuscripts that were eventually produced in both ancient faiths. Cultures with an oral history take great measures to preserve it, but rabbinic Judaism possesses a much greater motivation to preserve the Oral Torah because it guides the everyday functions of personal and community life. In modern times, with the invention of the printing press, libraries, computer databases, and the Internet, the ability to memorize information is no longer valued. But in a culture that relied on memory instead of manuscript, training in Torah involved rigorous memorization and practical application. The organization of the Oral Torah, and even its wording, reveal memory devices that aid in recitation by heart. Does an eagle scout forget the scout oath? Can a Christian recite the

---

[4] Gerhardsson, *Memory and Manuscript,* 30. In the new edition, Jacob Neusner has written the foreword. Earlier, Neusner sharply criticized Gerhardsson, arguing that rabbinic transmission is largely unreliable. He now recognizes Gerhardsson's contribution: "Seeing the rabbinic literature and the Gospels alike as models of phenomena, we then take the sources for what they are and value them for what they contain and exemplify....To see what is right, read this book."

Lord's prayer? How many children can still remember the Pledge of Allegiance to the United States? If someone changes the wording, another who knows the right wording will offer a correction. What child does not love to correct a parent who skips a line in a favorite bedtime story? In liturgical churches, congregants regularly affirm the Apostles' Creed, and would be offended if someone tried to change the words to suit their own purposes. Still, our powers of memory are seldom used in this age where answers are at our fingertips.

The rabbis, however, demanded memorization from their disciples.[5] No one was allowed to change the wording of the Oral Torah to suit their own purposes. The sages could debate the issues and seek a fresh interpretation and application of the oral law in practice, but they could not purposely change the teachings. Torah scholars not only would remember the teachings accurately but also would refer to their sources by referencing the sage who taught it, or they would note that the saying was "a halakhah [practical law] from Moses on Mount Sinai," "a commandment of the Elders," or "a tradition received from the fathers."[6] So in rabbinic Judaism one was not only allowed but encouraged to go beyond the plain meaning of the text to find the deeper meaning.[7] The Oral Torah aided in this search, and its authority was linked to the revelation of God to Moses upon Mount Sinai.

Torah Learning Takes Precedence over Sacrifices

Torah learning is even more pleasing to the Omni-Present than burnt sacrifices. After all if a person studies Torah he or she knows the will of the Omni-Present, as it is written, "Then you will understand the fear of the LORD and find the knowledge [or the will] of God (Proverbs 2:5)."

Fathers according to Rabbi Nathan, Version A, ch. 4

---

[5] Shmuel Safrai told me about his teacher, Gedalia Alon, who had memorized the Jerusalem Talmud. Safrai watched Alon write academic articles, using his memory when quoting extensively from primary source material in the rabbinic literature. When Safrai checked the quotations against the printed editions, Alon had not made one mistake.

[6] See Patte, *Early Jewish Hermeneutic,* 15. See especially the discussion of Jacob Epstein, *Mevoot Lesifrut Hatannaim* (Jerusalem: Magnes, 1957), 15–70, where he deals with the early sources of the Mishnah. Compare Wiesel, *Wise Men,* xvii.

[7] See Abraham Jacob Heschel's work in Hebrew, *Torah Men Hashamayim* (3 vols.; New York: Soncino, 1972–1990), 1:212–19; ET: *Heavenly Torah,* 1:254–56.

Three Insights into Christians and Jews

"As a child I received instruction both in the Bible and in the Talmud. I am a Jew, but I am enthralled by the luminous figure of the Nazarene. . . . No one can read the Gospels without feeling the actual presence of Jesus. His personality pulsates in every word. No myth is filled with such life."

Albert Einstein, as quoted by George Viereck, "What Life Means to Einstein," *Saturday Evening Post,* October 29, 1929.

"If Christians were Christians, there would be no anti-Semitism. Jesus was a Jew. There is nothing that the ordinary Christian so dislikes to remember as this awkward historical fact. But it happens, nonetheless, to be true."

John Haynes Holmes, Protestant theologian and minister (1879–1964)

"Whoever meets Jesus Christ meets Judaism."

Pope John Paul II, Mainz Germany, April 28, 1980

CHAPTER 13

Utopia or Plan of Action?

After probing early Jewish thought, introducing rabbinic literature, and meeting the rabbis, the time is right for viewing the teachings of Jesus in the Sermon on the Mount through the eyes of His contemporaries, and to make practical application. Jesus' sermon cannot be understood divorced from the Judaism of His day. So difficult-to-understand sayings of Jesus in the Gospels can better be understood in the light of the Hebrew texts from rabbinic literature. The opposite is also true. Teachings from rabbinic literature can better be understood when compared to similar teachings in the Gospels. The Jewish sources connected with the message of the kingdom of heaven are better understood in the light of the Greek in the Gospels. Jewish, Catholic, Protestant, Eastern religious, Agnostic, and Atheist readers will come to value the substance and content of the Sermon on the Mount when the teachings are based deeply upon the root that nourishes the branch. Modern Judaism and Christianity are branches sprouting from the root of ancient Judaism.

The Sermon on the Mount is not describing a utopian society of disciples, one that sounds good in theory but could never ever be attained in reality. Jesus did not ask his followers to do something beyond their capabilities. But for most Christians his teaching remains an unattainable challenge. The Sermon on the Mount is only there to show how much we need forgiveness of sins, taught the reformer and spiritual leader, Martin Luther, and many like him in church history.[1] It is not, then, considered a practical approach to daily living. We must cross-examine these prevailing Christian teachings concerning the message of the Sermon on the Mount. Did Jesus not teach a way of life for disciples serving in the kingdom of God? Jesus' kingdom of heaven message should not be viewed as an unattainable utopia, but rather as a plan of action.[2]

---

[1] See Georg Strecker, *The Sermon on the Mount* (Nashville: Abingdon, 1988), 16. See also the fine work of Craig S. Keener, *A Commentary on the Gospel of Matthew* (Grand Rapids: Eerdmans, 1999), 160–63.

[2] See the work of Lapide, *The Sermon on the Mount,* which asks the same question. I am grateful to Lapide's insightful analysis. Lapide writes, "For me Jesus is less

It is not that the Sermon on the Mount has been tried and found wanting. It has not been tried. The redemptive work of the kingdom is accomplished through small steps: praying to God, helping those in need, and repenting through fasting pave the way for the manifestation of the divine reign.[3] These actions lead the disciple into a right relationship with God through thoughtful obedience.

The ethical and moral teachings of the Sermon on the Mount derive from the deep spirituality of first-century Judaism; its message is not understandable except within the context of ancient Jewish faith and practice. Rabbinic literature contains a treasure store of pertinent resource material. The force of God's reign is experienced in small steps. Acts of worship such as prayer, giving charity directly to the needy, and repentance, which often in Jesus' day included fasting, are all activities devoted to God in a spiritual walk of true faith. Especially when they are done in secret, these actions push forward the redemptive plan. Loving your enemies, forgiving those who have wronged you, giving a helping hand to those who are less fortunate, seeking the face of God in daily life by doing the will of God in every circumstance, obeying the commandments, and acting on faith, all release the force of God's reign for the disciple who lives out the Sermon on the Mount in daily practice.

CREED OR COMMANDMENT?

There is no mention of what to believe in the Sermon on the Mount. The focus rather is on action: what to do and thereby fulfill the meaning of Torah. Early in its development, Christianity became focused more on belief as expressed in creeds. The Apostles' Creed, for instance, as crucial as it is for pronouncing the fundamental doctrines of the early church, does not even mention action or obedience to the commandments. One does not have to obey commandments to believe the creeds of Christendom. While living a moral and ethical lifestyle may be assumed in the act of reciting the creeds of the church, the practical side of how to fulfill the commandments through

---

the founder of Christianity than the instigator of a Christian way of life that has its great manifesto in the Sermon on the Mount: a Christian way of life that at bottom amounts to a Jewish way of life and, like it, unfortunately, finds far too few imitators in either community of faith" (ibid, 7). See also Daniel Patte, *The Challenge of Discipleship: A Critical Study of the Sermon on the Mount as Scripture* (Harrisburg, Penn.: Trinity International, 1999), 3, where Patte asks, "How does the Sermon on the Mount affect Christian believers in the concreteness of their lives?"

[3] See Lapide, *The Sermon on the Mount*, 35–36.

holy living is not explained in detail or emphasized as necessary demonstrations of these sacred beliefs. Divine grace through forgiveness of sins was never intended to be a license to neglect the ethical teachings Jesus emphasized. In contrast to the Creeds stands the Great Commission, where the risen Lord instructs his followers to raise up disciples in all the nations of the world, "teaching them to observe all that I have commanded you" (Matt 28:19–20).[4] The disciple expresses true love for the Master by obeying the commandments. Jesus' commandments in the Sermon on the Mount do not abolish the Torah, but rather express the deeper meaning of the divine revelation by explaining how to observe the law in a way that is pleasing to God.

If one violates a minor commandment like anger, this will lead to violating a major commandment, "Thou shalt not murder" (Exod 20:13; Deut 5:17). Not controlling one's thoughts about another man's wife will lead to violating the commandment, "Thou shalt not commit adultery" (Exod 20:14; Deut 5:18; on the relationship between minor and major commandments, see Chapter Three, pp. 45–46, and Chapter Ten, pp. 170–72). If one obeys the minor commandments, one builds a fence around the major ethical teachings of Scripture.[5] The disciple should run away from wrongdoing and seek the presence of God through active obedience. Jesus teaches, "Judge not so that you will not be judged" (Matt 7:1–2), which is similar to Hillel's teaching, "Do not judge your neighbor until you put yourself into his or her place" (*Avot* 2:7). Notice that Jesus uses the divine passive voice: "so that you will not be judged." Because the Jewish people held the name of God to be sacred, they refrained from pronouncing it in common usage, lest they misuse or profane the name. To avoid making direct reference to God they used the passive voice. People understood from the passive voice that, "If I pass judgment against another person, God himself will judge me in a similar way." God is the active personality behind the passive voice.

Moreover, Hillel's saying makes the listener assume the position of the one being judged. His approach makes reference to the summary of Torah requirements dealing with interpersonal relationships between individuals, "Love your neighbor as yourself." Indeed, every individual is created in the divine image and is accountable to God. How can one pass judgment against one's neighbor when each individual is in the same condition of need? One should not pass judgment on another because no one wishes to be judged harshly by others. Hillel also taught, "My humiliation is my exaltation and

---

[4] See also David Flusser, "The Conclusion of Matthew in a New Jewish Christian Source," *ASTI* 5 (1967): 300–310.

[5] See Young, *Jesus the Jewish Theologian*, 267–69.

my exaltation is my humiliation" (*Leviticus Rabbah* 1:5).[6] This teaching focuses attention on how an individual causes himself or herself to be put to shame. By seeking honor, one loses respect. By practicing humility, one actually gains the respect and esteem of others, thereby causing oneself to be exalted. Jesus gives a similar teaching using the divine passive voice. When he teaches, "The one who humbles himself will be exalted" (Luke 14:11; cf. Matt 23:12), he is saying that God will cause the one who practices humility to be honored and respected. The moral and ethical heritage of both Judaism and Christianity is rooted in the religious piety of Second Temple period Jewish faith and practice.

The resistance to teaching the commandments of God in Christian thought may be observed in the attitude toward the Sermon on the Mount. Often it is said that Jesus is the Second Moses, who goes up to the new Mount Sinai in order to teach the new Torah for the messianic age and replace the worn out and obsolete teachings of the Old Testament.[7] This interpretation is problematic. It is doubtful that Jesus could ever have intended that the Sermon on the Mount would become a replacement for the teachings of the Torah and prophets that he esteemed and lived out in his life through faithful obedience. In Matt 5:17 Jesus says, "Do not think that I have come to destroy the Torah and the prophets, I have not come to destroy but to fulfill." Jesus lived with the awareness that the Torah was still in force. He viewed his teaching of the commandments as upholding the true and original meaning of Torah. His interpretation intensifies the application.

A first-century Jewish audience would never interpret these words, "I have come to fulfill the Torah," as teaching that the old Torah was replaced with a new one. The obvious meaning is that Jesus is giving the proper interpretation of the Torah and the prophets, and the correct explanation will enable each individual to be prepared better to observe the commandments of God. Proper obedience to the commandments is a spiritual practice that makes living life a sacred duty pleasing to one's Creator. In fact, in the context of the Gospels, the Sermon is directed toward the disciples who are learning Jesus' teachings and putting them into practice. The setting for the

---

[6] See the discussion of the sources by David Flusser, "Hillel and Jesus: Two Ways of Self-Awareness," in James H. Charlesworth, *Hillel and Jesus* (Minneapolis: Fortress, 1997), 77.

[7] Certainly there are many different views of the mountain among interpreters, see William D. Davies and Dale C. Allison, *A Critical and Exegetical Commentary on The Gospel According to Saint Matthew* (3 vols.; Edinburgh: T&T Clark, 1988–1991), 1:423; also William D. Davies, *The Setting for the Sermon on the Mount* (Atlanta: Scholars Press, 1989), 93–108. Compare the earlier work of William. D. Davies, *Torah in the Messianic Age and/or the Age to Come* (Philadelphia: Society of Biblical Literature, 1952).

Sermon upon the mountain may well have recalled the setting for the giving of Torah on Mount Sinai, but this is only intended to validate Jesus' interpretation of the authentic meaning of Torah and how its message can be lived out through active discipleship. A chair where a rabbi teaches in the synagogue might even be compared to Mount Sinai. Hence Rabbi Joshua described the stone chair upon which his colleague, Rabbi Eliezer, sat to teach Torah: "This stone is like Mount Sinai" (*Song of Songs Rabbah* 1:3).[8] The idea is that the Rabbi's teaching fulfills the message of Torah from Mount Sinai by giving it its true and authentic meaning in everyday life.

In a similar way, Hillel the Elder would have believed that his teachings upheld the true meaning of the Torah and the prophets. For example, in a commentary on the Jewish teaching to "cover yourself with the dust of your Master's feet," Torah learning received from one's rabbi is compared to receiving the Law from Mount Sinai.[9] Disciples would eagerly walk alongside their master and listen to the message being taught from the distinct perspective of their Rabbi's approach to Torah. They would sit at their teacher's feet as he explained the meaning of Torah for daily life. They observed their mentor in practical situations, and learned from his conduct and behavior in the mundane circumstances of everyday living. The rabbinic imagery of covering oneself with the dust of one's teacher's feet focuses on the activity of disciple making, in which a mentoring relationship is firmly established. Learning Torah by covering oneself with the dust stirred up from the road one's rabbi is walking upon, or by sitting in the dirt at his feet, means that the committed disciple stays in close proximity. The intensity of desire for Torah education is expressed by the nearness of the disciple to his rabbi. To receive Torah learning in this way, was to listen intently to "every word that proceeds from his lips with awe, fear, terror, and trembling in the same way that your ancestors received Torah from Mount Sinai, with awe, fear, terror, and trembling."[10] Like the rabbis, Jesus viewed his teachings on Torah as fulfilling the original purpose of the divine revelation from Mount Sinai.

In fact, Jesus' interpretation does not make Torah observance easier. Often his approach is more stringent. It is based on the Jewish principle,

---

[8] See also Yitzhak Gilat, *R. Eliezer ben Hyrcanus: A Scholar Outcast* (Ramat Gan, Israel: Bar Ilan University, 1984), 139–41. Compare also Young, *Jesus the Jewish Theologian,* 186–88.

[9] See *Ethics of the Fathers (Avot)* 1:4: "Let your house be a meeting place for the wise; cover yourself with the dust of their feet, and drink in their words with thirst." The Hebraic imagery of the idiom recalls the instruction of Jesus for his disciples "to shake the dust from their feet" when their message is rejected (compare Matt 10:14).

[10] *Avot R. Nat.,* vers. A, ch. 6; vers. B, ch. 11.

"Run away from evil and everything that resembles evil."[11] If one really wants to sanctify life, then one must build a fence around the Torah.[12] If one stays far away from sin by not crossing the boundary line, then one will not transgress a commandment. Hence if one is to avoid committing adultery, one must control the thought processes. If one crosses the boundary by thinking about adultery, this thought process, though not a literal transgression of the Ten Commandments, will lead the person into dangerous terrain where the sin of actually committing adultery will be much easier. So Jesus urges his followers to control their thoughts as well as their actions. The one who commits adultery in the heart and mind will eventually do so in action. In a fascinating Jewish parallel, the sage Rabbi Joshua, teaches, "The one who commits adultery with the eye, commits adultery with the body" (*Pesikta Rabbati* 24).

Turn the Other Cheek

On retaliation, Jesus taught his disciples to "turn the other cheek" (Matt 5:39; Luke 6:29), which paved the way for non-violent resistance, and restricted the interpretation of the words "an eye for an eye" in the Torah (Exod 21:23–25; Lev 24:17–21; Deut 19:21) to limiting acts of vengeance and reprisals for an injury caused. Mahatma Gandhi and Dr. Martin Luther King Jr. championed the concept of passive resistance and peaceful demonstration in the face of extreme moral evil.[13] In Mosaic legislation, the concept of equal compensation prevented an injured party from seeking the death of the one who caused the injury in a spiral of violent blood revenge. The "eye for an eye" principle limited retaliation and prevented calling for the death of one who had caused an injury. The teachings of Jesus encouraged peaceful, non-violent solutions to moral decadence and personal injustices. While the message of the Sermon on the Mount calls upon the disciple to overcome wrong by doing good, one should question whether it restricts

---

[11] See M. Higger, *Massekhet Derekh Eretz,* 1:78–79 and 2:38. See also the *Didache* 3:1–6, Huub van de Sandt and David Flusser, *The Didache: Its Jewish Sources and Its Place in Early Judaism and Christianity.* (Minneapolis: Fortress, 2002), 170–75.

[12] See *Ethics of the Fathers (Avot)* 1:1, "raise up many disciples, and make a fence around the Torah." Compare, Finkelstein, "Introductory Study to Pirke Abot," 30–32, who argues that making a fence around the Torah actually means that once a decision of halakhah has been established, additional proofs to show its correctness are the fence that strengthens a ruling.

[13] See Patte, *Challenge of Discipleship,* 188, who observes that by turning the other cheek, "their reality was transformed . . . the shame of racism was now upon the racists and could be replaced by Black pride."

self-defense altogether, or even restrains protection of loved ones against a harmful attack. The NASB which is often considered a very literal translation, renders Matt 5:39 as, "But I say to you, do not resist him who is evil; but whoever slaps you on your right cheek, turn to him the other also." The concept of not resisting an evil person, or even wickedness in general, is also brought out in the RSV rendering, "Do not resist one who is evil."

Does the Sermon on the Mount instruct followers of Jesus not to resist evil or a person who does evil? The major force of the kingdom of heaven teachings is confrontation, not retaliation.[14] The small-steps approach of the Sermon on the Mount is a way of combating evil in a world of suffering people. The translation, "Do not resist" is less than adequate.[15] The Greek word *anthistēmi,* which is the basis of the English rendering "not to resist," is better translated, "do not compete." It is similar in thought and wording to Ps 37:1, which is usually translated, "Fret not yourself because of the evil doers" (compare verses 7 and 8). In Hebrew, the text reads *al titchar bameraim* and would be better translated, "Do not compete with evil doers."[16] The root word for *titchar* is *charah,* and it has a wide range of meanings. Sometimes it means "to burn with jealousy." The idea of jealousy probably comes from the meaning of competition; one is jealous of one's competitor and wants to overtake him or her in a contest. For instance, the Jewish Bible commentator Rashi calls attention to Jer 12:5, "If you have raced with men on foot, and they have wearied you, how will you compete with horses?"[17] Similarly, Rashi explains that one should not compete with evil (Ps 37). Just so, Jesus is saying that his disciples should not compete with evil, but seek to overcome wrong by doing good.

Furthermore, a slap on the right cheek is very different from being struck with all a person's might. Jesus specifically states that he is dealing

---

[14] See Betz, *The Sermon on the Mount,* 280: "the answer to the problem can only be that the issue is nonretaliation and that *antistanai* ['Do not resist evil'] must be translated as 'Do not retaliate.'" Betz refers to other passages that teach Christians to resist evil (e.g., Rom 12:9; 1 Cor 5:13; 1 Thess 5:22; 2 Thess 3:3; Eph 6:13).

[15] See the definition given in BDAG, 80, "be in opposition to, *set oneself against, oppose,*" which really lends itself to the understanding of competition. I am grateful to Robert Lindsey who first called my attention to the importance of Ps 37:1 in interpreting Matt 5:39 (private communication). See also Lapide, *The Sermon on the Mount,* 134.

[16] See the recent English translation in Mordechai Breuer and Raphael Jospe, *Keter Crown Bible* (New York: Feldheim, 2004) on Ps 37:1, "Do not compete with evildoers . . ." (779). See also N. Scherman, ed., *Stone Tanach* (New York: Masorah, 2005), 1467.

[17] See Rashi's insightful comment on Ps 37:1 (in Hebrew). On Rashi's Bible commentary, see Pearl, *Rashi,* 24–62.

with a slap to the right cheek, which probably indicates that he is discussing an insult to a person's dignity rather than an attack intended to do serious injury.[18] Jesus is describing a back-handed slap with a person's right hand, delivered to the right cheek of the victim. Such a slap to the face was considered a serious insult and could result in a heavy fine (*m. Baba Kamma* 8:6).[19] Turning the other cheek is a small step, but it was very difficult for most people to take, especially in a culture oriented around the concepts of shame and honor, as Jesus' was. The act of turning the other cheek appeals to the higher virtue of dignity in the offender, who may well be moved to reconcile. One should not sue for financial damages to character, although one is entitled to such after suffering this sort of indignity. Rather, one should turn the other cheek and seek reconciliation, thus avoiding a vindictive spirit.

The principle of saving life, however, which is highly valued in Jesus' teachings and rooted in the Torah, required one to defend oneself and others against a life-threatening attack. In a Sabbath controversy, for instance, Jesus reminds his critics that it is right "to save life" rather than to lose it. Healing on the Sabbath was considered to be preserving life and therefore was permitted (Mark 3:4; Matt 12:9–14; Luke 6:6–11). Also, in John's Gospel, Jesus makes reference to the thief who breaks into the house to kill and destroy (John 10:10). In rabbinic thought, as in modern jurisprudence, if a burglar breaks into a home it may be assumed that he will kill as well as steal. In such a case one is justified in using deadly force to protect oneself and loved ones in the home. Jesus seems to be aware of this rule of conduct. He did not come to cancel accepted Torah principles. Even so, Jesus stresses that one must love one's enemy (Matt 5:43–48; Luke 6:27–28, 32–36).

Jesus was saying, "Do not compete with evil," or a person who does wrong. This translation is supported by the Hebrew meaning behind the Greek text. Since Jesus spoke Hebrew, and the Gospels are derived from a Semitic source text, the work of translation must explore the Hebrew nuance of Greek terms (for more on this see Chapter One, pp. 9–11). Jesus warns against retaliation and revenge which often harms the spiritual life of the offended individual who seeks to even the score with an enemy. The disciple must not be caught up into the spirit of competition with revenge in the heart. Desiring retaliation for an offence negates the commandment to "love your neighbor as yourself" (Matt 5:43; 19:19; 22:39; Mark 12:31).

---

[18] Samuel T. Lachs, *A Rabbinic Commentary on the New Testament: The Gospels of Matthew, Mark, and Luke* (Hoboken, N.J.: KTAV, 1987), 104, and Thomas W. Manson, *The Sayings of Jesus: As Recorded in the Gospels According to St. Matthew and St. Luke* (London: SCM Press, 1977), 51, "But with a right-handed assailant the first blow would normally be to the left cheek of the victim."

[19] See Lachs, *A Rabbinic Commentary,* 104, and Manson, *Sayings,* 51.

The rabbinic literature contains significant parallels that demonstrate this attitude against competing with wrong doing through retaliation and revenge. The rabbis asked, "Who is the strong person?" Many would respond by assessing an individual's physical strength. The sages explain that the strong individual is the one who can turn an enemy into a friend (*Avot R. Nat.*, vers. A, ch. 23).[20] Winning over an enemy is considered a sign of great moral strength. The Talmud also praises an attitude of humility and long-suffering when an individual has to endure personal insult: "Our Rabbis taught: Those who are insulted but do not insult, hear themselves reviled without seeking reprisal, act through love and rejoice in suffering, of them the Scripture teaches, 'But they who love him are as the sun when it goes forth in its might' (Judg 5:31)" (*b. Shabbat* 88b). It is not a sign of weakness to turn the other cheek, rather, it demonstrates an inner strength that transforms the disciple in the midst of suffering and possesses the power to transform the aggressor who may decide to change.

The honor and dignity of each individual, created in the divine image, are highly prized in Jewish thought. The act of turning the other cheek can appeal to the noble qualities inherent in each person created by God, even if that individual has allowed violence and abuse to overwhelm basic goodness and fundamental decency. Respecting that God-given honor and dignity is crucial for learning to esteem others and for building self-worth. The rabbis taught that a person who embarrasses another in public is guilty of murder (*b. Baba Metzi'a* 58b). One should seek ways to give honor and esteem to others rather than shame or embarrassment.

The rabbis praised the attitude of humility so valued in the Sermon on the Mount. Jesus' commandment to love one's enemies was based upon Jewish principles taught in Torah education. Moreover, the Amoraic teacher, Rabbi Chama taught that one should feed one's enemy in literal fulfillment of the commandment in Prov 25:12–22. While this teaching came sometime after the Sermon on the Mount, it is deeply rooted in Scripture and could arise at any time in Jewish thought. In the Hebrew Bible, Elisha the prophet commands the king of Israel to feed the enemy army of the king of Aram, which had been sent to capture the prophet, and send them home (2 Kgs 6:21–23). The concept added to the text in Prov 25:21–22, by way of rabbinic commentary, is that God himself will work to establish peace between enemies. Because the would-be victim shows kindness in obedience to Scripture, God will cause one's enemy to be at peace, thus turning one's would-be murderer into a friend.

---

[20] See the parallel idea to this passage in *b. Shabbat* 88b.

FEEDING ONE'S ENEMIES

> Rabbi Chama son of Chanina taught, "Even if [your enemy] rises early to kill
> you, and comes to your house hungry and thirsty, you should give him food and
> drink. Why? [Because it is written,] 'If your enemy is hungry, give him or her
> bread to eat. If your enemy is thirsty, give him or her water to drink. By doing so,
> you will heap coals of fire upon his or her head, and the LORD will make your
> enemy to be at peace with you' (Proverbs 25:21–22). Hence you should not read
> and interpret the verse to mean, 'the LORD will reward [yishalem] you.' Rather
> you must read and interpret the verse to mean, 'the LORD will make your enemy
> to be at peace with you [yashlimenu]'" (Midrash Proverbs 25).[21]

While the rabbinic attitude to feed one's enemies and expect God to
cause them to be reconciled is very close to the teachings of Jesus in the Sermon on the Mount, the Talmud also expresses another opinion. Some Christians mistakenly characterize the rabbis as being legalistic and one-sided,
demanding everyone to agree with one opinion, but the Talmud works hard
to give numerous opinions on almost every subject. The rabbis were realists
on the subject of self-defense when a murder was about to be committed. In
a different opinion, they taught, "If someone is going to come and kill you,
get up early, and kill him or her first" (b. Sanhedrin 72a).[22] Preservation of
life, as a moral principle based on scriptural authority, requires self-defense
against a would-be murderer.

The teachings of Jesus in the Sermon on the Mount deal with peace
and reconciliation between individuals. They do not, however, reflect the
only acceptable methods for achieving justice between nations. While
peaceful solutions must be thoroughly exhausted in the search for reconciliation in an international crisis, and the principles outlined in the Sermon
on the Mount provide a solid foundation for ending disputes, the teaching
does not rule out establishing justice by all means necessary to save and
preserve life. [23]

---

[21] Visotzky, Midrash on Proverbs, 168 (Hebrew Edition), Yalkut Hamachiri, on
Prov 25:21–22, 58b, cf. b. Megilah 15b, as quoted by Abrahams, Studies in Pharisaism, 165.

[22] See Telushkin, Jewish Wisdom, 421.

[23] See Claude G. Montefiore, The Synoptic Gospels (2 vols.; New York: KTAV,
1968), 2:71: "Jesus was not thinking of public justice, the order of civic communities, the organization of states, but only how the members of his religious brother-
hood should act towards each other and towards those outside their ranks. Public
justice is outside his purview. Moreover, he believed that the old order was coming
soon to a catastrophic end. What would even be the use of the old methods for the
cure of evil? Wickedness can only be cured by goodness, or annihilated by the inter-
vention of God."

Disciples of Jesus will seek the higher moral principle of establishing peace and seeking reconciliation between individuals rather than choosing the path of revenge and retaliation. The Sermon on the Mount was never intended to replace Torah but rather fulfill it in practical application of principles. It is a plan of action. Interpreting the message of the Sermon on the Mount properly, and encouraging others to obey its teachings, may well do more to further the Great Commission (Matt 28:18–20) than preaching an evangelistic sermon. Gandhi sought to implement Jesus' Sermon on the Mount to end British colonial rule in India. His radical adherence to the principle of peace put him in danger, but he was never persuaded to compromise. When asked what he as a Hindu admired most in Christianity, he responded, "Jesus." When asked what disturbed him most in Christianity, Ghandi responded, "Christians."[24]

Dr. Martin Luther King Jr., as a Baptist minister opposing inequality, prejudice, and racism, successfully applied the small-step approach of the Sermon on the Mount in the civil rights movement. One might contrast the approach of Malcolm X, who advocated violence to achieve the same goals. One may wonder if progress toward equality in American society would have been advanced so dramatically if Malcolm X's approach to the problem had been pursued instead of the dream proclaimed by Dr. King. It is never enough to share the same belief system. Action must take precedence over words. While it is important for Jesus' followers to ascribe belief to like-minded creeds, faith should never be allowed to cause neglect in regard to living the message of the Sermon on the Mount in faithful obedience. Action must accompany belief. But action must be based upon knowledge. One cannot obey commandments that are not understood properly. The Sermon on the Mount teaches an approach to living based upon a fresh and insightful interpretation of the Torah and commandments. The interpretation is Jewish to the core, and best understood in the authentic context of ancient Judaism.

STUDY OR ACTION?

For the follower of Jesus, study must lead to action and action take precedence over learning. In Judaism, a life dedicated to fulfilling the

---

[24] See Louis Fischer, *Gandhi: Indian Leader and World Influence* (New York: Mentor Books, 1954), 131. Compare E. Stanley Jones, *Gandhi: Portrayal of a Friend* (Nashville: Abingdon, 1948), 51–77 and Charles F. Adams, *Mahatma Gandhi's Ideas* (New York: Macmillan, 1930), 85–99. Adams quotes Gandhi as saying, "to my mind much of what passes for Christianity is a negation of the Sermon on the Mount" (93–94).

commandments is based solidly on theology and belief. Indeed the community and religious leaders of the Jewish people possessed a solid theology rooted in biblical revelation, but they did not take a creedal approach to belief (for more on this see pp. 206–10 above). The influential rabbi and educator Solomon Shechter explains, "The Old Rabbis seem to have thought that the true health of a religion is to have a theology without being aware of it."[25] Certainly learning based upon the Bible and the collective historical experience of the people was a crucial foundation for rabbinic Judaism. As Samuel Sandmel observes, "The Bible was the adhesive that held the Jews together, that fed and nurtured their loyalty to the notion of being Jewish, and provided them with the basis from which they inferred their own understanding of what God and man and events meant."[26] But learning based upon the Bible and the theological meaning of historical events and human experience is not sufficient. The study of Scripture and oral interpretation of the divine revelation have to be put into practice through active obedience. Study must lead to action.

The rabbis debated the question of whether study should take precedence over learning or whether action really should be considered of higher value than education. In some ways, a similar debate raged among early Christians. What was really of primary significance, faith or works? While James bluntly declares that faith alone, without works, is dead (Jas 2:14–18), the Apostle Paul is more ambivalent, stressing the experience of faith as leading to a righteous way of living (Rom 4:1–16; 6:15–18).[27] In reality, both James and Paul believe that the Christian lifestyle must embrace faith *and* works, but they differ in stressing what is of chief significance. Paul stresses that where there is true faith, works will result. At times James seems to say that if one really works at obeying God, faith will follow. But both James and Paul teach the essential necessity of both faith and works.

In ancient Judaism, Rabbi Tarfon stressed that works are more important than learning. His influential colleague, Rabbi Akiva, took a different approach. Rabbi Akiva argues that study will lead to good works, and so learning takes precedence. His view prevailed within the religious community. This inter-Jewish debate is also reflected in rabbinic parables, which try to demonstrate the relationship between learning and doing. The same idea emerges in Jesus' teachings from the Sermon on the Mount. In the parable of the Two Builders that concludes the Sermon on the Mount (Matt 7:24–27;

---

[25] Solomon Shechter, *Aspects of Rabbinic Theology* (New York: Schocken, 1961), 12.

[26] Samuel Sandmel, *Judaism and Christian Beginnings* (New York: Oxford University Press, 1978), 17.

[27] See Young, *Paul the Jewish Theologian,* 70–105.

cf. Luke 6:46–49), Jesus describes the wise person as the one who both hears the teaching and puts it into practice. Between hearing and doing comes decision making. The parable is designed to force the right decision. The parallel rabbinic parable also stresses decision making (see below). One must not merely become consumed with study and the acquisition of wisdom, but must seek to practice what has been learned.

COMPARING A GOSPEL AND RABBINIC PARABLE

Let us compare the conclusion of the Sermon on the Mount, specifically the parable that contrasts the wise and the foolish builders, with the illustration of Rabbi Elisha ben Avuyah.

The Gospel Parable of the Two Builders

Therefore everyone who hears these words of mine and puts them into practice is like a wise man who built his house upon the rock. The rain came down, the waters flooded, the winds blew, and beat against that house. But it did not fall down because it was built upon the rock. Everyone, however, who hears these words of mine and does not do them, is like a foolish man who built his house upon the sand. The rain came down, the waters flooded, the winds blew, and beat against that house. It fell down and great was the crash of it. (Matt 7:24–27)

The Rabbinic Parable of the Two Builders

Rabbi Elisha the son of Avuyah told this parable, "A person who has done good works and has also learned much Torah, to what is this individual like? To one who builds a house by laying a foundation with large stones below and then builds with bricks above, in order that no matter how much water may flood against its foundation, the house will not wash away. But the person who has not done good works even though he or she has learned much Torah, to what is this individual like? To one who builds a house by laying a foundation with bricks below and then stones above, so that even if a little water flows against the foundation, it will at once destroy the house." (*The Fathers According to Rabbi Nathan,* Version A, Chapter 24)

The Gospel parable is similar in imagery and content to the rabbinic parable. In fact, both illustrations deal with the theme of putting good teaching into practice. Another rabbinic parable, told by Rabbi Eleazar the son of Azaryah, compares the one who has wisdom but no good works to a tree with many branches and no root; such a tree will be uprooted by the wind during a storm (*Avot* 3:22). The rabbinic parables seem to argue against the prevailing view espoused by Rabbi Akiva; namely, that learning takes

Jesus and the Last Supper Passover Meal
(Wood Engraving by Bernard A. Solomon)

precedence over good deeds. Certainly the parable of the Two Builders at the conclusion of the Sermon on the Mount also stresses doing, above and beyond, mere learning. But parables are designed to drive home the message and prompt the listener to decide. The kingdom message in the Sermon on the Mount requires immediate attention, without delay. Putting the Torah teaching as explained by Jesus into practice is of quintessential urgency.

Jesus brought Judaism to the world. The content of the Sermon on the Mount is intimately connected to the concepts of the old Judaism practiced by the Jewish people during the days of the Second Temple period. Jesus instructs his followers to make disciples and to teach commandments. His interpretation of the Torah and the commandments show his followers how to live a life of purposeful obedience through a deeply spiritual walk and inner life.

How ironic it is, then, that the world has invented its own brand of Christianity. Some Christians want Christianity to be distinctively different from any vestige of the old Judaism. Their brand of faith and belief often is devoid of commandments and good works. They build a wall of separation between the Christianity that Jesus revealed in the Sermon on the Mount and the Judaism lived by Jewish people in daily life. They neglect the fact that Jesus was a Jew. Contrary to popular opinion, Jesus never converted to Christianity. He provided an example to all by living the Jewish faith in daily life. He reverenced the Torah and its commandments. The faith in Jesus proclaimed by Christianity should never undermine the need to observe the teachings of Jesus.

Seeking first the kingdom of heaven must be translated into action. Taking the small steps of love, forgiveness, and reconciliation cause the healing power of God's reign to be released in a suffering world. Learning theology is not enough, the disciple of Jesus must walk in obedience. True Christianity that honors the life and teachings of Jesus must be rooted in the best of true Judaism.

The Two Great Commandments

Love the LORD your God with all your heart,
with all your soul and with all your strength. (Deut 6:5)

Love your neighbor as yourself. (Lev 19:18)

If you would enter life, keep the commandments. (Matt 19:17)

Does Jesus the Jew—as a Jew—have any impact on Christian theology and on Jewish-Christian relations? . . . To wrench Jesus out of his Jewish world destroys Jesus and destroys Christianity, the religion that grew out of his teachings. Even Jesus' most familiar role as Christ is a Jewish role. If Christians leave the concrete realities of Jesus' life and of the history of Israel in favor of a mythic, universal, spiritual Jesus and an otherworldly kingdom of God, they deny their origins in Israel, their history, and the God who loved and protected Israel and the church. They cease to interpret the actual Jesus sent by God and remake him in their own image and likeness. The dangers are obvious. If Christians violently wrench Jesus out of his natural, ethnic and historical place within the people of Israel, they open the way to doing equal violence to Israel, the place and people of Jesus.

Anthony Saldarini, "What Price the Uniqueness of Jesus?"
Bible Review (June 1999): 17.

PART IV

Study Helps

Most of the study helps provided for the reader in this Part Four will be self-explanatory. Although Christians and Jews read the same Bible, they view the canon differently. At a basic level, this can be seen in a different order of books in the Jewish and Christian canons. Moreover, even though the Jewish people, the Catholic Church, and all Protestants accept the Ten Commandments, each community of faith has counted them according to divergent methods. The seven laws for the children of Noah, universal demands God makes on all human beings, are well known in the Jewish community. Additionally, Israel must observe all the 613 commandments in the Torah. Non-Jews, however, must live up only to the seven commands and, then, they will have a place in the world to come. As we shall see below, the rabbis stressed saving life above all other commandments. There are three commands, however, so crucial for belief that each individual should choose death before violating them in public.

I have also provided a brief overview of the Jewish calendar which can be so confusing for the uninitiated. These Holy Days are essential in Jewish life. Included here is the complete list of the Davidic lineage for the Presiding Leader of the Sanhedrin. The dates for some of these leaders are approximate. As has been seen, the rabbis demonstrate the continuity of transition from one generation to another by building living links in a chain of transmission for Oral Torah. They were more interested in the process and the result than in precise chronology. Students of the New Testament might compare it to the Genealogies of Christ (see Matt 1:1–17; Luke 3:23–38). Few scholars would dare attempt to give precise dates for each person mentioned in the family tree of Jesus or to produce an exact historical record. Nonetheless, readers discover a clear overview of history from the perspective of a faith tradition. Here in the study helps, the reader has a glossary for unfamiliar terms, and indexes. The suggested reading list gives the reader an annotated bibliography of books that could be the next step for further study. The bibliography not only provides important works for study used in the book but also major editions of rabbinic sources and grammatical tools necessary for further research.

The One Law that Overrides All Others

The principle of saving life, *pikuach nefesh,* overrides all other laws.

"A person must live by them [the commandments]" (Lev. 18:5), but the individual must not die by them!

b. Yoma 85b

The one who saves one life, it is as if that one had saved an entire world.

m. Sanhedrin 4:5

Of Books, Commandments, Laws, Holy Days, and Lineage

THE BOOKS OF THE HEBREW BIBLE IN JUDAISM

The Jewish Bible contains the same canonical books as the Christian Old Testament, but they are ordered differently and the number of books differs because some are combined. For example, the twelve relatively short books known in the Christian church as the "minor prophets" (Hosea-Malachi) are one book in the Hebrew Bible. Thus, in the Hebrew Bible there are not thirty-nine, but twenty-four books as outlined below.

There are, moreover, three divisions of the Hebrew Bible: Torah (Revelation), Nevi'im (Prophets), and Ketuvim (Writings). These are often referred to as the Tanak (or Tanakh), where the "T" is from Torah, the "N" is from Nevi'im, and the "K" is from Ketuvim with the vowel "a" separating the consonants to make a pronounceable word.

TORAH (Revelation)

1. Genesis
2. Exodus
3. Leviticus
4. Numbers
5. Deuteronomy

NEVI'IM (Prophets)

6. Joshua
7. Judges
8. 1 & 2 Samuel (counted as one book)
9. 1 & 2 Kings (counted as one book)
10. Isaiah
11. Jeremiah
12. Ezekiel
13. The book of the Twelve: Hosea, Joel, Amos, Obadiah, Jonah, Micah, Nahum, Habakkuk, Zephaniah, Haggai, Zechariah, Malachi (counted as one book)

KETUVIM (Writings)

14. Psalms
15. Proverbs
16. Job
17. Song of Songs
18. Ruth
19. Lamentations
20. Ecclesiastes
21. Esther
22. Daniel
23. Ezra and Nehemiah (counted as one book)
24. 1 & 2 Chronicles (counted as one book)

THE TEN COMMANDMENTS IN JUDAISM

In Jewish tradition, numeration of the Ten Commandments begins with "I am the LORD your God," emphasizing the divine character and the act of salvation. Catholics and Protestants, however, understand Exod 20:3—"You shall have no other gods before me"—as the beginning of the first commandment. Protestants make up for the loss of the first commandment in the Jewish numbering of the ten by breaking the second commandment into two separate commands, "You shall have no other gods before me," and "You shall not make for yourself a sculptured image." Catholics, on the other hand, count this commandment as one. They make up for the loss of the first commandment by dividing the tenth commandment into two separate commandments, "You shall not covet your neighbor's house," and "you shall not covet your neighbor's wife."

EXODUS 20:1–14 (NJPS)

Commandment 1

I the LORD am your God who brought you out of the land of Egypt, the house of bondage:

Commandment 2

You shall have no other gods besides Me. You shall not make for yourself a sculptured image, or any likeness of what is in the heavens above, or on the earth below, or in the waters under the earth. You shall not bow down to them or serve them. For I the LORD your God am an impassioned God, visiting the guilt of the parents upon the children, upon the third and upon the fourth generations of those who reject Me, but showing kindness to the thousandth generation of those who love Me and keep My commandments.

Commandment 3

You shall not swear falsely by the name of the LORD your God; for the LORD will not clear one who swears falsely by His name.

Commandment 4

Remember the sabbath day and keep it holy. Six days you shall labor and do all your work, but the seventh day is a sabbath of the LORD your God: you shall not do any work—you, your son or daughter, your male or female slave, or your cattle, or the stranger who is within your settlements. For in six days the LORD made heaven and earth and sea, and all that is in them, and He rested on the seventh day; therefore the LORD blessed the sabbath day and hallowed it.

Commandment 5

Honor your father and your mother, that you may long endure on the land that the LORD your God is assigning to you.

Commandment 6

You shall not murder.

Commandment 7

You shall not commit adultery.

Commandment 8

You shall not steal.

Commandment 9

You shall not bear false witness against your neighbor.

Commandment 10

You shall not covet your neighbor's house: you shall not covet your neighbor's wife, or his male or female slave, or his ox or his ass, or anything that is your neighbor's.

SEVEN UNIVERSAL MORAL LAWS FOR THE CHILDREN OF NOAH

Following the story of the flood told in Gen 6–9, it was thought that God had established seven great moral laws by which all of humankind would be judged. Though implicit, there is no record of this in the biblical account.

These seven laws for the children of Noah are considered by Jewish people to be a universal moral and ethical code that should be observed by all people, while the 613 commandments enumerated from the Torah were given specifically to Israel. According to the rabbis, non-Jews who observe this universal code will have a place in the world to come.

1. Thou shalt not serve other gods.

2. Thou shalt not blaspheme the name of God.

3. Thou shalt not murder.

4. Thou shalt not commit forbidden sexual practices.

5. Thou shalt not steal.

6. Thou shalt not eat meat from a limb severed from an animal that is living.

7. Thou shalt live in a society which sets up courts of justice. (*b. Sanhedrin* 56a)

EXCEPTIONS TO THE LAWS

As the following teachings taken from the Talmud and the Mishnah demonstrate, there are overriding laws, both those that must be observed which might cause one to violate one of the 613 laws given in the Torah, and those which must be observed, even if it violates these exceptions.

> "There is no action that can stand before saving life, in precedence, except: idolatry, forbidden sexual transgressions and murder." (*b. Ketubot* 19a)

> "In all other laws of the Torah, if a person is commanded, 'You must break this law or suffer death,' that one must transgress [the law of the Torah and live], except in the case of idolatry, forbidden sexual trnasgressions and murder." (*b. Sanhedrin* 74a)

The three exceptions to the principle of saving life—a principle which must be upheld even if it means one's own death—are:

1. Idolatry;

2. Murder;

3. Forbidden sexual transgressions.

HOLY DAYS IN THE JEWISH CALENDAR

There are sacred days which are to be celebrated in Judaism. Many months have such a sacred day of commemoration, a high holy (sacred) day set aside for special activities and celebration. Below is the Hebrew name of each month followed by the names of the various sacred days that fall within that month. In addition, one day each week is a sacred day. The Sabbath is discussed below this calendar.

The Jewish Calendar

Tishrei [alternate English spelling, *Tishri*] (September–October)	Holy Days: New Year (Rosh Hashanah), Day of Atonement (Yom Kippur), Feast of Tabernacles (Sukkot)
Cheshvan [alternate English spelling, *Heshvan*] (October–November)	There are no Holy Days
Kislev (November–December)	Holy Day: Feast of Dedication (Hanukhah)
Tevet [alternate English spelling, *Tebet*] (December–January)	Holy Days: The Fast on the 10th of *Tevet*
Shvat [alternate English spelling, *Shevat*] (January–February)	Commemoration: The 15th of *Shvat* (*Tu Beshvat*)
Adar (February–March)	Holy Day: The Feast of Esther (Purim)
	*Adar Sheni** (February–March) Holy Day: The Feast of Esther (Purim)
Nisan (March–April)	Holy Day: The Feast of Passover (Pesach); Modern Commemoration: Holocaust Memorial Day (*Yom Hashoah*)
Iyar (April–May)	Modern Commemoration: Israel Independence Day (*Yom Haatzmaut*)
Sivan (May–June)	Holy Day: The Feast of Pentecost (*Shavuot*)
Tammuz (June–July)	Holy Day: Fast of the 17th of Tammuz

Av (July–August)   Holy Day: Fast of the 9th of *Av* (*Tisha Beav*) (Tishah-b'Ab)

Elul (August–September)   Month dedicated to Prayer in order to start New Year

*Literally Second Adar, for "leap month" which occurs in seven years out of nineteen.

In addition to these sacred periods and days, within Judaism, the Sabbath is set apart for special observance. It begins every Friday night at sundown and lasts through Saturday until nightfall. The major Jewish holy days listed above are commanded in the Bible and are found in Lev 23:1–44 and Deut 16:1–16. The commandment for the Sabbath is a refuge in time that provides a paradigm for the other Jewish commemorations during the liturgical year and is found in the Ten Commandments (Exod 20:8–11; Deut 5:12–15).[1] A Torah portion (*parashah*) is read in the synagogue every Sabbath. The entire Pentateuch will be read, passage by passage, over the period of a year.

THE DAVIDIC LINEAGE OF THE PRESIDING LEADER OF THE GREAT SANHEDRIN

Jewish tradition holds that the lineage of the rabbis descends from the great and righteous King of Israel, David, son of Jesse, of the tribe of Judah. It is held to be as follows:

King David (died ca. 970 B.C.E.)

Rabban Hillel the Elder (20 B.C.E.–20 C.E.)

The Tannaitic Period

Rabban Simeon (ca. 20–25 C.E.)
Rabban Gamaliel the Elder (25–65 C.E.)
Rabban Simeon ben Gamaliel I (65–85 C.E.)

Destruction of the Temple in 70 C.E.

(Rabban Yochanan ben Zakhai acted for a time as Presiding Leader after 70 C.E.)
Rabban Gamaliel of Yavneh (85–114 C.E.)*

---

[1] See also Michael Strassfeld, *The Jewish Holidays* (New York: Harper & Row, 1985).

Bar Kokhba Revolt in 132–135 C.E.

> Rabban Simeon ben Gamaliel II (150–180 C.E.)
> Rabbi Judah the Prince (180–220 C.E.)

Compilation of the Mishnah 220 C.E.

The Amoraic Period

> Gamaliel III (220–235 C.E.)
> Judah Nesiah II (235–255 C.E.)
> Gamaliel IV (255–285 C.E.)
> Judah III (285–305 C.E.)
> Hillel II (305–355 C.E.)
> Gamaliel V (355–380 C.E.)
> Judah IV (380–395 C.E.)
> Gamaliel VI (395–425 C.E.)

The End of the Patriarchate

> (For a time, Rabban Gamaliel of Yavneh was deposed and replaced by Rabbi Eleazar ben Azaryah. He was later reinstated.)

Dancing with God

During the Holocaust, a group of young Jews were about to be sent to the gas chamber in Auschwitz. The Nazis had put them in an adjacent room where the Jews' ornaments and clothes were taken and the valuable gold teeth were removed from their mouths.

While they were waiting for what would happen some of these young Jewish men remembered that it was Simhat Torah [rejoicing over the gift of Torah] that day. "It's Simhat Torah," they said, "so we have to rejoice! We don't have a Torah scroll to dance with, we don't even have a printed copy of the Five Books of Moses or a prayer book with us. But the Creator of the world is with us, so we can dance with Him!"

They all began to dance, so to speak with God Himself.

> Y. Buxbaum, *Jewish Tales of Mystic Joy* (San Francisco: Jossey-Bass, 2002), 162.

Glossary of Terms

Agadah   Hebrew term meaning "storytelling." It is the name given to the story sections of the Talmud and midrash. Whatever is not midrash or Halakhah, is Agadah. Agadic teachings may contain stories, anecdotes, legends, folklore, parables, and maxims. Other spellings are *aggadah, haggadah,* and *agada.*

Amidah   Hebrew term meaning "standing." It refers to the prayer that is prayed while standing. This is "the Prayer" made up of eighteen benedictions. The Amidah is also called the *Shemoneh Esreh* ("Eighteen") prayer, and is prayed three times a day.

Amora   Hebrew and Aramaic term meaning "speaker, interpreter" (plural, *Amoraim,* adjectival form, *Amoraic*). It refers to the person who loudly repeated the teaching of the sage as he spoke to the students in the academy. The term is also applied to the post-Mishnaic scholars (from 220 C.E. to about 500 C.E.). They were influential in writing the Gemara in the Talmud.

Amoraic Period   The period of post-Mishnaic scholarly activity from approximately 220 C.E. to about 500 C.E.

Amoraic Midrash   A commentary from the Amoraic period, when midrashic activity reached its zenith. The teachings in the Amoraic midrash often start with a *proem,* or "introductory text," from the Psalms, lead into a teaching from the Torah, and conclude with a message from the prophets.

Baraita   Hebrew and Aramaic term meaning "outside" (plural, *Baraitot*). These are sayings and teachings of the Tannaim that were not incorporated into the Mishnah but were included in later sources, such as the Tosefta, Tannaitic midrashim, and even the Talmuds.

Bet [Beit] Din   Hebrew term meaning "House of Law" (plural, *Batei Din*). It is the rabbinic court of law.

Bet [Beit] Midrash   Hebrew term meaning "House of Study" (plural, *Batei Midrash*). It is the college or academy for higher rabbinic studies.

Exegesis   Based on the Greek terms *ex* and *ago,* which together mean "to lead out," and refers to Bible commentary and correct interpretation. The interpreter leads out the proper meaning of a text of Scripture. Adjectival form is *exegetical.*

Gemara   Hebrew and Aramaic term meaning "completion, study of tradition." A commentary on the Mishnah contained in the Talmud, the Gemara was written by the Amoraim and appears in both the Babylonian and Jerusalem Talmuds.

Halakhah   Hebrew term meaning "walk, manner of conduct" (plural, *halakhot*). It refers to how one walks or conducts one's life. It can mean a legal decision on a matter of religious law itself, as recorded in the Mishnah and Talmud. The adjectival form is *halakhic* and means "according to (Jewish) law."

Homily   A sermon or exposition usually intended to teach a moral lesson. A homily may contain stories, illustrations, and discussions of Jewish law.

Midrash   Hebrew term meaning "Bible commentary, sermon on Scripture" (plural, *midrashim*). A collection of rabbinic expositions that interpret the Bible in order to bring out legal or moral truths. Adjectival form is *midrashic.*

Midrashe Halakhah   The Tannaitic midrashim based upon four books of the Pentateuch: Exodus, Leviticus, Numbers, and Deuteronomy. These biblical expositions are the foundation of Oral Torah, and they seek to mine the deeper meaning of the way one should live as revealed in the Bible. (See "Tannaitic Midrash")

Mishnah   The *oral law* that was memorized. Rabbi Judah Ha-Nasi edited this collection of laws into six divisions and sixty-three tractates.

Mishnayot   The plural form of *Mishnah.* Mishnayot are the individual religious laws or codes of conduct in the *oral tradition.* A synonym for *mishnayah* (singular form of *mishnayot*) is *halakhah.*

Mishnaic Period   The time from about 20 B.C.E. to 220 C.E. This was for the era of the Tannaim sages.

Oral Law   A synonym of Oral Torah.

Oral Torah   The second Torah, revealed to Moses on Mount Sinai, which explained and interpreted the Written Torah. The collection of laws passed from generation to generation in oral form. A synonym of *oral tradition* or Oral Torah.

Oral Tradition   A synonym of Oral Torah.

Pharisees   The term is probably derived from the meaning "to be set apart, or separate." It refers to the pious group of sages from the Second Temple period who believed in the Oral Torah. They were often involved in disputes with the Sadducees. The rabbis were the successors to the Pharisees.

Pilpul   A type of Talmudic discussion using dialectic argument, legal casuistry, sophisticated case analysis, and hypothetical possibilities. *Pilpul* is derived from the Hebrew word meaning "pepper."

Rabban   The title given to the heads of the Sanhedrin during the Mishnaic and Talmudic periods from the second to the sixth centuries C.E.

Rabbi(s)   The word *rabbi* actually means "my teacher, who has great learning" (in Hebrew, *rab* means "great"). These were the spiritual heirs of the Pharisees. In Talmudic times this title was given to sages in the land of Israel when they were ordained for service. The Babylonian sages were called rav. The word Rabbi, or rav, is often abbreviated with R. when occurring before a name.

Rabbinic   The adjectival form of *rabbi*. It often refers to the periods of the Mishnah and Talmud, after the destruction of the Temple in 70 C.E. It also refers to literary and communal activities of the sages. It may be used in reference to the rabbinic period, rabbinic Judaism, and rabbinic literature. Already in the New Testament Jesus is called Rabboni, meaning "my teacher" (John 20:16). In Jesus' day it was a polite address or title of honor and esteem. Judah ben Bava laid hands on the five disciples of Rabbi Akiva, ordaining them for public service as rabbis (120 C.E.). Little is known of ordination of rabbis in antiquity. But the reference to rabbi or rabbinic refers to these scholarly community leaders. In modern times rabbis are ordained by their academies of learning for community service.

Rebbetzin   The term refers to the wife of the rabbi. She is accorded great honor for her wisdom and noble example.

Sadducees   An influential group within the Jewish people during the Second Temple period who opposed the Pharisees. They accepted only the

Written Law; they rejected the *oral law* and the authority of the sages. Almost all of the priests were Sadducees. In the New Testament, they seem to be the primary opponents of Jesus and the early Christians because of their political ties to the Roman government.

Sage   A wise teacher who was knowledgeable in all areas of Jewish law and literature. Sages preached and taught the Torah during the Talmudic and Mishnaic periods. The term may refer to both rabbis from the land of Israel as well as Babylonian ravs.

Second Temple Period   The Second Temple period begins with the dedication of the reconstructed Temple in 515 B.C.E. The exiled Jewish people returned from Babylonian captivity to their national homeland. The Temple was the place ordained in Scripture for sacrifice, worship each day, and pilgrimage festivals. It was destroyed in 70 C.E.

Shema   Meaning "hear or obey," Shema is the first Hebrew word from Deut 6:4: "Hear, O Israel, the LORD our God is one." This verse is recited along with Deut 6:5–9; 11:13–21; and Num 15:37–41 as a prayer in synagogue worship.

Siddur   Meaning "order," the term refers to the order of prayers in Jewish liturgy. The Siddur is the Daily Prayer Book. The prayers are set in Order. They must be prayed from the heart.

Synagogue   Meaning "gathering together," the term is actually from Greek and reflects the Hebrew, *Bet Keneset* or "House of Gathering." The synagogue was a place of gathering together to study Torah. Today the focus of the synagogue is more on prayer. In the Second Temple period, the focus was more on study.

Talmud   Hebrew term meaning "study." The term comes from a root word that also forms the Hebrew word for "disciple." It is a form of study and education. The Mishnah, together with its written commentary, Gemara, form the Talmud. It is the quintessential encyclopedia of Jewish knowledge. A version of the Talmud was written in Israel (Jerusalem Talmud) and in Babylon (Babylonian Talmud).

Tanna   Hebrew and Aramaic term meaning "repeater," referring to the scholar who memorized the Oral Torah and repeated the teachings for later generations. The Tannaim (plural form) flourished from the time of Hillel in 20 B.C.E. to the time of Rabbi Judah HaNasi in 220 C.E. They developed sophisticated methods for accurately preserving the Oral Torah in memory and transmitting it to the next generation.

Tannaitic Midrash   A commentary from the time of the Tannaim (20 B.C.E. to 220 C.E.). The Tannaim emphasized proper method in interpreting the Written Torah. Their interpretations greatly influenced Oral Torah and practical application of the deeper meaning of the biblical text. Their commentaries mainly deal with four books of the Pentateuch: Exodus, Leviticus, Numbers, and Deuteronomy. (See "*Midrashe Halakhah*")

Tannaitic Period   The time period from the activities of Hillel and Shammai around 20 B.C.E. to the compilation of the Mishnah in 220 C.E.

Torah   Torah is derived from the Hebrew root meaning "to reveal" or "to instruct." In reality, it has little to do with the traditional English translation of the term as "law." It is much more closely connected to God's revelation of Himself with mercy and compassion than a legal code. So Torah means "revelation" or "instruction." The Torah includes the Ten Commandments, ethical teachings, and proper conduct. Depending on the context, Torah can refer to the first five books of Moses in the Bible, but may also refer to *oral tradition*.

Written Torah   The term refers to the five books of Moses: Genesis, Exodus, Leviticus, Numbers, and Deuteronomy.

Yeshiva   Hebrew term meaning "sitting together," referring to the academy of learning where disciples of Torah would gather together to study from the sages.

Zugot   Hebrew term meaning "pairs" or "couples." The singular form of the term is *Zug*. In Jewish literature the term designates two community leaders, the presiding leader of the Sanhedrin and the Chief Magistrate of the Court. These were their functions, at least according to traditional explanations. The community leadership provided by the Zugot, however, spans a long period of history and thus their roles and functional service evolved over time. In rabbinic thought the Zugot bridge the historical gap between the Bible and the Mishnah. They originate in the period of the return to Zion under Ezra and Nehemiah and the dedication of the Second Temple in 515 B.C.E., and span the period to the beginning of the work of the Tannaim (20 B.C.E.), during the community service of Hillel and Shammai. The five Zugot mentioned in the first chapter of the *Ethics of the Fathers* therefore span the historical period from the Bible to the Tannaim.

Bibliographic Helps

ANNOTATED BIBLIOGRAPHY FOR FURTHER STUDY

Abrams, Judith. *Prayer.* Vol. 1 of *The Talmud for Beginners.* Northvale, N.J.: Jason Aronson, Inc., 1993.

————. *Text.* Vol. 2 of *The Talmud for Beginners.* Northvale, N.J.: Jason Aronson, Inc., 1993.

————. *The Women of the Talmud.* Northvale, N.J.: Jason Aronson, Inc., 1995.

Judith Abrams' gives the reader a fine start in learning how to read, study, and understand the Talmud. The texts selected for study and the organized discussions help the student apply principles of learning to other passages from the Talmud. Her consideration of women in the Talmud is of particular interest for those exploring the significance of women in Jewish life.

Bader, Gershom. *The Encyclopedia of Talmudic Sages.* Translated by Solomon Katz. Northvale, N.J.: Jason Aronson, Inc., 1988.

Gershom Bader explores the life and teachings of Talmudic leaders in a fascinating study. Students will gain a familiarity with key Talmudic figures.

Baeck, Leo. *Judaism and Christianity: Essays by Leo Baeck.* Translated by Walter Kaufmann. Philadelphia: The Jewish Publication Society of America, 1960, 5720. [The 5720 date is the time of publication based on the Jewish calendar.]

Leo Baeck was a world leader during and after World War II, and his spiritual insight will assist anyone desiring to know the true heart of Judaism. In 1948 he began teaching at Hebrew Union College and was recognized as a leading scholar in progressive Judaism. During the holocaust he became a "witness for his faith" in Theresienstadt concentration camp, where he encouraged fellow prisoners. After the war, he worked for interfaith reconciliation. This volume will be of special interest to those wanting to learn the relationship between Judaism and Christianity.

Blackman, Philip. *Mishnayoth*. 2d ed. 7 vols. Gateshead: Judaica Press, 1990.

Philip Blackman has produced a scholarly seven-volume edition of the Mishnah with the Hebrew text, lucid English translation, textual notes, and concise commentary. The supplemental volume is a rich source of information with brief biographies of leading rabbis, a glossary, specialized indexes, and numerous other study helps. This is the very best study edition of the Mishnah for the English reader ever produced.

Blech, Benjamin. *The Complete Idiot's Guide to Understanding Judaism*. New York: Alpha Books, 1999.

Benjamin Blech is an Orthodox Rabbi who wrote this volume in the popular series, "The Complete Idiot's Guide to . . ." The book assumes little knowledge and gives a broad overview of Judaism's practice, from the Bible to the present. A true scholar, Blech is able to write for the general reader in a way that is both authoritative and easy to understand.

Buxbaum, Yitzhak. *Jewish Spiritual Practices*. Northvale, N.J.: Jason Aronson, Inc., 1990.

————. *The Life and Teachings of Hillel*. Northvale, N.J.: Jason Aronson, Inc., 1994.

Yitzhak Buxbaum is a fine writer with a gift for seeing the more important aspects of Jewish life and giving them meaning. The book on Hillel's life is a must-read that not only provides access to the primary sources but also brings out the spiritual meaning and application of the texts.

Cohen, Abraham. *Everyman's Talmud: The Major Teachings of the Sages*. New York: Schocken Books, 1975.

Abraham Cohen's book has become a classic for anyone desiring to learn about the Talmud. If you read only one book on the Talmud, this is probably the one you should select for study and reflection. Though the book is old and dated, it retains its relevance and is a joy to read.

Danby, Herbert. *The Mishnah*. New York: Oxford University Press, 1977.

Herbert Danby's English translation of the Mishnah is an excellent work of scholarship that will be an invaluable reference tool for serious students.

Flusser, David. *Jesus.* Jerusalem: Magnes, 1997.

For readers desiring a better understanding of Jesus' place in Second Temple period Judaism, David Flusser's research and analysis of the primary source material, from the perspective of this world-class scholar, will be a worthy investment of time and energy.

Guttman, Alexander. *Rabbinic Judaism in the Making: A Chapter in the History of the Halakhah from Ezra to Judah I.* Detroit: Wayne State University Press, 1970.

Though this book was written for scholars and teachers of Judaism, it is a very helpful introduction to the primary sources from the perspective of a progressive Judaism scholar.

Hertz, Joseph H. *The Authorized Daily Prayer Book.* New York: Bloch, 1985.

Rabbi Hertz served the Jewish communities in Great Britain and has produced outstanding works of scholarship. The Siddur, or Daily Prayer Book, is one of the very best places to begin a study of Jewish thought, faith, and action. This edition provides the Hebrew text of the prayers, a fine English translation, and insightful commentary. The notes are very informative and go into more detail than the concise commentary most other Jewish prayer books provide. Nonetheless, each Jewish prayer book is a treasure store of information that will reveal so much about the practice of Judaism throughout history. Everyone needs to study the prayer book.

Heschel, Abraham Joshua. *God in Search of Man: A Philosophy of Judaism.* Northvale, N.J.: Jason Aronson, 1987.

Abraham Joshua Heschel's book is a must-read for anyone desiring to understand the character of God as revealed in the Bible. Heschel is a powerful author who is profoundly knowledgeable in every area of Jewish learning but he is also a deeply spiritual person who penetrates the meaning of the text with an over arching theology and philosophy of Judaism. His writings have had a remarkable impact upon Christian theologians. An activist, Heschel did not merely write about his beliefs, he took to the streets and marched with Dr. Martin Luther King Jr. to campaign for civil rights. Heschel illuminates Jewish thought, rabbinic literature, anthropology, theology, philosophy, and the true nature of God's commandments.

———. *Heavenly Torah as Refracted through the Generations.* Edited and Translated by Gordon Tucker with Leonard Levin. 3 vols. New York: Continuum, 2005.

In my opinion, this is Heschel's greatest book and perhaps the finest introduction to Jewish thought and spirituality ever written. The three-volume set was translated from Hebrew into English and published in 2005. Readers will be led along a path into the heart of rabbinic Judaism. The deep spirituality of the rabbis emerges from this engaging work of excellent scholarship.

Jungreis, Esther Rebbetzin. *The Committed Life: Principles for Good Living from Our Timeless Past.* New York: Harper Collins, 1998.

Esther Jungreis is a holocaust survivor, as well as the daughter of a highly esteemed rabbi and the widow of a rabbi who died of cancer. Her book is an inspirational account of her experiences, along with Torah study, and the application of Talmud in an Orthodox woman's life. Her book is an easy read and very educational for learning the way of life practiced by the religious Jewish faithful. She shows how the wisdom of the Talmud is practiced in daily living.

Katz, Michael, and Gershon Schwartz. *Swimming the Sea of Talmud: Lessons for Everyday Living.* Philadelphia: The Jewish Publication Society, 1998.

This is one of the finest introductions for the basic study of the Talmud available today. Katz and Schwartz give selections from the major divisions of the Talmud and guide the learner through an interactive study approach.

Kolatch, Alfred. *Masters of the Talmud: Their Lives and Views.* Middle Village, N.Y.: Jonathan David Publishers, 2003.

Rabbi Kolatch writes popular books for the general reader on Jewish themes. This book is a scholarly treatment of the life and teachings of important rabbis in the Talmud. The book also gives pertinent information about the contents, make-up, and design of the rabbinic literature in an eighty-page introduction on the origin and development of the Talmud.

Neusner, Jacob. *Dictionary of Ancient Rabbis: Selections from the Jewish Encyclopaedia.* Peabody, Mass.: Hendrickson, 2003.

This dictionary is an informative reference work, especially for the general reader who does not have the *Jewish Encyclopaedia* or the *Encyclopaedia Judaica* readily available. This dictionary collects biographies of the rabbis mentioned in rabbinic literature from the *Jewish Encyclopedia.* The *Jewish Encyclopaedia* is an incredible piece of scholarship. Some of these biographies on rabbis in the Talmud were written by Wilhem Bacher, one of the greatest rabbinic scholars of all time. The reader will discover references to the primary sources from the Talmudic literature in the biographical sketches and a basic outline for the life of many of the teachers. Neusner provides a critical preface to the collection that will introduce the reader to his post-modern school of interpretation.

Parry, Aaron. *The Complete Idiot's Guide to The Talmud.* Indianapolis: Alpha Books, 2004.

Aaron Parry covers the main themes of Talmud study in this popular book in the "Complete Idiot's Guide to . . ." series, which is written for the reader with little or no prior knowledge. He not only covers the Talmud but also discusses current issues of public discourse, such as cloning and abortion, as well as touching upon Jewish mysticism and spirituality.

Pearl, Chaim. *Theology in Rabbinic Stories.* Peabody, Mass.: Hendrickson, 1997.

Chaim Pearl has produced a delightful book exploring rabbinic theology based upon story narratives. The stories he selects are illustrative of the spiritual themes that he treats for developing a concise theology of Judaism. Everyone will enjoy his insightful overview of Jewish theology in rabbinic story.

Robinson, George. *Essential Torah: A Complete Guide to the Five Books of Moses.* New York: Schocken Books, 2006.

George Robinson is a New York film critic who has used his ability as a writer to explain and introduce Judaism to a wide spectrum of interested readers. His earlier book, *Essential Judaism,* introduced the world of the synagogue and now his *Essential Torah* gives fresh insight into the meaning of the biblical text which is the foundation of Jewish practice.

Safrai, Shumel, ed. *The Literature of the Sages.* Philadelphia: Fortress, 1987.

Shumel Safrai was a Talmudic genius and brilliant Jewish historian. This is one of the most comprehensive and in-depth works of scholarship dealing with the rabbinic literature ever produced. The book is written for scholars, but all serious students and general readers will gain much insight from Safrai's sound scholarship.

Schiffman, Lawrence. *From Text to Tradition: A History of Second Temple and Rabbinic Judaism.* Hoboken, N.J.: KTAV, 1991.

Lawrence Schiffman's book is especially helpful in understanding the history and development of Jewish thought. He gives an historical overview from the Bible to the Talmud, examining the most important issues.

Steinsaltz, Adin. *The Essential Talmud.* Translated by Chaya Galai. New York: Basic Books, 1976.

Adin Steinsaltz is one of the foremost orthodox Talmudic scholars today, having written commentary and lucid explanations for the entire encyclopedic text of the Babylonian Talmud. This is his perceptive introduction for the general reader. His breadth of knowledge and solid scholarship will be of great help for everyone who studies his work.

———. *The Talmud: The Steinsaltz Edition: A Reference Guide.* New York: Random House, 1989.

This book is Steinsaltz's reference guide for the entire Talmud series he produced, first in Modern Hebrew, and now, volume by volume, in English. This is one of the most helpful books available for the reader who wants to study the Talmud and learn how to interpret the text with sound scholarly method. It is a must for the serious student of the Talmud, and a valuable reference tool for the general reader.

Strack, Hermann L., and Günter Stemberger. *Introduction to the Talmud and Midrash.* Translated by Markus Bockmuehl. Edinburgh: T&T Clark, 1991.

Herman Strack produced one of the best systematic treatments of the Talmud and midrash in 1887. Günter Stemberger has updated this classic introduction and discussed the current critical editions of rabbinic texts. This is a well-organized introductory study and an unparalleled reference guide for the serious student.

Telushkin, Joseph. *Jewish Wisdom: Ethical, Spiritual, and Historical Lessons from the Great Works and Thinkers.* New York: William Morrow & Co., 1994.

Rabbi Joseph Telushkin is a gifted communicator who can summarize the main points of rabbinic teachings in the Talmud and make practical application that will benefit all readers, Jewish and non-Jewish alike. This book on Jewish wisdom quotes from a wide spectrum of primary sources. The texts are interpreted in light of a comprehensive theology and thought-provoking wit, with an eye toward how Talmudic values can enhance one's life in practical ways. Readers will enjoy other works by Rabbi Telushkin, as well.

Trepp, Leo. *The Complete Book of Jewish Observance: A Practical Manual for the Modern Jew.* New York: Behrman House/Summit Books, 1980.

Leo Trepp has produced a very readable guide for anyone desiring to apply Talmudic wisdom for everyday living. It answers many questions the general reader has about keeping the commandments in a religious Jewish household, such as how to observe the Sabbath and Jewish holidays, and keep a kosher kitchen.

Wilson, Marvin H. *Our Father Abraham: Jewish Roots of the Christian Faith.* Grand Rapids: Eerdmans, 1989.

Marvin Wilson is an evangelical scholar who has pioneered meaningful dialogue with the Jewish community. His book lays the biblical foundation of Christian faith and explores the Jewish roots of the New Testament. This book has become a classic and is a must read for anyone who desires to understand the continuity between the Old and New Testaments in Christian experience.

Witty, Abraham, and Rachel J. Witty. *Exploring Jewish Tradition: A Transliterated Guide to Everyday Practice and Observance.* New York: Doubleday, 2001.

Rabbi and Rebbetzin Witty have written an engaging account of Jewish tradition that explores the wisdom of the rabbinic literature. Their well-written overview provides an insightful analysis of the Bible, Talmudic sources, the Prayer Book, life-cycle events, Jewish holidays, and religious observance from the past to the present.

PRIMARY SOURCES, EDITIONS, AND TRANSLATIONS

Albeck, Chanoch, ed. *Mishnah.* 6 vols. Jerusalem: Bialik Institute, 1978.

Albeck, Chanoch, and Julius Theodor, eds. *Midrash Bereshit Rabbah.* 3 vols. Jerusalem: Wahrmann, 1965.

Black, Matthew. *The Book of Enoch.* Leiden: Brill, 1985.

Blackman, Philip, ed. and trans. *Mishnayoth.* 7 vols. New York: Judaica, 1990.

Braude, William G. *The Midrash on Psalms.* 2 vols. New Haven: Yale University Press, 1959.

———. *Pesikta Rabbati.* 2 vols. New Haven: Yale University Press, 1968.

———. *Tanna Debe Eliyyahu.* Philadelphia: Jewish Publication Society, 1981.

Braude, William G., and Israel Kapstein. *Pesikta de Rab Kahana.* Philadelphia: Jewish Publication Society, 1975.

Buber, Salomon, ed. *Midrash Ekha Rabbah.* Wilna, Lithuania: Wittwa & Gebrüder Romm, 1899.

———. *Midrash Lekach Tov.* Wilna, Lithuania: Wittwa & Gebrüder Romm, 1880.

———. *Midrash Mishle.* Wilna, Lithuania: Wittwa & Gebrüder Romm, 1891.

———. *Midrash Shemuel.* Cracow: Joseph Fischer, 1893.

———. *Midrash Tanchuma.* Wilna, Lithuania: Wittwa & Gebrüder Romm, 1885.

———. *Midrash Tehilim.* Wilna, Lithuania: Wittwa & Gebrüder Romm, 1891.

———. *Pesikta Derav Kahana.* Elk, Poland: L. Silbermann, 1868.

———. *Yalkut Hamakiri.* Berdyczew, Ukraine: Ch. J. Schefftel, 1899.

Charles, Robert H., ed. *The Apocrypha and Pseudepigrapha of the Old Testament.* 2 vols. Oxford: Clarendon, 1998.

Charlesworth, James. H., ed. *The Old Testament Pseudepigrapha.* 2 vols. Garden City, N.Y.: Doubleday, 1983–1985.

Clark, E. G. *Targum Pseudo-Jonathan of the Prophets.* Hoboken, N.J.: KTAV, 1984.

Cohen, Abraham. *Midrash Rabbah.* 13 vols. London: Soncino, 1939.

Cohen, Abraham, and Israel Brodie, eds. *The Minor Tractates of the Talmud.* 2 vols. London: Soncino, 1971.

Diez Macho, Alejandro. *Neophyti I.* 6 vols. Text and translations into Spanish, French, and English. Madrid: Consejo Superior de Investigaciones Cientificas, 1968–1979.

Donski, Shimshon, ed. *Midrash Shir Hashirim Rabbah.* Tel Aviv: Davir, 1980.

Eisenstein, Judah D., ed. *Otzav Midrashim.* 2 vols. Jerusalem: Hillel, 1969.

Epstein, Isidore, ed. *The Babylonian Talmud.* 35 vols. London: Soncino, 1935–1978.

Epstein, Jacob N., and Ezra Z. Melamed, eds. *Mekilta Derabbi Shimeon Bar Yochai.* Jerusalem: Hillel, 1980.

Finkelstein, Louis, ed. *Sifra.* 5 vols. New York: Jewish Theological Seminary, 1984.

———. *Sifre Devarim.* New York: Jewish Theological Seminary, 1969.

Freedman, Harry, and Maurice Simon, eds. *Midrash Rabbah.* 9 vols. London: Soncino, 1951.

Friedlander, Gerald. *Pirke de Rabbi Eliezer.* New York: Hermon, 1981.

Friedmann, Meir, ed. *Mekhilta Derabbi Ishmael.* n.p. 1870. Repr., Jerusalem: Old City, 1978.

———. *Pesikta Rabbati.* Vienna: Josef Kaiser, 1880.

———. *Seder Eliyahu Rabbah.* Jerusalem: Wahrmann, 1969.

———. *Sifra* (incomplete). 1915. Repr., Jerusalem: Old City, 1978.

————. *Sifre Debe Rav.* Vienna: Be-hosta'ot ha-motsi le-or uvi–defus Holtsvorth,1864. Repr., Jerusalem: Old City, 1978.

Gaster, Theodor H. *The Dead Sea Scriptures.* New York: Anchor, 1976.

Goldin, Judah. *The Fathers According to Rabbi Nathan.* New Haven: Yale University Press, 1955.

Goldschmidt, Ernest D. *Machazor Leyamin Noraim.* New York: Leo Black Institute, 1970.

Goldschmidt, S. *Seder Haselichot.* Jerusalem: Mosad Derav Kook, 1975.

Goldwurm, H. *Schottenstein Edition Talmud Bavli.* 73 vols. New York: Masorah Publications, 2000.

Grant, Robert M. *Miracle and Natural Law in Graeco-Roman and Early Christian Thought.* Amsterdam: North Holland, 1952.

Greenup, Albert W., ed. *Yalkut Hamakiri.* Jerusalem: Hameitar, 1968.

Grunhut, Eliezer Halevi, ed. *Midrash Shir Hashirim.* Jerusalem: n.p., 1897.

Guggenheimer, H. *The Jerusalem Talmud.* Berlin: de Gruyter, 2005.

Haberman, A. *Megillot Midbar Yehuda.* Tel Aviv: Machbarot Lesifrut, 1959.

Hammer, Reuven. *The Classic Midrash: Tannaitic Commentaries on the Bible.* New York: Paulist, 1995.

————. *Sifre: A Tannaitic Commentary on the Book of Deuteronomy.* New Haven: Yale University Press, 1986.

Herford, R. Travers. *Pirke Aboth: The Ethics of the Talmud: Sayings of the Fathers.* New York: Schocken, 1975.

Higger, Michael. *Masechet Sofrim.* Jerusalem: Makor, 1970.

————. *Masechtot Kallah.* Jerusalem: Makor, 1970.

————. *Massekhtot Derekh Eretz.* 2 vols. New York: Moinester, 1935.

————. *Otzar Habaraitot.* 10 vols. New York: Shulsinger, 1938.

————. *Treatise Semahot.* New York: Bloch, 1931.

Higger, Michael, ed. *Masekhet Semachot.* Jerusalem: Makor, 1970.

Hoffmann, D., ed. *Midrash Tannaim.* Berlin: Defus T. H. Ittskovski, 1909. Repr., Jerusalem: Books Export, n.d.

Hollander, Harm W., and Marinus de Jonge. *The Testaments of the Twelve Patriarchs: A Commentary.* Leiden: Brill, 1985.

Horovitz, Hayyim S., ed. *Sifre Al Bemidbar Vesifre Zuta.* Jerusalem: Wahrmann, 1966.

Horovitz, Hayyim S., and Ch. Rabin, eds. *Mekhilta Derabbi Ishmael.* Jerusalem: Wahrmann, 1970.

Horst, Pieter W. van der. *The Sentences of Pseudo-Phocylides.* Leiden: Brill, 1978.

Hyman, Aaron. *Torah Haketubah Vehmasurah.* 3 vols. Tel Aviv: Davir, 1979.

————. *Toldoth Tannaim Veamoraim.* 3 vols. Jerusalem: Boys Town, 1964.

James, Montague R. *The Apocryphal New Testament.* Oxford: Clarendon, 1924.

Jellinek, Aharon, ed. *Bet Hamidrash*. Jerusalem: Wahrmann, 1967.

Josephus. Translated by H. St. J. Thackeray et al. 10 vols. Loeb Classical Library. Cambridge: Harvard University Press, 1926–65.

Kasher, Menahem, ed. *Torah Shelemah*. 45 vols. New York: Talmud Institute, 1951–1992.

Kister, Menahem. *Avoth de-Rabbi Nathan*. Jerusalem: Jewish Theological Society, 2005.

Klein, Michael L. *The Fragment-Targums of the Pentateuch*. 2 vols. Rome: Pontifical Biblical Institute, 1980.

———. *The Geniza Manuscript of the Palestinian Targum to the Pentateuch*. 2 vols. Jerusalem: Hebrew Union College Press, 1986.

Lauterbach, Jacob, ed. and trans. *Mekhilta Derabbi Ishmael*. Jacob. 3 vols. Philadelphia: Jewish Publication Society, 1976.

Lerner, M., ed. "Midrash Rut Rabbah." PhD diss. Hebrew University, Jerusalem, 1971.

Levertoff, Paul trans. *Midrash Sifre on Numbers*. London: SPCK, 1926.

Licht, Jacob. *Megilat Hahodayot*. Jerusalem: Bialik Institute, 1957.

———. *Megilat Haserachim*. Jerusalem: Bialik Institute, 1965.

Liebermann, Saul, ed. *Midrash Devarim Rabbah*. Jerusalem: Wahrmann, 1974.

———. *Tosefta Kefushutah*. 15 vols. New York: Jewish Theological Seminary, 1955–1977.

Luria, David, ed. *Pirke Derabbi Eliezer*. Warsaw: Bomberg, 1852.

Mandelbaum, B., ed. *Pesikta Derav Kahana*. New York: Jewish Theological Seminary, 1962.

Margulies, Mordecai, ed. *Midrash Hagadol*. 5 vols. Jerusalem: Mosad Harav Kook, 1975.

———, ed. *Midrash Vayikra Rabbah*. 5 vols. Jerusalem: Wahrmann, 1979.

Midrash Rabbah. 2 vols. Wilna, Lithuania: Wittwa & Gebrüder Romm, 1887.

Midrash Tanchuma. Lublin: Bi-defus Y. Hershenhorn [u]-M Shnaydmesir, 1879. Repr., Jerusalem: Lewin-Epstein, 1975.

Mirkin, Moshe, ed. *Midrash Rabbah*. 11 vols. Tel Aviv: Yavneh, 1977.

Mishnah Torah. Jerusalem: Mosad Derav Kook, 1986.

Nelson, D. *Mekhilta De-rabbi Shimon Bar Yochai*. Philadelphia: Jewish Publication Society, 2006.

Neusner, Jacob, trans. *Sifra: An Analytical Translation*. 3 vols. Atlanta: Scholars, 1985.

———. *Sifre to Numbers*. 2 vols. Atlanta: Scholars, 1986.

———. *The Talmud of the Land of Israel*. Chicago: University of Chicago Press, 1984.

————. *The Tosefta.* New York: KTAV, 1981. Repr., Peabody, Mass.: Hendrickson, 2002.

Pearl, Chaim, Hayyim N. Bialik, and Yehoshua H. Rawnitzky. *Sefer Ha-aggadah: The Book of Jewish Folklore and Legend.* Tel Aviv: Dvir, 1988.

Philo. Translated by Francis H. Colson and George H. Whitaker. 10 vols. and 2 supps. Loeb Classical Library. Cambridge: Harvard University Press, 1981.

Rabbenu Hillel, ed. *Sifra Debe Rav Hu Sefer Torah Kohanim.* Jerusalem: Schachne Koleditzky, 1971.

Raskin, Saul. *Pirke Aboth.* New York: Academy of Photo Offset, 1940.

Ratner, Dov B., ed. *Midrash Seder Olam.* New York: Talmudic Research Institute, 1966.

Reed, Stephen A., Marilyn J. Lundberg, Emanuel Tov, and Stephen J. Pfann, eds. *The Dead Sea Scrolls on Microfiche.* Leiden: Brill, 1993.

Rieder, D. *Targum Jonathan ben Uzziel.* 2 vols. Jerusalem: Naveh Simchah, 1984–1985.

Saldarini, Anthony J. *The Fathers according to Rabbi Nathan.* Leiden: Brill, 1975.

Schechter, Solomon, ed. *Aboth de Rabbi Nathan.* Vienna: Lippe, 1887.

Schmidt, Francis. *Le Testament grec d'Abraham.* Tübingen: J. C. B. Mohr, 1986.

Segal, Moses H. *Sefer Ben Sira Hashalem.* Jerusalem: Bialik Institute, 1972.

Shapiro, Y. ed. *Yalkut Hamakiri.* Jerusalem: Makor, 1964.

Shinan, Avigdor. *Midrash Shemot Rabbah.* Jerusalem: Dvir, 1984.

Sperber, Alexander. *The Bible in Aramaic.* 5 vols. Leiden: Brill, 1959–1968.

Steinberger, Avraham, ed. *Midrash Rabbah Hamevuar.* Jerusalem: Hanachal, 1983.

Steinsaltz, Adin. *The Talmud.* New York: Random House, 1989.

Stone, Michael, trans. *The Testament of Abraham: The Greek Recensions.* Missoula, Mont.: Society of Biblical Literature, 1972.

Sussman, Yaacov. *Talmud Yerushalmi.* Jerusalem: Hebrew Language Academy, 2001.

Tal, Abraham. *The Samaritan Targum of the Pentateuch.* Tel Aviv: Tel Aviv University Press, 1980.

Tal, Shlomo, *Machazor Rinat Israel.* Jerusalem: Yad Shapira, 1982.

Talmud Babli. Wilna, Lithuania: Wittwa & Gebrüder Romm, 1835.

Talmud Jerushalmi. Krotoshin, Poland: Dov Baer Monash, 1866.

Taylor, Charles. *Sayings of the Jewish Fathers.* 2 vols. Cambridge: Cambridge University Press, 1877.

Vermes, Geza. *The Complete Dead Sea Scrolls in English.* New York: Penguin, 2004.

Visotzky, Burton. *The Midrash on Proverbs.* New Haven: Yale University Press, 1992.
Visotzky, Burton, ed. *Midrash Mishle.* New York: Jewish Theological Seminary, 1990.
Wacholder, Ben Zion, and Martin G. Abegg. *A Preliminary Edition of the Unpublished Dead Sea Scrolls.* Washington, D.C.: Biblical Archaeological Society, 1991–1995.
Weiss, Isaac H., ed. *Sifra.* Vienna: Salsberg, 1862.
Wengst, Klaus. *Schriften des Urchristentums.* Munich: Köstel, 1984.
Wertheimer, Abraham J. *Batei Midrashot.* 2 vols. Jerusalem: Ketav Vesefer, 1980.
Wertheimer, Solomon A., ed. *Batei Midrashot.* Jerusalem: Ketav Vesefer, 1980.
Yalkut Shimoni. Wilna, Lithuania: Wittwa & Gebrüder Romm, 1898.
Zlotnick, Dov. *The Tractate Mourning.* New Haven: Yale University Press, 1966.
Zuckermandel, Moses, ed. *Tosefta.* Jerusalem: Wahrmann, 1937.

GENERAL BIBLIOGRAPHY

Abrahams, Israel. *Studies in Pharisaism and the Gospels.* Series 1. New York: KTAV, 1967.
Adams, Charles F. *Mahatma Gandhi's Ideas.* New York: Macmillan, 1930.
Alon, Gedalia. *The Jews in Their Land in the Talmudic Age.* 2 vols. Jerusalem: Magnes, 1980–1984.
Bacher, Wilhelm. *Die Agada der Palästinischen Amoräer.* 3 vols. Strassburg: Karl Tübner, 1892–1899. [Translated into Hebrew by Alexander Rabinovitz. *Agadot Amore Eretz Israel.* Jerusalem: Davir, 1926.]
———. *Die Agada der Tannaiten.* Strassburg: Karl Tübner, 1890. Translated into Hebrew by Alexander Rabinovitz. *Agadot Hatannaim.* Jerusalem: Davir, 1919.
———. *Die Exegetische Ternlinologie der jüdischen Traditionsliteratur.* Leipzig: Hinrich, 1905. Translated into Hebrew by Alexander Rabinovitz. *Erche Midrash.* Jerusalem: Carmiel, 1970.
———. *Tradition und Tradenten.* Leipzig: Gustav Fock, 1914.
Betz, Hans. D. *The Sermon on the Mount.* Minneapolis: Fortress, 1995.
Bialik, C., and J. Rabnitzki. *Sefer Haagadah.* Tel Aviv: Davir, 1973.
Bickerman, Elias. *The Jews in the Greek Age.* New York: Jewish Theological Seminary, 1988.
Binder, Donald D. *Into the Temple Courts: the Place of the Synagogue in the Second Temple Period.* Atlanta: Society of Biblical Literature, 1999.

Bivin, David. "'And' or 'in order to' Remarry." *Jerusalem Perspective* 50 (1996): 10–17.

———. *New Light on the Difficult Words of Jesus.* Holland, Mich.: En-Gedi Resource Center, 2005.

Bivin, David, and Roy Blizzard. *Understanding the Difficult Words of Jesus.* Arcadia, Calif.: Makor Foundation, 1983.

Black, Matthew. *An Aramaic Approach to the Gospels and Acts.* 3d ed. Oxford: Clarendon, 1967. Repr., Peabody, Mass.: Hendrickson, 1998.

Bleich, J. David. *With Perfect Faith: The Foundation of Jewish Belief.* New York: KTAV, 1983.

Borgen, Peder and Søren Giversen, eds. *The New Testament and Hellenistic Judaism.* Peabody, Mass.: Hendrickson, 1997.

Boring, M. Eugene, Klaus Berger, and Carsten Colpe. *Hellenistic Commentary to the New Testament.* Nashville: Abingdon, 1995.

Boteach, Shumely. *Judaism for Everyone: Renewing your Life through the Vibrant Lesson of the Jewish Faith.* New York: Basic Books, 2002.

Bowker, John. *Jesus and the Pharisees.* Cambridge: Cambridge University Press, 1973.

Braun, Shony Alex. *My Heart Is a Violin.* Los Angeles: Shony Music, 2003.

Breuer, Mordechai, and Raphael Jospe, *Keter Crown Bible.* N.Y.: Feldheim, 2004.

Brown, Raymond E. *The Birth of the Messiah: A Commentary on the Infancy Narratives in Matthew and Luke.* New York: Doubleday, 1977.

Buber, Martin, with afterword by David Flusser. *Two Types of Faith.* New York: Syracuse University Press, 2003.

Büchler, A. "Learning and Teaching in the Open Air in Palestine," *Jewish Quarterly Review* 4 (1914): 485ff.

———. *Die Priester und der Cultus im letzten Jahrzehnt des jerusalemischen Tempels.* Vienna; Holder, 1895.

———. *Types of Jewish-Palestinian Piety for 70 B.C.E. to 70 C.E.* London: Jews' College Press, 1922.

Bultmann, Rudolf. *History of the Synoptic Tradition.* Rev. ed. Peabody, Mass.: Hendrickson, 1994. Reprint of *History of the Synoptic Tradition.* Translated by John Marsh. Oxford: Basil Blackwell, 1963. Translation of *Geschichte der Synoptischen Tradition.* Göttingen: Vandenhoeck & Ruprecht, 1921.

———. *Jesus and the Word.* 1st Scribner/Macmillian Hudson River ed. New York: Scribner, 1989. Reprint of *Jesus and the Word.* Translated by Louise Pettibone Smith and Erminie Huntress Lantero. New York: Scribner, 1934. Translation of *Jesus.* Berlin: Deutsche bibliothek, 1926.

Buth, Randall. "Luke 19:31–34, Mishnaic Hebrew and Bible Translation." *Journal of Biblical Literature* 104 (1985): 680–85.

Chajes, Zebi. H. *The Student's Guide through the Talmud.* Translated and annotated by J. Schachter. New York: Feldheim, 1960.

Chancey, Mark A. *The Myth of a Gentile Galilee.* Cambridge: Cambridge University Press, 2002.

Charlesworth, James H. *Hillel and Jesus: Comparisons of Two Major Religions.* Minneapolis: Fortress, 1997.

———. *Jesus within Judaism.* Garden City, N.Y.: Doubleday, 1988.

Charlesworth, James H., ed. *Jesus and the Dead Sea Scrolls.* New York: Doubleday, 1993.

———. *The Messiah.* Minneapolis: Fortress, 1992.

Chwolson, Daniel A. *Das letzte Passamahl Christi und der Tag seines Todes.* Leipzig: H. Haessel, 1908.

Cornfeld, Gaalyahu, ed. *The Historical Jesus: A Scholarly View of the Man and His World.* New York: Macmillan, 1982.

Dalman, Gustaf. *Jesus-Jeshua.* London: SPCK, 1929.

———. *Sacred Sites and Sacred Ways.* London: SPCK, 1935.

———. *The Words of Jesus Considered in the Light of Post-Biblical Jewish Writings and the Aramaic Language.* Edinburgh: T&T Clark, 1909.

Daube, David. *The New Testament and Rabbinic Judaism.* Jordan Lectures in Comparative Religion, 2. London: University of London, Athlone Press,1956. Repr., Peabody, Mass.: Hendrickson, 1994.

———. "Rabbinic Methods of Interpretation and Hellenistic Rhetoric." *Hebrew Union College Annual* 22 (1949): 239–64.

Davies, William D. *The Setting of the Sermon on the Mount.* Atlanta: Scholars, 1989.

———. *Torah in the Messianic Age and/or the Age to Come.* Philadelphia: Society of Biblical Literature, 1952.

Davies, William D., and Dale C. Allison. *A Critical and Exegetical Commentary on The Gospel according to St. Matthew.* 3 vols. International Critical Commentary. Edinburgh: T&T Clark, 1988–1991.

Deissmann, Gustav Adolf. *Bible Studies.* Edinburgh: T&T Clark, 1901.

———. *Light from the Ancient East: The New Testament Illustrated by Recently Discovered Texts of the Greco-Roman World.* Translated by Lionel R. M. Strachan. New and Completely Revised Edition. New York: George H. Doran, 1927. Repr., Peabody, Mass.: Hendrickson, 1995.

Di Sante, Carmine. *Jewish Prayer and the Origins of Christian Liturgy.* New York: Paulist, 1985.

Doeve, Jan W. *Jewish Hermeneutics in the Synoptic Gospels and Acts.* Assen, Netherlands: Van Gorcum, 1954.

Donin, Hayim. *To Pray as a Jew: A Guide to the Prayer Book and the Synagogue Service.* New York: Basic Books, 1980.

Dresner, Samuel H. *I Asked for Wonder: A Spiritual Anthology.* New York: Crossroads, 2000.

Edersheim, Alfred. *The Life and Times of Jesus the Messiah.* Rev. ed. Peabody, Mass.: Hendrickson, 1993.

Elbogen, Ismar. *Jewish Liturgy: A Comprehensive History.* Translated by Raymond P. Scheindlin. Philadelphia: Jewish Publication Society, 1993.

Epstein, Jacob. N. *Mevoot Lesifrut Hatannaim.* Jerusalem: Magnes, 1957.

Finkelstein, Louis. *Akiba: Scholar, Saint, and Martyr.* New York: Atheneum, 1975.

———. "The Development of the Amidah." *Jewish Quarterly Review* 16 (1925–1926): 1–43, 127–70.

———. *Haperushim Veanshe Keneset Hagedolah.* New York: Jewish Theological Seminary, 1950.

———. "Introductory Study to Pirke Abot" *Journal of Biblical Literature* 58 (1938): 13–50.

———. *Mevo Lemesechtot Avot Veavot Derabbi Natan.* New York: Jewish Theological Seminary, 1950.

———. *New Light from the Prophets.* New York: Basic, 1969.

———. *The Pharisees.* Philadelphia: Jewish Publication Society, 1940.

Fischel, Henry A. *Rabbinic Literature and Greco-Roman Philosophy.* Leiden: Brill, 1973.

Fischer, Louis. *Gandhi: Indian Leader and World Influence.* New York: Mentor Books, 1954.

Fitzmyer, Joseph. A. *Essays on the Semitic Background of the New Testament.* Missoula, Mont.: Society of Biblical Literature, 1974.

———. *The Gospel according to Luke.* 2 vols. Anchor Bible 28. New York; Doubleday, 1981–1985.

———. *A Wandering Aramean.* Chico, Calif.: Scholars, 1979.

Flannery, Edward H. *The Anguish of the Jews: Twenty-Three Centuries of Anti-Semitism.* Mahwah, N.J.: Paulist, 1985.

Flusser, David. "Blessed Are the Poor in Spirit." *Israel Exploration Journal* 10 (1960): 1–10.

———. "The Conclusion of Matthew in a New Jewish a Christian Source." *Annual of the Swedish Theological Institute* 5 (1967): 300–310.

———. "The Crucified One and the Jews." *Immanuel* 7 (1977): 25–37. Reprinted in *Judaism and the Origins of Christianity.* Jerusalem: Magnes, 1989.

———. "Hillel and Jesus: Two Ways of Self-Awareness," Pages xx–xx in James H. Charlesworth, *Hillel and Jesus.* Minneapolis: Fortress, 1997.

———. "The House of David on an Ossuary." *Israel Museum Journal* 5 (1986): 37–40.

———. *Judaism and the Origins of Christianity.* Jerusalem: Magnes, 1988.

———. "Prayer at the Time of the Second Temple." Pages 19–24 in *Society and Religion in the Second Temple* Jerusalem: Massada Publishing, 1977.

———. "Sanktus und Gloria." Pages 9–151 in *Abraham unser Vater: Festschrift für Otto Michel zum 60. Geburtstag.* Edited by O. Betz, M. Hengel, and P. Schmidt. Leiden: Brill, 1963.

———. "To Bury Caiaphas, Not to Praise Him." *Jerusalem Perspective* 33/34 (1991): 23–28.

———. "Die Versuchung Jesu und ihr jüdische Hintergrund." *Judaica* 45 (1989): 11–28.

———. *Yahadut Umekorot Hanatzrut.* Tel Aviv: Sifriyat Poalim, 1979.

Fraade, Steven. *From Tradition to Commentary: Torah and Its Interpretation in the Midrash Sifre to Deuteronomy.* Albany: State University of New York Press, 1991.

Fridrichsen, A. "Exegetisches zum Neuen Testament," *Symbolae Osloeneses* 13 (1934): 28–46.

Gafni, Yeshayahu, and Yaron Tsur, with English editor Isaac Gottlieb. *Jerusalem to Jabneh: The Period of the Mishnah and Its Literature.* Ramat Aviv, Israel: Everyman's University, 1980.

Gerhardsson, Birger: *Memory and Manuscript: Oral Tradition and Written Transmission in Rabbinic Judaism and Early Christianity.* Lund, Sweden: Gleerup, 1964. Repr., Grand Rapids, Mich.: Eerdmans, 1998.

———. *The Testing of God's Son.* Lund, Sweden: Gleerup, 1966.

Gilat, Yitzhak. *R. Eliezer ben Hyrcanus: A Scholar Outcast.* Ramat Gan, Israel: Bar Ilan University Press, 1984.

Ginzberg, Louis. "The Religion of the Jews at the Time of Jesus." *Hebrew Union College Annual* 1 (1924): 305–21.

Glatzer, Nahum. *Hillel the Elder: The Emergence of Classical Judaism.* New York: B'nai B'rith Hillel Foundations, 1956.

Goldin, J. "The Two Versions of Abot de-Rabbi Nathan. " *Hebrew Union College Annual* 19 (1945): 97–120.

Goodspeed, Edgar J. *The Complete Bible: An American Translation.* Chicago: University of Chicago Press, 1957.

Graetz. Heinrich. *Popular History of the Jews.* 6 vols. New York: Hebrew Publishing, 1949.

Grintz, Jehoshua. "Hebrew as the Spoken and Written Language of the Second Temple." *Journal of Biblical Literature* 79 (1960): 32–49.

Gros, M. *Otzar Haagadah.* 3 vols. Jerusalem: Mosad Harav Kook, 1977.

Halperin, David. *The Merkabah in Rabbinic Literature.* New Haven: American Oriental Society, 1980.

Harnack, Adolf. *The Sayings of Jesus.* New York: Williams & Norgate, 1908.

Harrington, Daniel J. *The Gospel of Matthew.* Collegeville, Minn.: Liturgical, 1991.

Heinemann, I. *Darche Haagadah.* Jerusalem: Masada, 1970.

Heinemann, Joseph. *Agadot Vetodotehen.* Jerusalem: Keter, 1974.

Heinemann, Joseph and Dov Noy, eds. *Studies in Aggadah and Folk-Literature.* Scripta Hierosolymitana 22. Jerusalem: Magnes, 1971.

Hengel, Martin. *Judaism and Hellenism.* London: SCM, 1974.

———. *Studies in the Gospel of Mark.* London: SCM, 1985.

———. *The Zealots.* Edinburgh: T&T Clark, 1989.

Heschel, Abraham Joshua. *The Insecurity of Freedom.* New York; Schocken, 1972.

———. *Maimonides.* New York: Farrar, Straus and Giroux, 1982.

———. *Man's Quest for God: Studies in Prayer and Symbolism.* New York: Scribner's, 1966.

———. "Protestant Renewal: A Jewish View." Pages 301–8 in *Jewish Perspectives on Christianity.* Edited by E. Rothschild. New York: Crossroad, 1990.

———. *Torah Men Hashamayim.* 3 vols. New York: Soncino, 1972–1990.

Heschel, Susannah, ed., *Moral Grandeur and Spiritual Audacity.* New York: Farrar, Straus & Giroux, 2001.

Hestrin, Ruth, and Yael Israeli, eds. *Inscriptions Reveal: Documents from the Time of the Bible, the Mishna, and the Talmud.* Jerusalem: Israel Museum, 1972.

Higger, Michael. *Seven Minor Tractates.* New York: Bloch, 1930.

———. *The Treatises Derek Erez.* Brooklyn: Moinester, 1935.

Hoenig, Sidney H. *The Great Sanhedrin.* New York: Yeshiva University Press, 1953.

Horbury, W. "The Messianic Associations of 'the Son of Man.'" *Journal of Theological Studies* 36 (1985): 34–55.

Horst, Peter. W. van der. *Ancient Jewish Epitaphs: An Introductory Survey of a Millennium of Jewish Funerary Epigraphy (300 B.C.E.–700 C.E.).* Kampen, Netherlands: Pharos, 1991.

Hruby, Kurt. "The Proclamation of the Unity of God as Actualization of the Kingdom." Pages 183–93 in *Standing Before God.* Edited by A. Finkel and L. Frizzel. New York: KTAV, 1981.

Idelson, Abraham Z. *Jewish Liturgy.* New York: Schocken, 1975.

Jaubert, Annie. *The Date of the Last Supper.* Staten Island, N.Y.: Alba House, 1965.

Jeremias, Joachim. *Jerusalem in the Time of Jesus: An Investigation into Economic and Social Condition during the New Testament Period.* London: SCM, 1969.

———. *New Testament Theology* London: SCM, 1981.

———. *The Prayers of Jesus.* Philadelphia: Fortress, 1984.

Jones, E. Stanley. *Gandhi: Portrayal of a Friend.* Nashville: Abingdon, 1948.

Jonsson, Jakob. *Humour and Irony in the New Testament: Illuminated by Parallels in Talmud and Midrash.* Leiden: Brill, 1985.

Kadushim, Max. *The Rabbinic Mind.* New York: Bloch, 1972.

———. *Theology of Seder Eliahu: A Study in Organic Thinking.* New York: Bloch, 1932.

Keener, Craig S. *A Commentary on the Gospel of Matthew.* Grand Rapids: Eerdmans, 1999.

Kensky, Allan. "Moses and Jesus: The Birth of a Savior." *Judaism* 42 (1993): 43–49.

Kistemaker, Simon. *Exposition of Acts.* New Testament Commentary 17. Grand Rapids: Baker, 1990.

Kister, Menahem. "Plucking on the Sabbath and Jewish-Christian Polemic." *Immanuel* 24/25 (1990): 35–51.

Klausner, Joseph. *From Jesus to Paul.* London: George Allen & Unwin, 1946.

———. *Jesus of Nazareth.* New York: Macmillan, 1945.

———. *The Messianic Idea in Israel.* New York: Macmillan, 1955.

Klostermann, Erich. *Das Lukasevangelium.* Tübingen: J. C. B. Mohr, 1950.

———. *Das Markusevangelium.* Tübingen: J. C. B. Mohr, 1950.

Kobelski, Paul J. *Melchizedek and Melchireša'.* Catholic Biblical Quarterly Monograph Series 10. Washington, D.C.: Catholic Biblical Association, 1981.

Kohler, Kaufman. *Hebrew Union College and other Addresses* (Cincinnati: Ark Publishing, 1916.

Lachs, Samuel T. *A Rabbinic Commentary on the New Testament: The Gospels of Matthew, Mark, and Luke.* Hoboken, N.J.: KTAV, 1987.

Ladd, George. E. *The Presence of the Future.* Grand Rapids: Eerdmans, 1980.

———. *A Theology of the New Testament.* Grand Rapids: Eerdmans, 1974.

Lapide, Pinchas. *The Sermon on the Mount.* New York: Orbis, 1986.

Lapide, Pinchas and Ulrich Luz. *Jesus in Two Perspectives.* Minneapolis: Augsburg, 1971.

Lauterbach, Jacob. *Rabbinic Essays.* Cincinnati: Hebrew Union College Press, 1951.

Lerner, M. "The External Tractates," Pages 367–409 in *The Literature of the Sages.* Edited by Shmuel Safrai. Philadelphia: Fortress, 1987.

Lerner, M. with English editor I. Gottlieb. *The World of the Sages.* Ramat Aviv, Israel: Everyman's University, 1983.

Levine, Lee. *Ancient Synagogues Revealed.* Jerusalem: Israel Exploration Society, 1981.

———. *The Galilee in Late Antiquity.* New York: Jewish Theological Seminary, 1992.

———. *The Rabbinic Class of Roman Palestine in Late Antiquity.* New York: Jewish Theological Seminary, 1989.

Lieberman, Saul. *Greek in Jewish Palestine*. New York: Feldheim, 1965.

———. *Hellenism in Jewish Palestine*. New York: Jewish Theological Seminary, 1962.

———. *Mechkarim Betorat Eretz Yisrael*. Jerusalem: Magnes, 1991.

———. *Texts and Studies*. New York: KTAV, 1974.

Lightfoot, John. *A Commentary on the New Testament from the Talmud and Hebraica Matthew—1 Corinthians*. 4 vols. Grand Rapids: Baker, 1979.

Lindsey, Robert L. *A Hebrew Translation of the Gospel of Mark*. Jerusalem: Baptist House, 1973.

———. *Jesus, Rabbi and Lord*. Oak Creek, Wis.: Cornerstone, 1990.

———. *The Jesus Sources*. Tulsa, Okla.: HaKesher, 1990.

Lindsey, Robert L., and E. dos Santos. *A Comparative Greek Concordance of the Synoptic Gospels*. 3 vols. Jerusalem: Baptist House, 1985–1989.

Loewenstamm, Samuel E. "Beloved Is Man in That He Was Created in the Image." Pages 48–50 in *Comparative Studies in Biblical and Ancient Oriental Literature*. Vluyn, Germany: Neukirchener, 1980.

———. "Chaviv Adam Shnivra Betzelem." *Tarbiz* 27 (1957–1958): 1–2.

Mann, C. S. *The Gospel according to Mark*. Anchor Bible 27. New York: Doubleday, 1986.

Mann, Jacob. "Jesus and the Sadducean Priests: Luke 10:25–37." *Jewish Quarterly Review* 6 (1914): 415–22.

Manns, Frédéric. *Jewish Prayer in the Time of Jesus*. Jerusalem: Franciscan Printing, 1994.

Manson, Thomas W. *The Sayings of Jesus: As Recorded in the Gospels According to St. Matthew and St. Luke*. London: SCM, 1977.

———. *The Teachings of Jesus*. Cambridge: Cambridge University Press, 1951.

Mantel, Hugo. "Sanhedrin." Pages 836–39 in volume 14 of *Encyclopaedia Judaica*. Edited by Cecil Roth. 17 vols. Jerusalem: Keter, 1972.

———. *Studies in the History of the Sanhedrin*. Cambridge, Mass.: Harvard University Press, 1965.

Marmonstein, A. "Das Motiv vom veruntreuten Depositum in der jüdischen Volkskunde." *Monatschrift für Geschichte und Wissenschaft des Judentums* 78 (1934): 183–95.

Marshall, I. Howard, *The Gospel of Luke*. New International Greek Testament Commentary. Grand Rapids: Eerdmans, 1978.

McArthur, Harvey K. and Robert M. Johnston. *They Also Taught in Parables*. Grand Rapids: Zondervan, 1990.

McGinley, Laurence. *Form-Criticism of the Synoptic Healing Narratives*. Woodstock, Md.: Woodstock College Press, 1944.

McNamara, Martin. *The New Testament and the Palestinian Targum to the Pentateuch*. Rome: Pontifical Biblical Institute, 1966.

McNeile, Alan H. *The Gospel according to St. Matthew.* London: Macmillan, 1949.

Meyer, Ben. *Aims of Jesus.* London: SCM, 1979.

Milikowsky, Chaim. "Gehenna and 'Sinners of Israel' in the Light of Seder Olam." Hebrew. *Tarbiz* 51 (1986): 311–43.

Montefiore, Claude G. *Rabbinic Literature and Gospel Teachings.* New York: KTAV, 1970.

———. *The Synoptic Gospels.* 2 vols. New York: KTAV, 1968.

Montefiore, Claude G. and Herbert Loewe. *A Rabbinic Anthology.* New York: Schocken, 1974.

Moore, George F. "Christian Writers on Judaism." *Harvard Theological Review* 14 (1921): 197–254.

———. *Judaism in the First Centuries of the Christian Era.* New York: Schocken, 1975.

Mowinckel, Sigmund. *He That Cometh.* New York: Abingdon, 1954.

Murphy, Frederick. *The Religious World of Jesus.* Nashville: Abingdon, 1991.

Newman, Louis and Samuel Spitz. *The Talmudic Anthology: Tales and Teachings of the Rabbis.* New York: Behrman House, 1945.

Nolland, John. *Luke.* 3 vols. Word Biblical Commentary 35. Dallas: Word, 1989–1993.

Noth, Martin. "The 'Re-presentation' of the Old Testament in Proclamation." Pages 76–88 in Claus Westermann, ed., *Essays on Old Testament Hermeneutics.* Richmond, Va.: Westminster John Knox, 1963.

Novak, David. "The Mind of Maimonides." *First Things* (Feburary, 1999): 27–33.

Patte, Daniel. *The Challenge of Discipleship: A Critical Study of the Sermon on the Mount as Scripture.* Harrisburg, Penn.: Trinity International, 1999.

———. *Early Jewish Hermeneutic in Palestine.* Missoula: Scholars, 1975.

Pearl, Chaim. *Rashi.* New York: Grove Press, 1988.

Plaut, W. Gunther. *Growth of Reform Judaism.* New York: World Union for Progressive Judaism, 1965.

———. *The Torah a Modern Commentary.* New York: Union of American Hebrew Congregations, 1981.

Pritz, Ray. *Nazarene Jewish Christianity.* Jerusalem: Magnes, 1988.

Raphael, Simcha P. *Jewish Views of the Afterlife.* Northvale, N.J.: Jason Aronson, 1994.

Resch, Alfred. *Die Logia Jesu: nach dem griechischen und hebräischen Text wiederhergestellt: ein Versuch.* Leipzig: J. C. Hinrichs, 1898.

Riches, John. *Jesus and the Transformation of Judaism.* London: Darton, Longman & Todd, 1980.

Rosner, Fred. *Moses Maimonides.* New York: Feldheim, 1975.

Roth, Cecil., ed. *Encyclopaedia Judaica.* 17 vols. Jerusalem: Keter, 1972.

Rothschild, Fritz A, ed. *Jewish Perspectives on Christianity: Leo Baeck, Martin Buber, Franz Rosenzweig, Will Herberg, and Abraham J. Heschel.* New York: Crossroad, 1990.

Rubenstein, Jeffrey. *Culture of the Babylonian Talmud.* Baltimore: Johns Hopkins University Press, 2003.

Safrai, Shmuel. ". . . all is according to the increase of works performed." *Tarbiz* 53 (1984): 33–40.

———. "Amoraim" Pages 865–75 in vol. 2 of the *Encyclopaedia Judaica.* Edited by Cecil Roth. 17 vols. Jerusalem: Keter, 1972.

———. *Beyame Habayit Uveyame Hamishnah.* Hebrew. Jerusalem: Magnes, 1994.

———. "Chasididm Venashe Maaseh." Hebrew. *Tzion* 16 (1985): 134–54.

———. "The Jewish Cultural Nature of Galilee in the First Century." *Immanuel* 24/25 (1990): 147–86.

———. *Rabbi Akiva Ben Yosef Chayav Umishnato.* Jerusalem: Bialik Institute, 1970.

———. "The Synagogue and its Worship" Pages 78–89 in *Society and Religion in the Second Temple Period.* Edited by Michael Avi–Yonah and Zvi Baras. Jerusalem: Massada, 1977.

———. "Teaching of Pietists in Mishnaic Literature." *Journal of Jewish Studies* 16 (1965): 15–33.

Safrai, Shmuel, M. Stern, David Flusser, and Willem C. van Unnik, eds. *The Jewish People in the First Century: Historical Geography, Political History, Social, Cultural, and Religious Life and Institutions.* 9 vols. Amsterdam: Van Gorcum, 1974–1993.

Sanders, E. P. *The Historical Figure of Jesus.* London: Penguin, 1991.

———. *Jesus and Judaism.* London: SCM, 1985.

———. *Jewish Law from Jesus to the Mishnah.* Philadelphia: Trinity, 1990.

———. *Judaism Practice and Belief 63 B.C.E. to 66 C.E.* London: SCM, 1992.

———. *Paul and Palestinian Judaism.* London: SCM, 1977.

Sanders, James A. *The Psalms Scroll of Qumran Cave 11.* Discoveries in the Judean Desert of Jordan, 4. New York: Oxford University Press, 1965.

Sandmel, Samuel. *Judaism and Christian Beginnings.* New York: Oxford University Press, 1978.

———. "Parallelomania." *Journal of Biblical Literature* 81 (1962): 1–13.

Sandt, Huub van de, and David Flusser, *The Didache: Its Jewish Sources and Its Place in Early Judaism and Christianity.* Minneapolis: Fortress, 2002.

Schäfer, Peter, and Catherine Hezser. *The Talmud Yerushalmi.* Tübingen: J. C. B. Mohr, 2000.

Schofer, Jonathan. *The Making of a Sage.* Madison: University of Wisconsin Press, 2005.

Schechter, Solomon. *Aspects of Rabbinic Theology.* New York: Schocken, 1961.

Schürer, Emil. *The History of the Jewish People in the Time of Jesus Christ.* 5 vols. New York: Scribner, 1891. Repr., Peabody, Mass.: Hendrickson, 1994.

———. *The History of the Jewish People in the Time of Jesus Christ.* Revised and edited by Geza Vermes and Fergus Millar. 3 vols. Edinburgh: T&T Clark, 1974–1987.

Sigal, Phillip. *The Halakah of Jesus of Nazareth.* Lanham, Md.: University Press of America, 1986.

Skehan, Patrick, and Alexander Di Lella. *Wisdom of Ben Sira.* Anchor Bible 39. Garden City, N.Y.: Doubleday, 1987.

Smith, Morton. "A Comparison of Early Christian and Early Rabbinic Tradition." *Journal of Biblical Literature* 82 (1963): 169–76.

———. *Tannaitic Parallels to the Gospels.* Journal of Biblical Literature Monograph Series 6. Philadelphia: Society of Biblical Literature, 1951.

Soloveitchik, Joseph B. *Halakhic Man.* Philadelphia: Jewish Publication Society, 1983.

Stein, S. "The Influence of Symposa Literature on the Literary Form of the Pesah Haggadah." *Journal of Jewish Studies* 8 (1957): 13–44.

Steinsaltz, Adin. *A Guide to Jewish Prayer.* New York: Schocken, 2000.

Stern, M. "Aspects of Jewish Society: The Priesthood and Other Classes." Pages 2:561–603 in *The Jewish People in the First Century.* Edited by Shmuel Safrai, M. Stem, David Flusser, and Willem C. van Unnik. 9 vols. Amsterdam: Van Gorcum, 1974–1993.

———. "The Greek and Latin Literary Sources." Pages 1:18–36 in *The Jewish People in the First Century.* Edited by Shmuel Safrai, M. Stem, David Flusser, and Willem C. van Unnik. 9 vols. Amsterdam: Van Gorcum, 1974–1993.

———. *Mechkarim Betoldot Yisrael Beyame Bayit Sheni.* Hebrew. Jerusalem: Yad Izhak Ben Zvi, 1991.

Stoldt, Hans-Herbert. *History and Criticism of the Marcan Hypothesis.* Macon, Ga.: Mercer, 1980.

Strack Hermann, L. and Paul Billerbeck. *Kommentar zum Neuen Testament aus Talmud und Midrasch.* 6 vols. Munich: C. H. Beck, 1922–1961.

Strassfeld, Michael. *A Book of Life: Embracing Judaism as a Spiritual Practice.* N.Y.: Schocken, 2002.

———. *The Jewish Holidays.* New York: Harper & Row, 1985.

Strecker, Georg. *The Sermon on the Mount.* Nashville: Abingdon, 1988.

Thoma, Clemens. *A Christian Theology of Judaism.* Mahwah, N.J.: Paulist, 1980.

Tomson, Peter J. *Paul and the Jewish Law.* Assen, Netherlands: Van Gorcum, 1990.

Turner, Nigel. *Grammatical Insights into the New Testament.* Reissued paperback ed. Edinburgh: T&T Clark, 2004.

Urbach, Ephraim E. *Class-Status and Leadership in the World of Palestinian Sages.* Jerusalem: Israel Academy of Sciences and Humanities, 1966.

―――. *The Halakhah: Its Sources and Development.* Jerusalem: Yad Latalmud, 1986.

―――. *The Sages: Their Concepts and Beliefs.* 2 vols. Jerusalem: Magnes, 1975.

VanderKam, James. *The Dead Sea Scrolls Today.* Grand Rapids: Eerdmans, 1994.

Vermes, Geza. *Jesus and the World of Judaism.* London: SCM, 1983.

―――. *Jesus the Jew.* London: Collins, 1973.

―――. *The Religion of Jesus the Jew.* Minneapolis: Fortress, 1993.

―――. "Sectarian Matrimonial Halakhah in the Damascus Rule." *Journal of Semitic Studies* 25 (1974): 197ff.

Wiesel, Elie. *Sages and Dreamers: Biblical, Talmudic, and Hasidic Portraits and Legends.* New York: Summit Books, 1991.

―――. *Wise Men and their Tales.* New York: Schocken Books, 2003.

Windisch, Hans. *The Meaning of the Sermon on the Mount.* Philadelphia: Westminster, 1950.

Winter, Paul. *On the Trial of Jesus.* Berlin: Walter de Gruyter, 1961.

Wolpe, David. *Healer of Shattered Hearts: A Jewish View of God.* New York: Henry Holt, 1990.

―――. *In Speech and Silence: The Jewish Quest for God.* New York: Henry Holt, 1992.

Wünsche, August. *Erläuterung der Evangelien aus Talmud und Midrasch.* Göttingen: Vandenhoeck & Ruprecht, 1878.

Yadin, Yigal. *Tefillin from Qumran.* Jerusalem: Israel Exploration Society, 1969.

Young, Brad H. "The Ascension Motif of 2 Corinthians in Jewish, Christian, and Gnostic Texts." *Grace Theological Journal* 9 (1, 1988): 73–103.

―――. "The Cross, Jesus, and the Jewish People." *Immanuel* 24/25 (1990): 23–34.

―――. *Jesus and His Jewish Parables.* Tulsa, Okla.: Gospel Research Foundation, 2000.

―――. *Jesus the Jewish Theologian.* Peabody, Mass.: Hendrickson, 1995.

―――. *The Jewish Background to the Lord's Prayer.* Tulsa, Okla.: Gospel Research Foundation, 2000.

―――. *The Parables: Jewish Tradition and Christian Interpretation.* Peabody, Mass.: Hendrickson, 1998.

————. *Paul the Jewish Theologian.* Peabody, Mass.: Hendrickson, 1997.

Young, Brad H., and David Flusser. "Messianic Blessings in Jewish and Christian Texts." Pages 280–300 in *Judaism and the Origins of Christianity,* by David Flusser. Jerusalem: Magnes, 1989.

GRAMMATICAL AND LEXICAL AIDS

Bauer, Walter, William Arndt, Felix W. Gingrich, and Frederick W. Danker. *A Greek-English Lexicon of the New Testament and Other Early Christian Literature.* 3d ed. Chicago: University of Chicago Press, 2000.

Ben Yehuda, Eliezer. *Milon Halashon Haevrit.* 17 vols. Jerusalem: General Federation of Jewish Labor in Eretz Israel, 1959.

Blass, Friedrich, and Albert Debrunner. *A Greek Grammar of the New Testament and Other Early Christian Literature.* Translated and revised by Robert Funk. Chicago: University of Chicago Press, 1961.

Brown, Francis, S. R. Driver, and Charles A. Briggs. *The Brown-Driver-Briggs-Gesenius Hebrew and English Lexicon.* Boston: Houghton Mifflin, 1906. Repr., Peabody, Mass: Hendrickson, 2004.

Dalman, Gustaf. *Aramäisch-neuhebräisches Handwörterbuch.* Frankfurt am Main: J. Kaufmann, 1922.

————. *Grammatik des jüdisch-palästinischen Aramäisch.* 2d ed. Leipzig: J. C. Hinrichs, 1905. Repr., Darmstadt: Wissenschaftliche, 1981.

Golomb, David. *A Grammar of Targum Neofiti.* Chico, Calif: Scholars, 1985.

Howard, Wilbert E. "Semitisms in the New Testament." Pages 2:418–19 in *A Grammar of New Testament Greek.* 2.418–19. Edited by James. H. Moulton. 4 vols. Edinburgh: T&T Clark, 1930.

Jastrow, Marcus. *A Dictionary of the Targumim, the Talmud Bahli and Yerushalmi, and the Midrashic Literature.* 2 vols. London: Luzac & Co., 1886–1903. Repr., Peabody, Mass.: Hendrickson, 2005.

Kittel, Gerhard, ed. *Theological Dictionary of the New Testament.* Translated by Geoffrey Bromiley. 10 vols. Grand Rapids: Eerdmans, 1964–1976.

Koehler, Ludwig, and Walter Baumgartner. *Lexicon in Veteris Testamenti libros.* 2d ed. Leiden: Brill, 1958.

Kosovsky, B. *Otzar Leshon Hatannaim Lasifra.* New York: Jewish Theological Seminary, 1967.

————. *Otzar Leshon Hatannaim Lasifre Bemidbar Vedevarim.* New York: Jewish Theological Seminary, 1971.

————. *Otzar Leshon Hatannaim Lemekilta Derabbi Ishmael.* New York: Jewish Theological Seminary, 1965.

Kosovsky, Ch. *Otzar Leshon Hamishnah.* Tel Aviv: Massadah, 1967.

———. *Otzar Leshon Hatalmud*. Jerusalem: Ministry of Education and Culture, Government of Israel, 1971.

———. *Otzar Leshon Hatosefta*. New York: Jewish Theological Seminary, 1961.

Kosovsky, Moshe. *Otzar Leshon Talmud Yerushalmi*. Jerusalem: Israel Academy of Sciences and Humanities, 1979.

Kutscher, E.Y. "Aramaic." Pages 3:260–87 in *Encyclopaedia Judaica*. Edited by Cecil Roth. 16 vols. Jerusalem: Keter, 1978.

———. *Studies in Galilean Aramaic*. Ramat Gan, Israel: Bar Ilan University Press,1976.

Levias, Caspar. *A Grammar of Galilean Aramaic*. Hebrew. New York: Jewish Theological Seminary, 1986.

Levy, Jacob. *Chaldäisches Wörterbuch über die Targumim und einen grossen Theil des rabbinischen Schriftthums*. 2 vols. Leipzig: J. C. Hinrichs, 1867–1868.

———. *Wörterbuch über die Talmudim und Midraschim*. 4 vols. Berlin: Benjamin Harz, 1924.

Liddell, Henry G. and Robert Scott. *A Greek-English Lexicon*. Oxford: Clarendon, 1976.

Moulton, James H., ed. *A Grammar of New Testament Greek*. 4 vols. Edinburgh: T&T Clark, 1930.

Nathan ben Zechiel. *Aruch Completum*. Edited by A. Kohut. Vienna, n.p. 1878–1892. Repr., Jerusalem, Israel: Books Export Enterprises, n.d.

Sokoloff, Michael. *A Dictionary of Jewish Babylonian Aramaic*. Ramat Gan, Israel: Bar Ilan University Press, 2002.

Sokoloff, Michael. *A Dictionary of Jewish Palestinian Aramaic of the Byzantine Period*. 2d ed. Ramat Gan, Israel: Bar Ilan University Press, 2002.

Spicq, Ceslas. *Theological Lexicon of the New Testament*. Translated and edited by James D. Ernest. 3 vols. Peabody, Mass.: Hendrickson, 1994.

Stevenson, William B. *Grammar of Palestinian Jewish Aramaic*. Oxford: Clarendon, 1974.

Thackeray, Henry St. John *A Grammar of the Old Testament in Greek*. Cambridge: Cambridge University Press, 1909.

Index of Modern Authors

Index of Subjects

Index of Ancient Sources